CRISIS MANAGEMENT

CRISIS MANAGEMENT

Planning for the Inevitable

Steven Fink

American Management Association

This book is available at a special
discount when ordered in bulk quantities.
For information, contact Special Sales Department,
AMACOM, a division of American Management Association,
135 West 50th Street, New York, NY 10020.

Library of Congress Cataloging-in-Publication Data

Fink, Steven.
    Crisis management.

    Includes index.
    1. Crisis management. I. American Management
Association. II. Title.
HD49.F56   1986   658.4   85-48220
ISBN 0-8144-5859-9

Printing number

10 9 8 7 6 5 4 3 2 1

For my parents,
who rescued me from more
crises than I can recall,

And for my wife,
my most treasured turning point.

With love.

Be prepared.
    —*Motto of the Boy Scouts of America*

**I always view problems as opportunities in
work clothes.**
    —*Henry Kaiser*

Contents

Introduction

If Three Mile Island, Union Carbide's carnage in India, the Tylenol poisonings, the Ohio bank failures, and the Procter & Gamble/Rely tampon controversy—to name but a few recent crises—have taught the world anything, it is that a crisis in business can occur today with little or no warning, anywhere, anytime. And it can happen to any company, large or small, public or private.

It is, in other words, the safest of assumptions that a crisis looms on the horizon.

This is *not* necessarily bad news—merely reality.

And if you will accept that reality as a given—if you will acknowledge that in these complex and unpredictable times in which we live and work, *anything* is possible, including a crisis that may prove devastating to you *or* your business—then you will be in the right frame of mind to accept the contention that forms the basic foundation for this book: with proper advance planning, there can be a positive side to a crisis.

The Chinese have embraced this concept for centuries. The symbol for their word "crisis"—called *wei-ji*—is actually a combination of two words, "danger" and "opportunity."

While no one is saying that a crisis may not be perilous, this book will deal more with the preparation necessary for capitalizing on crises and creating achievement out of adversity, inspiration out of humiliation, opportunity out of danger.

But do not assume that you have to be the chief executive officer of a company to implement the ideas presented here. For almost any individual, on any rung of the management ladder, or even outside the business environment, can play a crisis to his or her advantage. This is true for *anyone* having *anything* to do with the operations of a business—even for customers, shareholders, or members of the community.

And the operative word here is "individual." While a crisis may strike at the heart of a corporation or a family, it is always an individual who must have the heart—and the courage—to respond. And that individual may be *you*.

In other words, you should view and plan for the inevitability of a crisis in much the same way you view and plan for the inevitability of death and taxes: not out of weakness or fear, but out of the strength that comes from knowing you are prepared to face life and play the hand that fate deals you.

Fate dealt me an interesting hand early in 1979.

At that time, I accepted a position in the fledgling administration of Pennsylvania Governor Dick Thornburgh. In the private sector, this position would be something akin to vice president for marketing and communications, and my initial duty was to help package and market the entire Commonwealth of Pennsylvania as a product—marketing its travel and tourism and economic development programs. In the state's 300-year history, this had never before been attempted.

Thornburgh had been in office only 72 days—and I even less—when the Three Mile Island incident happened.

I was drafted (at the time, "shanghaied" seemed a more appropriate term) to serve as a member of the crisis management team in the Thornburgh administration. Nuclear power was not my strong suit, nor was it Thornburgh's, nor, for that matter, was it anyone else's in the governor's office. Everyone, though, became a quick study.

But it soon became apparent that a lack of knowledge about nuclear reactors did not prevent the administration from doing a good job managing its portion of the crisis, any more than an in-depth knowledge of nuclear reactors did not keep the Metropolitan Edison (Met Ed) utility company from doing a poor job with its portion. While Thornburgh's approval rating skyrocketed, Met Ed's suffered a "meltdown."

The unique experience of being on the inside of arguably the world's most riveting crisis forever altered the way I view crises. What I learned during and subsequent to Three Mile Island—and what I counsel corporate clients in today—is that crises need not be the seemingly uncontrolled and uncontrollable events that their victims too often allow them to become.

This will become clearer to you as we examine the mechanics of many well-known public crises, which are used throughout for illustrative, analytical, and interpretive purposes. Bear in mind an important point that will be repeated periodically: at no time in any discussion of a crisis is culpability on the part of an individual or company either stated or implied. It is irrelevant to our discussion. Our main concern is the management of the crisis: why was it managed well, or why was it managed poorly?

The ability to manage fluid situations and make good, vigilant decisions—just another way to view crisis management—is vital to achieving success at critical turning points in life, in business, in both.

It is crucial to remember that what happens in business affects what happens in your personal life. Conversely, a personal crisis can cloud your thinking and affect your decision-making judgment at work. Simply put, your two lives—business and personal—and the potential crises and stressful life events in each, are inextricably intertwined. One affects—and sometimes feeds on—the other.

For this reason, as you will observe, very little will be said about business crises that cannot be applied every bit as effectively to personal crises as well.

You can plan for, or at least respond to, personal crises in much the same way you plan for or respond to business crises.

And you should consider a personal crisis as filled with as much potential opportunity—and as much potential danger—as a business crisis.

When you think about it, you may see that the successfully handled crises in your personal life are sometimes much more dramatically felt than those in your business life and yield greater satisfaction. It is almost as though in business you have the power to turn danger into opportunity, but in your personal life you have the added ability to turn humiliation into inspiration.

But it helps if you understand exactly what it is that makes a crisis a crisis.

1

A Crisis Begins

From a tiny spark comes a great conflagration.

—*Ben Sirach,* Ecclesiasticus

You couldn't see it.

You couldn't touch it, taste it, smell it, or hear it coming.

Your lungs might be sucking it in right then and there and you wouldn't know it; this breath—maybe the next breath—might be your last.

Were your eyes starting to water? Was that a symptom of some kind?

Was it safe inside the house? Were the kids safe with the windows shut tight? Should you flee? If you held your breath as you ran from the house to the car, would you be all right?

Bombarded by a barrage of conflicting information from a variety of sources, how were you to know whom to believe?

These concerns were part of the invisible crisis known as Three Mile Island, the part that struck fear into the minds of adults, terror into the hearts of children.

Panic, for the most part, however, was averted. So were widespread chaos, evacuation, looting, burning, and death. There were no fatalities.

But for more than a week, it seemed the world stopped spinning and focused its collective attention on Three Mile Island, on the banks of the Susquehanna River, ten too-short miles from Harrisburg, Pennsylvania. In the shadows of the massive cooling towers of two nuclear reactors, as alarm bells pierced the 4 A.M. calm of a morning in late March 1979, it was impossible to avoid the fear.

If only one explanation could be applied to the reason for the enhanced fear, it might be because none of the human senses was usable during the Three Mile Island crisis. And when the senses don't work or are unable to provide satisfactory references, the imagination runs wild.

Potentially, there was *something* to be afraid of; but what, exactly?

Saying that a deadly, invisible cloud of radioactive gas was released from TMI would not provide the senses with enough information to process.

You couldn't see it if it was invisible.

If you inhaled it, you wouldn't be able to feel it or taste it or smell it. So how would you know if you had been . . . *zapped?*

Everybody knew that radioactive gas is colorless and odorless, isn't it? And that death would certainly not be instantaneous. No; first, in a couple of days (weeks? months? years?) your hair would fall out; then spots would appear on your skin, like liver spots. Then the pain would begin. Was that right?

Was any of this true? Or was it just mythology?

What *was* true was this: fear of the unknown caused a large part of the *human* crisis; fear of the truth caused almost all of the *business* crisis.

The fact that *The China Syndrome* had opened in movie theaters across the country just prior to the accident at TMI served only to compound the fears. So great was the public demand to view the Jane Fonda–Michael Douglas–Jack Lemmon movie, about a disaster at a fictitious nuclear power plant, that at least one Harrisburg-area movie theater screened the film around the clock throughout the TMI crisis.

Saul Kohler, editor of the Harrisburg *Patriot* and *Evening News,* had just put the paper to bed and was sitting in an all-night Howard Johnson's restaurant at 3:30 in the morning when hundreds of anxiety-ridden people rushed into the eatery. They had just come from seeing the film, and the entire place was soon abuzz about local implications. The accident happened on Kohler's first day on the job, and he quickly decided that he'd better see the film, too. Perhaps he went to learn something about nuclear reactors. Perhaps he was wondering whether it might be his *last* day on the job—*any* job.

"I gave all of my reporters and editorial staff immediate emergency leave if they wanted to evacuate their families," Kohler recalled. "But they had to promise to return."[1]

"I know reporters who spent a year in Saigon and turned down this assignment because they were afraid," remembered National Public Radio's Nina Totenberg, who did cover the story. "I've been shot at in Northern Ireland, but I never knew *this* level of fear before. And it got most frightening for me when I saw the science reporters get scared."[2]

And late on a Saturday night—just three days after the first alarm at TMI sounded, one day after the second alarm sounded and people began to realize that maybe there really *was* something to be concerned about, despite the utility company's pablum-filled assurances that everything was under control, and on the day after the Nuclear Regulatory Commission dispatched troubleshooter Harold Denton, the head of its Office of Nuclear Reactor Regulations, to the scene—on that Saturday night, a small group of "battle scarred" news reporters, some wearing dosimeters, burst into the governor's press office and demanded to know once and for all whether or not it was safe for them and their families to be in Harrisburg.

The fear was palpable and all-pervasive.

Long before the TMI crisis began—long before anyone ever heard the term "meltdown"—the crisis was in a prodromal, or warning, phase. Knowing how to recognize and manage the prodromes—from the Greek for "running before" and meaning the "warning signs," the "precrises," if you will—before they erupt into the far more serious acute crisis stage is often what spells the difference between a company (or an individual) that profits during a crisis (its or someone else's) and companies (or people) that suffer and sometimes fail.

Knowing how to spot prodromes in a crisis also has the capacity to create "overnight" heroes within a company. These are the people, the managers, who make quantum leaps in achievement within a company and promotional leaps over their colleagues.

You and your managers should understand that anytime you're not in a crisis, you are instead in a precrisis, or prodromal, mode.

Anytime. All the time. Be vigilant. Be prepared.

And if you operate in a prodromal, or vigilant, state, you may catch sight of something that needs to be addressed quickly, before it gets out of control. Before it becomes an acute crisis.

To understand and analyze the TMI crisis from a business and management perspective does not require a comprehensive understanding of the complexities and sophisticated technicalities of the workings of a nuclear power plant. In fact, as you will see as we examine a host of other crises, you will not need to know how tampons are manufactured to understand how Procter & Gamble managed the Rely crisis, nor do you need to be an expert in the manufacture of methyl isocyanate to appreciate Union Carbide's response to its crisis.

The Report of the President's Commission on the Accident at Three Mile Island (commonly referred to as the Kemeny Commission Report, after its chairman, John G. Kemeny) took six months to conclude that "a series of events—compounded by equipment failures, inappropriate procedures, and human errors and ignorance—escalated [the accident] into the worst crisis yet experienced by the nation's nuclear power industry."[3]

The report said:

> . . . While the major factor that turned this incident into a serious accident was inappropriate operator action, many factors contributed to the action of

the operators, such as deficiencies in their training, lack of clarity in their operating procedures, failure of organizations to learn the proper lessons from previous incidents, and deficiencies in the design of the control room.[4]

After examining all of the "deficiencies" and wading through six months of hearings and testimony, the commission resolved that ". . . we are convinced that an accident like Three Mile Island was eventually inevitable."

Government bureaucrats are not known for their creative writing flair. But even in monotonals, when you read the Kemeny Commission's account of the TMI accident, your pulse quickens as the almost incredible sequence of avoidable events unfolds.

Put yourself for a moment in the place of TMI shift supervisor William Zewe or shift foreman Fred Scheimann, or either of the two control-room operators, Edward Frederick and Craig Faust.

It is 4 A.M. on March 28, 1979. And your life—at a crucial turning point—is about to begin a roller-coaster ride into the unknown.

Here is how the Kemeny Commission report described just the first few *seconds* of the "inevitable" accident that should never have escalated beyond the nuisance stage:

In the parlance of the electric power industry, a "trip" means a piece of machinery stops operating. A series of feedwater system pumps supplying water to TMI-2's steam generators tripped on the morning of March 28, 1979. The nuclear plant was operating at 97 percent power at the time. The first pump trip occurred at 36 seconds after 4:00 A.M. When the pumps stopped, the flow of water to the steam generators stopped. With no feedwater being added, there soon would be no steam, so the plant's safety system automatically shut down the steam turbine and the electric generator it powered. The incident at Three Mile Island was 2 seconds old.

The production of steam is a critical function of a nuclear reactor. Not only does steam run the generator to produce electricity but also, as steam is produced, it removes some of the intense heat that the reactor water carries.

When the feedwater flow stopped, the temperature of the reactor coolant increased. The rapidly heating water expanded. The pressurizer level (the level of the water inside the pressurizer tank) rose and the steam in the top of the tank compressed. Pressure inside the pressurizer built to 2,255 pounds per square inch, 100 psi more than normal. Then a valve atop the pressurizer, called a pilot-operated relief valve, or PORV, opened—as it was designed to do—and steam and water began flowing out of the reactor coolant system through a drain pipe to a tank on the floor of the containment building. Pressure continued to rise, however, and 8 seconds after the first pump tripped, TMI-2's reactor—as it was designed to do—scrammed: its control rods automatically dropped down into the reactor core to halt its nuclear fission.

Less than a second later, the heat generated by fission was essentially zero. But, as in any nuclear reactor, the decaying radioactive materials left from the fission process continued to heat the reactor's coolant water. This heat was a small fraction—just 6 percent—of that released during fission, but it was still substantial and had to be removed to keep the core from overheating. When the pumps that normally supply the steam generator with water shut down, three emergency feedwater pumps automatically started. Fourteen seconds into the accident, an operator in TMI-2's control room noted the emergency feed pumps were running. He did not notice two lights that told him a valve was closed on each of the two emergency feedwater lines and thus no water could reach the steam generators. One light was covered by a yellow maintenance tag. No one knows why the second light was missed.

With the reactor scrammed and the PORV open, pressure in the reactor coolant system fell. Up to this point, the reactor system was responding normally to a turbine trip. The PORV should have closed 13 seconds into the accident, when pressure dropped to 2,205 psi. It did not. A light on the control room panel indicated that the electric power that opened the PORV had gone off, leading the operators to assume the valve had shut. But the PORV was stuck open, and would remain open for 2 hours and 22 minutes, draining needed coolant water—a LOCA [Loss of Coolant Accident] was in progress. In the first 100 minutes of the accident, some 32,000 gallons—over one-third of the entire capacity of the reactor coolant system—would escape through the PORV and out the reactor's let-down system. Had the valve closed as it was designed to do, or if the control room operators had realized that the valve was stuck open and closed a backup valve to stem the flow of coolant water, or if they had simply left on the plant's high pressure injection pumps, the accident at Three Mile Island would have remained little more than a minor inconvenience for Met Ed.[5]

In the final analysis, then, it was catalytic and cataclysmic human errors—"a severe deficiency in [TMI operator] training," according to the Kemeny Commission—that ultimately put Three Mile Island on the map and then came perilously close to taking TMI and a substantial chunk of Pennsylvania *off* the map; it was human error that caused the nation's worst nuclear power plant accident—and a worldwide crisis.

It has been said that if *nothing* had been done at all in the wee small hours of that infamous March morning—if the plant operators literally had been asleep at the switch, so to speak—nothing adverse or untoward would have occurred. The plant's built-in safety systems, designed by Babcock & Wilcox, would have satisfactorily handled *any* contingency. Humans, who caused the accident, were needed only as a fail-safe mechanism to prevent accidents.

(In dealing with crisis situations you may as well learn early that the fates can be cruel. As we shall see, they can also be exceedingly kind. But first, they can be cruel.)

As the dust begins to settle following any major crisis that commands megamedia attention, one of the first things to happen is "the investigation"—*all* of them. There were countless post-TMI investigations, including (besides the Kemeny Commission) congressional investigations, NRC investigations, investigations by Pennsylvania's governor (which actually were carried out by Lieutenant Governor William W. Scranton, III), investigations by Pennsylvania's State House and Senate, investigations and allegations by the Union of Concerned Scientists, and scores of investigations, exposés, features, and background pieces by national and local news media.

Some postcrisis investigations are legitimate in their concern for public safety and well-being; others are headline-grabbing witch hunts that are looking for scapegoats. But usually in the course of an investigation or a series of hearings, certain previously unknown information comes to light that may be considered damaging, or at least embarrassing, to the company involved.

It may be that this information sheds new light on the cause of the crisis. Or perhaps the information doesn't exactly explain any more about the cause of a crisis, but it reveals that the company tolerated or allowed shoddy workmanship, or inaccurate (or false) reporting to government agencies, or unfair hiring practices, and on and on.

It was during the TMI investigation, for example, that it became known that "human error" was really "management error"—meaning that the company simply had not been doing a good job of managing a nuclear power facility. General Public Utilities' Metropolitan Edison subsidiary* had been not just "deficient" in operating procedures, as the Kemeny Commission reported, but deceitful, too, as a plea of guilty to one of 11 federal indictments ultimately determined.

It is a very safe bet that anytime an individual or a company is put under anyone's microscope, *something* is going to come into focus.

And depending on the motivation of the group conducting the investigation, "findings" may get blown way out of proportion, even if the only "negative" or questionable revelations that come to light are minor.

During one of the post-TMI investigations, it was revealed that there was cheating on some of the exams required to become licensed to be an operator at the plant. The cheating that was first revealed happened *after* the TMI incident and involved TMI-1, the reactor that was *not* damaged in the accident (although, at the time of the accident, there was frequent "crossover" licensing from one plant to another). Then, after the accident,

---

*In 1979, General Public Utilities Corporation, headquartered in Parsippany, New Jersey, was the holding company for Metropolitan Edison, of Reading, Pennsylvania. Met Ed was the licensed operator of the Three Mile Island nuclear reactors. However, in 1982, Met Ed was relieved of operating responsibilities when General Public Utilities created a new subsidiary called GPU Nuclear Corporation, which was licensed specifically to operate TMI and one other nuclear reactor, Oyster Creek, at Forked River, New Jersey. Today GPU Nuclear supplies nuclear power to the Met Ed utility, which is still in existence. Met Ed just does not—and, by virtue of its lack of an operating license, cannot—have anything to do with generating nuclear power.

when the qualification tests were readministered under much closer supervision, one-third of the licensed operators failed the test. But most damaging of all, subsequent digging indicated—and a guilty plea from Met Ed ultimately confirmed—that inadequate, improper, and criminal procedures had been used for certain leak-rate tests at TMI-2 (the infamous reactor), *and* that these events had occurred *prior* to the accident.

The following conclusions or inferences may be drawn:

- Certain management procedures at Three Mile Island were lax.
- Lax procedures of any kind in any sort of operation—but certainly in a high-risk operation such as a nuclear power plant or a chemical plant—may be a precursor of a potential crisis.
- Recognizing and taking appropriate and necessary action in a prodromal situation *may* prevent a crisis just by making managers more vigilant.

It may be reasoned that had someone at TMI recognized the severity and potential repercussions of the cheating situation and blown the whistle early on, the crisis might never have occurred.

In sound crisis management planning, you must train yourself and your managers to examine *every* out-of-the-ordinary situation for what it is—a warning, a prodrome, a precrisis. And having recognized the prodrome, you then must question what, if anything, can or should be done about it.

This is managing a fluid situation by a process of vigilant decision making. It is contingency planning; it is asking "what if" questions.

However, when someone *does* recognize a prodrome and *does* sound the proper warning bells, but *no one listens,* then senior management must take a closer look inward to get to the root of the problem and shoulder the bulk of the blame for the consequences.

A full 13 months before the incident at Three Mile Island, a senior engineer at Babcock & Wilcox (the supplier of TMI's nuclear steam system) wrote a strongly worded warning memorandum in which he described an almost identical accident to the one that ultimately occurred at TMI—an accident in which operators at another plant* had mistakenly turned off the emergency cooling system. He detailed how this set of circumstances *almost* led to a serous accident—and warned how it *could* lead to a serious accident if these events were to occur again.[6] Despite his memo's urgings that clear safety instructions be passed on to all plant operators, *nothing happened.* The memo got sidetracked in the Babcock & Wilcox and NRC chains of command and channels of communication. Consequently, no

---

*The Davis-Besse plant near Toledo, Ohio.

action ever was taken by anyone, least of all by the TMI plant operators, who didn't even see the warning memo until after the accident.

As this story illustrates, recognizing a prodrome is only half the battle. If *you* are not the ultimate decision maker, you have to be certain that action is taken by the appropriate people.

Met Ed was fortunate in only one respect: no one died. Other situations for other companies did not turn out as well.

Union Carbide, at its Institute, West Virginia, plant, had some 71 prodrome situations, plus a responsible prediction of catastrophe, between 1980 and 1984, according to the Environmental Protection Agency and company officials.

(The Institute plant was once proudly hailed by Union Carbide as the "sister plant" to the one in Bhopal, India, where a deadly gas leak of methyl isocyanate on December 3, 1984, killed more than 2,000 people.)

The EPA also charged that Union Carbide did not routinely inform the regulatory agency of all the leaks at the Institute plant, as required by law, and that not all leaks that were reported were done so in a timely manner.

According to Union Carbide, during the same four-year period at this plant there also were 107 leaks of phosgene—which was used as a nerve gas during World War I—and 22 additional leaks of methyl isocyanate and phosgene *combined*.

To appreciate fully just how deadly methyl isocyanate can be, EPA regulations require the reporting of leaks of *just one pound* or more of the substance over a 24-hour period outside the grounds of the plant; in contrast, *5,000 pounds* of phosgene, the nerve gas, may leak before it has to be reported.

Union Carbide, while it acknowledged the leaks, took issue with the EPA's claim of lack of, or improper, reporting.

But Union Carbide did *not* take issue with the claim that no one in Institute, West Virginia, and no one at the *Fortune* 500 company's Danbury, Connecticut, corporate headquarters, thought to alert any of the Bhopal managers of the leaks; nor even to alert them to a damaging internal company report that screamed in the loudest possible language that a "catastrophic failure" was a distinct possibility at the U.S. plant.

Less than two months after the December 1984 disaster in India, and as a direct result of hearings held by the Congressional Subcommittee on Health and Environment, Subcommittee Chairman Henry Waxman released to the media an *internal* Union Carbide report which warned that the Institute plant faced a possible "runaway reaction" of methyl isocyanate. Waxman said that the report cautioned how potentially serious this incident could be.

The internal report was dated September 11, 1984—*three months before* the Bhopal nightmare.

The report spoke of the possibility of a "runaway reaction" if any methyl isocyanate storage tanks were contaminated by water; this was a distinct possibility, because a water cooling system was used at the plant, as well as in the catalytic materials used in a flare system specifically designed to burn off any escaping gas.

The apparently well-researched and well-reasoned report warned that because previous water-contamination incidents at the Institute plant had been "handled with little or no problem," this "may have created a degree of overconfidence or lack of concern that could allow a situation to proceed to the point where it isn't controllable." An inability to be able to respond in this type of crisis quickly and effectively, the report continued, could lead to a "catastrophic failure of the tank."[7]

Following Waxman's release of the report, Jackson B. Browning, Union Carbide's corporate director of health, safety, and environmental affairs, appeared on the "NBC Nightly News." He acknowledged the report but said it had not been forwarded to Bhopal as a warning, because "It was not immediately apparent that it would have been helpful."[8]

The most likely cause of the Bhopal leak was water contamination. If it is proved that Union Carbide did not take appropriate precautions, and that the company was lax in protecting the health and welfare of workers and residents in Bhopal, this would greatly (an understatement, to be sure) affect the outcome of the multibillion-dollar litigation in which the company will be immersed for some time.

By the way, prior to Bhopal, no corrective steps were taken at the Institute plant, either.

So, in the case of Union Carbide, as with TMI, there was a report or a memo that identified a prodrome—a precrisis situation—and properly and loudly sounded the crisis clarion.

Only, apparently, again as with TMI, to fall on deaf ears. And as we'll see later on, when we take a closer look at what went wrong at Union Carbide, such inaction can be devastating.

It does not appear that it would be excessively costly for a multibillion-dollar corporation with numerous and similar plants around the world to establish an internal "prodrome" link among its plant operators. This is part of crisis management planning, as well as part of a good crisis management plan.

Perhaps this hook-up could be in the form of a daily Telex or wire service in which one plant manager reports a possible prodrome situation he or she has uncovered and either warns fellow managers to take proper steps to avoid the same sort of situation or asks them whether they have experienced similar problems and, if so, how they managed them.

Given the highly volatile nature of crises, a high-speed prodrome link-up is far more pragmatic today than merely writing memos or "bringing it up" at the next meeting—whenever that may be.

And to be *really* effective, open lines of communications among competing, high-risk companies or through industry groups perhaps could be established to warn of impending dangerous situations. (The United States and the Soviet Union do it.)

This, after all, is the height of effective crisis management—crisis *avoidance* techniques. And when carried out successfully, the players involved may never even know they have sidestepped a potential crisis.

But what makes the recognition of a prodromal situation so imperative to successful crisis management is that *only* a prodrome can be aborted; only a precrisis can be averted.

Once the acute crisis hits, there is no turning back.

2

A Crisis Defined

Chance is the pseudonym God uses when He'd rather not sign His own name.

—*Anatole France*

Webster's defines a crisis as a "turning point for better or worse"; as a "decisive moment" or "crucial time."

It also defines a crisis as "a situation that has reached a critical phase."

A crisis is an unstable time or state of affairs in which a decisive change is impending—either one with the distinct possibility of a highly undesirable outcome or one with the distinct possibility of a highly *desirable* and extremely *positive* outcome. It is usually a 50–50 proposition, but you can improve the odds.

Anyone who can predict and plan for a crisis—substitute the phrase "turning point" if you have trouble putting the erroneously negative connotation of the word "crisis" out of your mind—anyone who can predict and plan for a *turning point* in his or her business or personal life stands a far better chance of capitalizing on that opportunity than someone who allows the crisis to sneak up on him or her unprepared.

Contrary to popular belief, a crisis, then, is not necessarily bad. It is merely characterized by a certain degree of risk and uncertainty.

Crisis management—planning for a crisis, a turning point—is the art of removing much of the risk and uncertainty to allow you to achieve more control over your own destiny.

From a practical, business-oriented point of view, a crisis (a turning point) is *any prodromal situation that runs the risk of:*

1. Escalating in intensity.
2. Falling under close media or government scrutiny.
3. Interfering with the normal operations of business.

4. Jeopardizing the positive public image presently enjoyed by a company or its officers.
5. Damaging a company's bottom line in any way.

If any or all of these developments occur, the turning point most likely will take a turn for the worse. (As Webster's stated: a turning point for better *or* worse.)

Therefore, there is every reason to assume that if a situation runs the risk of escalating in intensity, that same situation—if caught and dealt with in time—may not escalate. Instead, it may very conveniently dissipate, be resolved.

Instead of front-page exposés in the *Wall Street Journal,* the media may never link your name or the name of your company to any adverse condition or crisis.

Rather than interfere with your business operations, the phrase "business as usual" may become your watchword.

What you may not realize is that you probably avert prodromal situations every day of your business life, but you may not be aware of it because you do it so adroitly that it has become a part of your regular routine. You would notice it only if something really out of the ordinary were occurring. But when nothing adverse occurs, you may not be aware that your mundane, business-as-usual business is ahead of the game if only because the alternatives may be devastating.

Vic Braden, the tennis teacher, advises his students to watch the boring, repetitive strokes of the great tennis players. The ones, it seems, who constantly win are the ones who are content to return the ball over the net, time after time after time. Chris Evert Lloyd, one of the world's greatest women tennis players, has been accused of playing very boring tennis. She stands at the baseline and returns almost anything hit on her side of the net. For some it may be boring to watch, but her banker doesn't think so.

Braden tries to instill the same repetitive boredom in his students. It's called winning.

You are winning when you avert prodromal situations. You are practicing crisis management. You run your business or your department by certain tried and true measures. You keep your antennae up for anything out of the routine. Usually when something out of place or character develops, you are in a position to deal with it because you have handled similar situations routinely before.

Consider two alternative responses to the same prodromal situation—a potential situation common to many businesses.

SITUATION #1

You are the company treasurer, and one of your duties is to handle the payroll. It's two days before payday, but your accounts receivable have been running late this month and you won't be able to meet the payroll with current cash on hand. It's happened before. You call your banker, arrange a short-term loan (or draw down on an already established line of credit) to meet the payroll, and repay the note when your receivables come in.

The prodrome was the shortage of cash. The treasurer averted a crisis by perceptively spotting the prodrome and taking corrective crisis management measures.

No crisis; no turning point. But, let's consider the other alternative.

SITUATION #2

Assume the same cash flow situation as above. But, this time the company treasurer has suddenly been called out of town on a personal emergency.

You are the CEO, and the data processing manager has just brought you the computer-generated payroll checks for your signature, just the way she always does. You assume everything is fine and sign your name on the dotted line of a crisis.

The checks bounce.

Although it takes no time to realize what has happened and your banker immediately begins to cover the checks, rumors begin to fly that your company is going belly-up: "They can't even meet their payroll."

The next day a story appears in the newspaper and you are accurately quoted as having said, "While it is true that all of our employees' payroll checks bounced, it really was just a small problem that we took care of. All of our employees have been repaid. We have made good on every check. And these damn rumors that we are going out of business are just not true."

This protest only fuels the crisis fire.

Some of your suppliers see the story and begin to get nervous about the size of your account with them. They demand immediate payment on the outstanding balance and refuse to extend you additional credit. All further shipments will be C.O.D.

Without the credit—*every* company operates on credit—your cash flow does indeed get worse, and you have to borrow more money to meet expenses. Your debt ratio grows and your banker starts to apply pressure on you to reduce your debt with his bank.

Meanwhile, employee morale is at an all-time low. The internal rumors are worse than the external ones. Some of your key executives resign—some to work for your competitors, others to go into business against you.

You sue them all—old competitors, new competitors, and former employees—for a violation of the Trade Secrets Act and for a breach of fiduciary responsibilities.

The cost of the litigation is astronomical.

More stories appear in the media about the lawsuits and about how badly your business has been hurt. The stories are true.

Eventually, those once ill-founded rumors turn into gospel. Your company cannot escape the dire financial straits it has gotten itself into. Your company either (a) goes out of business; (b) files for Chapter 11 protection; (c) is taken over by the bank; (d) is taken over by outside financial interests. Take your pick.

Is any of this possible? All of it.

Is any of this *probable?* Not for an astute manager.

Such an executive is so adept at spotting potential trouble spots and prodromal situations that, if placed in this CEO's shoes, he or she would have made sure that the assistant treasurer or someone else was on top of things while the treasurer was out of town.

(Most likely the treasurer—being the responsible person and crisis manager he is—made certain before leaving town either that the situation was under control or that someone, either a superior or subordinate, would be vigilant for any untoward occurrence.)

But let's go back to that first scenario for a moment.

By making just one telephone call to the bank, the treasurer averted an acute crisis. He literally could be given credit for saving the company.

But is he? Certainly not. Part of his job is to make certain that no financial crises occur over such routine matters as meeting a payroll.

Does he realize how close he could have come to putting hundreds of employees out of work? Does he know the company could have teetered on the brink of financial ruin and collapse if he hadn't made that call? Not at all.

Nor is it likely that at any point when the company's financial systems were being developed did anyone envision a possible scenario such as Situation #2. Someone probably just said ". . . and let's make damn sure we don't ever have any screw-ups with our payroll," and that form of crisis management was good enough for them.

But is this *really* crisis management? Yes. Any measure that plans in advance for a crisis (or turning point)—any measure that removes the risk and uncertainty from a given situation and thereby allows you to be more in control of your own destiny—is indeed a form of crisis management.

Can you recall, from when you were young, being cautioned to bring two pencils to school on the day of a test? In the event one pencil point broke, you would be prepared to continue on with the exam, unfazed by the mishap.

That was a form of crisis management.

And when you prepare for a long automobile trip, do you remember to have the car checked over carefully, to fill up the gas tank, to check the tires and under the hood, and to be sure to wear your seat belt?

These, too, are forms of crisis management.

So crisis management in its most basic form—being prepared—is nothing new to most of us.

Then why is it so alien to so many managers and to so many businesses? Why do so many negative crises occur? Why are so many obvious warning signs missed?

Is it a case of not being able to see the forest for the trees?

Or of not being able to see the prodromes for the profits?

It's hard to tell because the content of every crisis changes, as do the players. But the four phases of a crisis are almost always the same. And knowing these phases will give you an important edge.

3

Anatomy of a Crisis

Life is lived in the vast complexity of the gray.

—*Thomas Merton*

A crisis can consist of as many as four different and distinct phases. And if their names sound medically rooted, it is because a crisis can be viewed as a disease. The phases are:

Prodromal crisis stage
Acute crisis stage
Chronic crisis stage
Crisis resolution stage

In many illnesses, the duration and intensity of the symptoms will be a function of several variables, such as the strain of the virus, the age and medical condition of the patient, the potency of the medication or treatment, and the skill of the physician. Sometimes, all four phases may occur within a very short space of time, as in the case of the 24-hour flu. At other times, there is an extended, long-fused prodrome. The same is true of crises.

And, whereas in some cases the acute flu stage passes but a chronic cough lingers for a while before the patient recovers, a crisis can follow a similar path toward its resolution.

But, as we know, there are times when the acute flu stage develops into pneumonia and the patient dies. And there are times when a crisis has no resolution, except for the demise of the company involved.

A crisis is a fluid, unstable, dynamic situation—just like an illness. And it must be ministered to in much the same way. With both an illness and a crisis, things are in a state of constant flux.

When you recognize the prodromes of a possible medical ailment, such as the flu, you intervene as soon as possible by taking aspirin or some other medication, drinking fluids, and getting into bed. The operative word, of course, is *recognize*. You have to recognize the prodrome in order to intervene proactively.

Not all crises have all four of these stages, but they can't have any more. By dissecting a crisis and taking a closer, microscopic look at each phase, you may be better able to spot these stages in the future.

THE PRODROMAL CRISIS STAGE

As discussed previously, the prodromal crisis stage is the warning stage, if there is any warning stage. In many instances, this is the real turning point, too. And (as with Union Carbide, as we shall see later), if the turning point, the prodrome, is missed entirely, the acute crisis can strike with such swiftness that so-called crisis management after the fact is, in reality, merely damage control.

Occasionally the prodromal crisis stage is referred to as the precrisis stage. But usually that appellation is used *after* the acute crisis has hit, when, in retrospect, people look back on a series of events and point to something as a "precrisis." ("If only we/they had/had not done such and such.")

But since everyone has 20–20 hindsight through the "retrospecto-scope," our task is to sharpen our antennae to be able to spot the prodromes before, not after, the acute crisis occurs.

A prodrome may be as obvious as a union leader telling management that unless a new contract is negotiated within a specified period of time, labor will strike. If you are the CEO of that company, or manager of the labor relations department, you recognize it as a warning—a prodrome—and the consequences of your actions, or nonactions, have been made clear to you.

A prodrome may be oblique and much harder to recognize, however. In the Three Mile Island episode, for example, one prodrome was cheating on tests.

And sometimes the prodrome is evident, but no action is taken and an acute crisis occurs—as with the warning memo written 13 months before the TMI accident. This may be as a result of "analysis paralysis" or obsessive decision making, both of which will be discussed.

The reason why prodromes are so important to catch is that it is so much easier to manage a crisis in the prodromal stage. As with many illnesses, while it is possible to save the patient's life during the acute stage, it is much safer and more reliable to take care of the problem before it becomes acute, before it erupts and causes possible complications.

But it is also important to remember that if you recognize the pro-drome but are unable to dispose of it for whatever reason, just knowing or having a sense of what is about to happen will help you to prepare for the acute crisis stage.

Sailors at sea who spot the ominous prodrome of fast-gathering storm clouds off in the horizon have no power to stop the acute storm. But knowing what is about to happen gives them the opportunity to batten down the hatches, head for shore, and just generally brace themselves and their ship for the inevitable acute crisis.

THE ACUTE CRISIS STAGE

In many ways, this is the point of no return. Once the warnings have ended and you have passed from the prodromal into the acute crisis stage, you can almost never recover the ground you lost. *Some* damage has been done; how much additional damage occurs depends on you.

It is usually the acute crisis stage which most people have in mind when they speak of a crisis.

Most people would tell you, for example, that the Three Mile Island "crisis" began on March 28, 1979, and ended about a week later. That is incorrect.

The Three Mile Island *crisis* began at least 13 months *before* March 28, 1979 (the warning, or prodrome, memo cited earlier), and the crisis *is still going on.*

However, the *acute crisis stage* of the overall TMI crisis did begin on March 28, 1979, and did end about a week later.

If the prodromal phase alerts you to the fact that a hot spot is brewing, the acute crisis phase tells you that it has erupted. With proper advance planning, it will not explode in your face. With proper advance planning, you may choose when and where *you* want it to erupt, giving yourself not only time to prepare, but more ability to control the flow, the speed, the direction, and the duration of the crisis.

Going back to our sailor friends for a moment, if they realize that they cannot make it back to shore before the storm hits, they at least have an opportunity to pick the spot where they feel they will be in the most advantageous position to weather the storm intact.

Perhaps they are too close to hidden reefs and they fear the raging storm may dash their ship against some rocks. They have the opportunity and the time to move to the open sea, if they calculate that as their best alternative.

The key is to control as much of the crisis as you can. If you can't control the actual crisis, see if you can exert some degree of influence over where, how, and when the crisis erupts.

The next time the White House press office releases some unfavorable news—not critical, fast-breaking news, just something that the Administration might like to have swept under the rug if it could—observe *when* the news is released. Is it released early in the morning at a 10 A.M. press briefing, which allows the media (especially the television network news reporters) the balance of the day to ferret out more facts and perhaps make the story even more unfavorable for the Administration?

Or is it released close to media deadlines quite late in the day (or even on a Friday afternoon), which may have the desired effect of forcing the media to go with the story "as is"—meaning as the White House wants the story controlled—or maybe not even using the story or giving it much "play"?

If you are a member of the news media, you may object to this manner of "controlling the news."

The White House, though, sees it as "damage control." If you are the White House and you perceive a prodrome in a story that you have to release, you have the option to choose when and where the story is released to minimize potential damage or get more control over the acute crisis phase of the story.

One of the major difficulties in managing a crisis during the acute phase—even if you are ready for it—is the avalanchelike speed and intensity that often accompany and characterize this stage. The speed is dependent primarily on the type of crisis, while the intensity is usually determined by the severity or value of the possible outcome(s).

If you can gauge both the potential speed and the intensity while you are still in the prodromal stage, you will be that much farther ahead in preparing for managing and controlling a crisis through the acute stage.

No matter how long you may feel you are in the eye of an acute crisis hurricane, this is often the shortest of the four phases. But, because of its intensity, it often may feel as though it is the longest phase.

That designation, however, usually belongs to phase three.

THE CHRONIC CRISIS STAGE

It is during this stage that the carcass gets picked clean. Assuming, of course, that a carcass remains to be picked.

This is sometimes called the clean-up phase, or the post-mortem. If there is to be a congressional investigation, or an audit, or a newspaper exposé, or a long period of interviews and explanations and *mea culpas,* this is when such lingering malignancies settle in.

This is also a period of recovery, of self-analysis, of self-doubt, and of healing.

With good crisis management skills, it also may become a time for congratulations and for plaudits and for testimonials.

Skillful managers will also use it wisely as a good time for further crisis management planning—analyzing what went right or what went wrong and taking appropriate actions.

Or it may be a time for financial upheaval, management shake-ups, hostile takeover attempts, or bankruptcy.

The chronic stage can linger indefinitely. But crisis management plans can, and do, shorten this phase. A survey of the *Fortune* 500 chief executive officers, taken for this book and reported on in detail in Chapter 8, revealed that those companies *without* a crisis management plan reported suffering lingering effects of a chronic crisis as much as two and a half times longer than companies that were prepared with a crisis management plan.

More than six years after the *acute* crisis at Three Mile Island, which the Philadelphia *Inquirer* called the "accident without an end," the chronic crisis stage lingers on. Just consider the following facts:[9]

• The clean-up on the damaged reactor, TMI-2, is *still* going on.

• The clean-up, originally estimated in 1979 to take two years and cost $200 million, now *may* be completed by the end of the 1980s and will cost at least five times as much: $1 billion. Already $500 million has been spent.

• The *un*damaged reactor, TMI-1, which was in a cold shutdown during the acute crisis, was not allowed to restart for *six and a half years*— until October 1985.

• TMI-related investigations are *still* in progress.

• It took almost six years (until February 1985) to settle 280 out of 300 injury claims against General Public Utilities Corporation. These claims were filed by residents who lived within 25 miles of the plant and who claimed damages from emotional stress.

• Two other claims—on behalf of children who allegedly suffered birth defects as a result of the radiation—also took more than six years to settle. The largest settlement, for $1.9 million, went to a child who was born with Down's syndrome within a year of the acute crisis at TMI. Another settlement, for $855,000, was awarded to an infant born with cerebral palsy.

• The disaster that *almost* occurred at Three Mile Island did more to spur nuclear protests and reexaminations, and to place the entire nuclear power industry under a high-powered microscope, than any other event in our history.

• An 11-count criminal indictment was returned against the utility by a federal grand jury, and, in a separate matter, one criminal indictment was returned against one employee. Met Ed pleaded guilty in 1984 to one of the 11 counts, a felony charge of falsifying plant records prior to the accident, and paid more than $1 million, both in fines and to establish a special emergency preparedness fund for the community. The company pleaded "nolo contendere" (no defense) on six of the other counts and plea-bargained the remaining four counts to dismissal. The employee, James Floyd (supervisor of operations at TMI-2 at the time of the accident, although he was not present when it happened), was convicted by a jury trial of cheating on an operator's exam. In lieu of a prison sentence, he received a two-year probationary sentence, was fined $2,000, and was ordered to perform 400 hours of community service.

• Since 1979 TMI has been cited more than 60 times in dangerous radiation-exposure instances.

The chronic phase for TMI's owners still goes on and on.

THE CRISIS RESOLUTION STAGE

It is this fourth and final stage that should be the crisis management goal during the preceding three phases. This is when the patient is well and whole again.

When a prodrome is spotted, your objective as a crisis manager is to seize control swiftly and calculate the most direct and expedient route to achieving a resolution of the crisis. Your goal is to turn the turning point into an opportunity for you.

But if the prodrome slips by unchecked, your actions and decisions during the acute and chronic crisis stages should be guided by the thought: "What can I do to speed up this phase and resolve this crisis once and for all?"

But beware and be advised: crises historically evolve in cyclical fashion, and a crisis sufferer almost never has the luxury of dealing exclusively with one crisis at a time.

In reality, as you may already have discovered, the light of resolution you begin to see at the end of one crisis tunnel usually is the prodromal light of an oncoming crisis.

That would be bad enough, if it weren't also for the acute whistle of another crisis sneaking up behind you in the same tunnel.

And the rumbling noise you hear all around you is the chronic crumbling of the tunnel itself.

As you can see, because crises are not tiered on a convenient plateau

Figure 1. What *one* crisis cycle *may* look like.

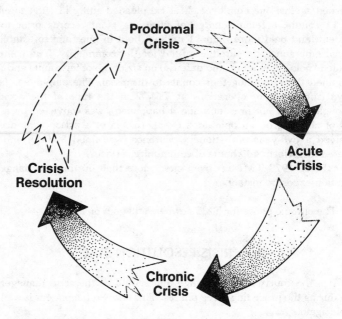

Figure 2. What you would *like* your crisis cycle to look like.

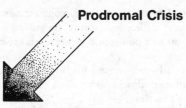

Figure 3. What *your* crisis cycles look or feel like to you.

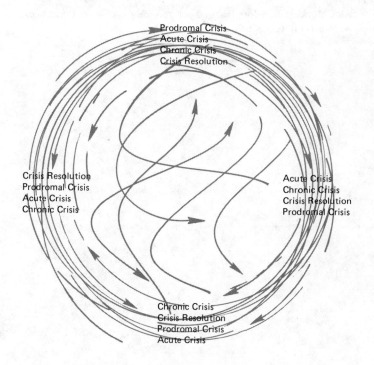

system, the crisis cycle makes it difficult to see where and when one crisis ends and another begins (see Figures 1–3). This is especially true in situations where the ripple-effect complications of one crisis set off other crises.

This is why, as we will discuss later, it is so critical to be able to identify the *real* crisis.

Because when crises come, they can come in pairs. Or bunches, or thundering herds.

And a crisis, like life itself, is almost never cut and dried; never black and white.

As Columbia Pictures learned not too long ago, a real crisis comes in full, wide-screen Technicolor.

4

Hollywoodgate

When you have eliminated all that is impossible, then whatever remains, however improbable, must be the truth.

—*Sherlock Holmes*

Alan Hirschfield was a man who was loved by his family, admired by his peers, and respected by the thousands of employees under his command.

His company, Columbia Pictures, was a leader in its field, at the time riding the crest of several highly publicized and immensely profitable business waves, such as the hugely successful worldwide opening of *Close Encounters of the Third Kind*.

He was bicoastal, owning luxurious homes in Beverly Hills and Scarsdale and well-appointed offices in Burbank and New York.

Hirschfield was highly regarded by Wall Street as an astute businessman. Profits were up; stock prices were up; everything, it seemed, was up.

Everything, that is, except one little nagging problem that just wouldn't go away.

It seemed that David Begelman, who was the head of the Columbia studio (Hirschfield was president and CEO of the corporate entity, and Begelman reported directly to him), had been caught with his hand in the company cookie jar. Begelman—one of Hirschfield's most valuable, trusted, and highly compensated employees, and a man who in many ways actually ran the company—was privately accused of misappropriating a small amount of company funds.

"Privately" means that, in the beginning and for an incredibly long period of time, only the smallest group of inner-circle people (who certainly wouldn't talk) knew about the situation.

"A small amount" was, at first, thought to be $10,000, which to most people is anything but a small amount. But to the people and the studio involved, it was only a notch or two above "insignificant." And Begelman certainly did not *need* the money.

And "misappropriation" was merely a euphemism for embezzlement.

Oh—and Begelman did this by forging actor Cliff Robertson's name on a Columbia check that he (Begelman) had feloniously issued to Robertson, without the actor's knowledge.

Let's briefly review what has been termed "Hollywoodgate" and trace it through the four phases of a crisis.

In early 1977 Cliff Robertson received an IRS 1099 form from Columbia Pictures, which showed that the actor had been paid $10,000 by the studio in 1976. Robertson knew this was incorrect and asked his secretary, Evelyn Christel, to investigate.

Christel's inquiries eventually brought the matter to the attention of Dick Caudillo, Columbia's accounts payable supervisor, who checked the Robertson file, examined an endorsed $10,000 check made out to Robertson, but thought the signature looked suspiciously like Begelman's.

Caudillo briefed his boss, Louis Phillips, the studio controller, who also was suspicious.

Phillips alerted his boss, James T. Johnson, vice president for administration.

Johnson had enough questions to bring into the picture *his* boss, Joseph A. Fischer, senior vice president and chief financial officer of Columbia Pictures Industries, the studio's parent company. Fischer took one look at the check and basically confirmed what everyone else either knew or suspected: it was Begelman's distinctive scrawl on the check.

Fischer told his boss about the check. His boss was Alan Hirschfield, chairman of the board of Columbia Pictures Industries.

And James Johnson raised the question with Begelman. Not that anyone suspected that he had forged a check; just that Cliff Robertson's people were making noises about this $10,000 on a 1099 form. Begelman said he'd handle it.

It was June 1977. Five months had elapsed since Cliff Robertson had first brought the matter to light.

At this point, the crisis was still in the prodromal stage. There were enough people in authority who knew, felt, believed, suspected—whatever—that something was fishy. One of them—Begelman—not only knew what was wrong, he decided to "fix" it.

On June 6, 1977, Begelman took the first step in bringing "Hollywoodgate" from the prodromal crisis stage into the acute crisis stage.

Columbia studio people had a hard time believing that Begelman would commit a crime. Even if he were going to commit a crime, why *that* type of crime?

Begelman certainly did not have to forge or embezzle to get $10,000 out of the studio if he needed it. There were so many other easier, legitimate ways.

With Begelman, it was the inconceivability of both the sort of crime and the person involved, measured against the small gain, that had people fooled for so long.

But on June 6, 1977, Begelman told his first lie: he told Cliff Robertson's accountant that a fictitious young man in Columbia's New York office had written a check to Robertson and forged the actor's endorsement; the accounting department had automatically issued the 1099 form, Begelman said. But the lad had been fired, the IRS would be issued a correction, and nobody really wants to prosecute the kid. OK?

OK.

Except that Robertson's insatiable curiosity demanded to know how a kid in New York would be able to:

1. Cut a check in the first place.
2. Cash—not deposit—it 3,000 miles away at a Beverly Hills bank.
3. Forge Robertson's well-known name and get away with it.

How indeed? Something was rotten at Columbia, and as the odor got stronger the prodromal crisis began rapidly escalating into an acute crisis.

Within a few months, the forgery, the embezzlement, the lies, and the cheating had all caught up with Begelman. Hirschfield confronted him, wanted to fire him, but didn't; couldn't. Begelman had strong, powerful friends on the Columbia board of directors, and they blindly rallied to his defense.

When Hirschfield confronted Begelman, the crisis was still prodromal and, surprisingly, still nonpublic. If Hirschfield had fired him and word got out why the termination took place, Columbia's response *could* have been quite candid: there were some irregularities with company funds, and, as a result, Begelman "resigned."

In reality, it is a virtual certainty that this sort of story never would have been issued—even if Hirschfield had fired Begelman at the first opportunity. Most likely there would have been a jointly approved announcement that nicely explained away Begelman's departure without ever mentioning or even hinting at the truth.

But Hirschfield did not fire him at that opportunity. And consequently Begelman's allies on the board started putting strong pressure on Hirschfield to give Begelman a second chance.

Alan Hirschfield, David Begelman, and Columbia Pictures were now closely intertwined in an acute crisis, during which time:

• Begelman confessed to the embezzlement but said it was the only time it had ever happened. He begged for a second chance and said he would seek professional help.

• Hirschfield, succumbing to the pressure of the board, gave Begelman another chance, but ordered an investigation to make sure that there were no "smoking pistols."

• The investigation revealed three additional improprieties similar to those in the Cliff Robertson affair. One involved a $5,000 check issued in 1975 to film director Martin Ritt. Another concerned a $35,000 contract and payment to a Peter Choate for acoustical work done on the motion picture *Tommy*. Choate was a local architect and house designer, and Begelman had recently hired him to design a screening room in his home. In the third and most elaborate scam, Begelman had the studio lawyers draw up a $25,000 contract for Pierre Groleau for marketing consulting services in connection with two French-made films. Begelman immediately opened a checking account in Monsieur Groleau's name and began writing checks on the account. Groleau knew nothing about the contract. He was the maître d' at the fashionable Ma Maison restaurant in Los Angeles.

• Hirschfield was repeatedly thwarted by the board in his attempts to oust Begelman.

• Hirschfield did agree to a Begelman "leave of absence" for a time.

• And the media finally began snooping around.

The full events of the Columbia Pictures/Begelman affair were well described in David McClintick's exposé, *Indecent Exposure*. In it, he quoted Rona Barrett's January 3, 1978, television report:

A comic scenario is currently being played out in the corporate corridors of Columbia Pictures that would make a dandy little film farce, should any producer like to do to movies what *Network* did to television. The situation in question centers around the return of David Begelman to the presidency of Columbia Pictures. His present reinstatement has caused executives who abandoned support of Begelman during the controversy to quickly learn some new routines now that all has been forgiven. The name of the game at Columbia now is: tell David we love him—and the refrain reads: and we always did. Just how many can fool some of the people enough of the time remains to be seen. What is for certain is that over the next few weeks and months, no less than seven major periodicals are planning in-depth reports on Begelman, the man and his machinations. Therefore, don't look for the heat to be out of this kitchen yet.[10]

Among the periodicals referred to were the *Wall Street Journal,* the Washington *Post,* the New York *Times,* and *Esquire* and *New West* magazines.

Unquestionably, this was the acute crisis. The turning point for Hirschfield—to fire Begelman or not—had come and gone. Now, Hirschfield was into damage control.

The story had gotten out. Oh, had it gotten out. And following this acute phase, the crisis got chronically worse. During this chronic phase of the crisis:

• The entertainment media had a field day with what they termed "Hollywoodgate."

• Because Columbia is a public company, other, more conventional news media (such as those just cited) ran major features on the scandal.

• Law enforcement agencies in Los Angeles and Beverly Hills either began or heated up their investigations into the original crime of forgery.

• Again, because Columbia is a public company, the Securities and Exchange Commission began its own investigation.

• Hirschfield had a near-impossible task of running the studio. There were occasions when people he wanted to hire wouldn't consider working at Columbia because of the internal fighting and the external investigations.

• The internal fighting, which consumed massive amounts of Hirschfield's time and energies, involved influential board members who were displeased with Hirschfield, with Hirschfield's handling of the Begelman affair, and with the way Hirschfield was running the studio. Actually, "running the studio" was something these board members were making it difficult for Hirschfield to do.

• Begelman, it seemed, was an on-again/off-again studio head. One day he was in, the next day he was out; then he was back in—as head of the studio or as an independent producer working with, or for, Columbia. Or not. It was not easy to follow this movement, even with a scorecard. And very few people had scorecards, although a lot of people were trying to keep score.

• The price of Columbia's stock grew anemic.

• Hirschfield perceived that there would be a power struggle on the board and that he stood a good chance of being ousted himself. More large chunks of his time were consumed by looking for a "White Knight"—a company that would acquire Columbia, install its own board, and, naturally, retain Hirschfield. Hirschfield also at one point considered waging a proxy fight and/or putting together backers to buy the studio himself. Although the company eventually was sold to Coca-Cola, this was not of Hirschfield's doing.

• Hirschfield's reputation was greatly damaged.

• Hirschfield's wife's moral character, integrity, and honesty were impugned. (There was no substantive basis for this, but it was a way to hurt Hirschfield.)

All of this happened because of one man's—Begelman's—actions and one man's—Hirschfield's—inactions, or, to be more precise, Hirschfield's lack of prompt action, or his inability to effect a swift and sure resolution to the crisis.

A crisis sufferer should be cautious about splintered, or spinoff, crises. One crisis tends to bring about other crises, which, although tied to the main crisis, may not necessarily be settled when the main crisis is resolved.

One major crisis resolution for Columbia came about at a July 1978 board of directors meeting when, by a vote of 5–2, the Columbia board voted not to renew Hirschfield's contract.

He had been fired. And the crisis of dealing with Hirschfield had been "resolved" by the board.

But Columbia still had to suffer certain lasting chronic effects of the crisis, such as ongoing investigations.

Begelman was originally fined $5,000 and sentenced to three years' probation for felony grand theft; however, the sentence was later reduced. As part of his punishment he also produced an antidrug film, *Angel Death,* about the drug PCP, or angel dust.

In terms of benchmarks, it is accurate to point to Columbia's sale to Coca-Cola as the real crisis resolution. The selling price—cash and stock in the soft-drink company—came to close to $800 million.

Begelman's chronic crisis was resolved when he wound up making movies at MGM.

Hirschfield's personal and business crises could be said to have been resolved when he landed on his feet at Twentieth Century–Fox.

So, was there a crisis? Certainly.

As a direct and indisputable result of Hirschfield not firing Begelman when he should have, the situation:

1. Escalated in intensity.
2. Fell under extremely close scrutiny of the news media, the Securities and Exchange Commission, and local law enforcement agencies.
3. Interfered tremendously with the normal operations of the studio.
4. Severely jeopardized Hirschfield's, Begelman's, and Columbia's reputations.
5. And hurt the company on Wall Street.

Furthermore, not only did the Begelman affair put Columbia under the microscope, but it attracted such attention that the Los Angeles District Attorney's office established an Entertainment Industry Task Force to investigate wrongdoing in the industry. A special hotline was installed in the event anyone wanted to make anonymous tips. Within two years, the task force had received more than 600 tips—some quite substantial—involving virtually every major film studio in Hollywood.

A crisis does not occur in a vacuum. Each crisis has a ripple effect on the lives of others.

It is well worth considering when making decisions in the midst of a crisis: how will your actions affect others?

In the epilogue to his book, McClintick wrote:

> In reflective moments, Begelman occasionally remarked to friends on the number of lives that had been affected directly or indirectly by the events the Cliff Robertson forgery had set in motion. The number surely was in the hundreds and perhaps the thousands. The entire entertainment community had been shaken. Four of the seven major studios—Columbia, Fox, MGM, and United Artists—had changed drastically. . . .[11]

And of all those hundreds or thousands whose lives had been so affected by Begelman's actions, Hirschfield—the man who at one time had the power to terminate the situation before it reached crisis proportions— clearly was the person whose life was the most affected by the crisis.

In McClintick's closing chapter, he had Hirschfield ruminating over the incredible events:

> Ten months of ugliness, ten months of infighting, ten months of secret maneuvering—the most horrific months of his [Hirschfield's] life. Was it possible that all of this had started with an IRS form and a forged check? To say it was farfetched was to understate the radical improbability of the whole affair.[12]

"The radical improbability of the whole affair" indeed.

Was that it? Did the crisis take place because of "the radical improbability of the whole affair"?

Does that "radical improbability" statement suggest that if Hirschfield had known precisely what the probabilities were in the equation, then the crisis would not have occurred? Or that if he had found a way to forecast the profound effect the crisis would have—on himself, on the studio, on *everyone*—then he would have taken proper preventive actions?

There *is* a model—a method of proaction/reaction—that may help if used properly.

5

Crisis Forecasting

Everyone talks about the weather, but no one does anything about it.

—*Mark Twain*

What is the worst thing that could happen?

Think about it seriously for a moment, or longer. Everybody is afraid of something. What are *you* afraid of?

Death (yours or anyone else's) aside, what is the single worst thing that you can envision happening that would cause you to say, "I'm (or "We're" or "My business is") ruined"?

If you were the President of the United States, you might say nuclear war.

If you were an executive working in a foreign country, you might consider the threat of a terrorist kidnapping to be the worst thing that could happen.

If you marshaled all of your company's financial resources behind a new product and set that product afloat in uncharted marketing waters, only to find that your flawed market research failed to reveal that a deep-pocket competitor was about to launch its own version of a similar product, you very well might consider that to be a devastating crisis with enormous consequences.

But how about you? What is the worst thing that could happen to *you*, your business, your division?

In order to create a worst-case/what-if scenario model for crisis forecasting, "You need people who can conceptualize about what-if questions; people who can see where the assumptions take you," according to Texaco's general manager for strategic planning, Clement B. Malin. "The imagination of man can be infinite in cases like this."

But, as Malin knows, it takes courage to make assumptions.

He went on to explain:

At Texaco, we ask questions like "What is the environment in which a situation is developing, and if you don't like what you see, how can you change it?" Or "What can go wrong and what would you do to change it?" Next, we present to management a variety of courses of actions designed to meet specific goals and objectives.[13]

This involves presenting a range of bracketed possibilities (for example, high/low, good/bad). But certain signposts are checked along the way to see what is happening at particular points and to enable management to fine-tune anything that may require a mid-course correction.

Let's assume you've assumed the worst. Now, how likely is it that the crisis that you have just envisioned for yourself will ever happen?

Is there a "slim chance" that it could happen?

How about a "once in a blue moon" chance?

Or would you call the odds "pretty good"?

Assume that it's possible to assign a numerical value to the weight, or impact, of your crisis. The number that we arrive at would be the Crisis Impact Value, or CIV, on a low-to-high impact scale of 0 to 10.

The Crisis Impact Value will tell us how damaging a crisis *may* be *if* there is *no* crisis intervention. If a crisis hits and nothing is done to stop it, avert it, control it, or abort it, the Crisis Impact Value will give us a reasonably close estimate of the effects, the ramifications, and the cost in dollars and/or the cost in lives.

How is this possible? By doing *before* a crisis hits what you certainly would do *after* a crisis strikes. And this may be done companywide by the CEO and senior management, or division by division, manager by manager.

After any crisis—a business crisis, a hurricane, an earthquake, a fire, and so on—someone calculates the damage estimate. This is a figure, often arrived at in the heat of the moment by a combination of company officials, government officials, and/or reporters—and then later calculated more accurately by cost accountants—that reports how much the crisis cost and how much it will cost to get back to business as usual.

Your task is simply to perform the damage estimate *now*, within certain parameters of confidence, well *before* the potential crisis strikes.

And within those parameters of confidence, you will be asked to make certain subjective evaluations on a series of 10-point scales. But despite the subjectivity, keep in mind that it is *your* subjective crisis that is under consideration.

What you may consider a crisis may be nothing of the kind to someone else. One person's crisis may be another's glory. Some people may think that it is devastating to have an exposé-type story appear in print; others may think that any publicity is good publicity as long as their name is spelled right.

So for accurate forecasting, as Shakespeare might have said, "To thine own crisis be true." Do not worry how some blip on a radar screen will affect your competitors; ask how it will affect *you*.

In so doing, you will be able to plot a Crisis Impact Value for a potential crisis and know, in advance, how badly it could turn out—or how well.

Take the potential crisis you were asked to consider at the start of this chapter and ask yourself these five questions:

QUESTION #1

If your crisis runs the risk of escalating in intensity, how intense might it get, and how quickly? What degree of intensity can you or your company endure, and for how long? What, in your opinion, constitutes "intense"? A flood of angry telephone calls? A burst of vitriolic hate mail? Mass resignations from employees? A sudden rise in your blood pressure? A suspicious pattern of canceled customer orders? You are the only one who can determine what levels or degrees of intensity are acceptable. How much heat can you take before you have to leave the kitchen?

Now score your response to the initial question: if your crisis escalates in intensity, how intense might it get *for you?* Score from 0 to 10, with 0 being lowest and 10 being highest.

QUESTION #2

To what extent would your crisis fall under someone's watchful eye, such as the news media or some government regulatory agency?

If yours is a public company, you already know that you operate in a fishbowl. Any irregularity may be written about by the *Wall Street Journal, Investor's Daily,* or the business sections of local newspapers or weekly business or news magazines.

And what sort of news coverage might ensue? A small "filler" item buried deep in the back pages of a newspaper, or a full-scale, multiseries exposé of the questionable way your business operates and why your crisis was inevitable?

If yours is a public company, you also know that you are at risk of having this "irregularity" investigated by the Securities and Exchange

Commission or other regulatory body. (You know also that, depending on the nature of the irregularity, you may be required by law to report it yourself to the SEC and/or other appropriate agency.)

But public company or private, large or small, how closely would the media and/or government agency scrutinize your crisis?

Again, rate your answer on a 10-point scale, with 0 indicating no scrutiny at all and 10 standing for extreme scrutiny.

QUESTION #3

To what extent would your crisis interfere with the normal operations of your business?

Might it affect your ability to get your product to market on time, or at all? Might you run short of stock or have too much inventory?

Might the crisis impair your ability to meet a routine payroll or pay your creditors on time?

Is it possible that you will have to spend so much time dealing with the crisis that you will be unable to tend to other, more routine functions of your job properly?

And do not forget that a personal crisis can take up so much of your time, or occupy so much of your mind, that you are unable to deal with business effectively.

Think about the potential crisis. Think about what you might have to do. Think about how it might affect your business, and ask yourself whether or not—even in the midst of the crisis—you will still be doing "business as usual."

Or will there, in fact, be some measurable interference? Score between 0 (no interference) and 10 (maximum interference) the extent to which the crisis would interfere with the normal operations of your business.

QUESTION #4

There are crises in which you (or your company) are the victim, and there are those in which you are the culprit. Knowing the difference will help you to determine whether you stand to jeopardize the positive public image you and/or your company presently enjoy.

If you are the manager of an oil refinery and your operation explodes one night in a deadly ball of fire, you are suddenly in the midst of an acute crisis.

If the event occurred as the result of sabotage on the part of some terrorist group, you are the victim. Your company's public image may not be at risk if you were an innocent target.

If, however, the tragedy was the result of your careless operation, for which you had been cited several times in the past by a host of such agencies as the Occupational Safety and Health Administration, the Environmental Protection Agency, or even your union's health and welfare committee, you now are the culprit. The cause of the accident is now laid at your feet.

You are both culpable and liable.

And your positive public image is at serious risk.

The importance of actively pursuing a positive public image cannot be overstated. It can be viewed as money in the bank: the more favorable your image, the more you can "draw on" when you need it.

For example, during the summer of 1984, 21 people died at a McDonald's restaurant in San Ysidro, California. Obviously, had McDonald's in any way caused, or contributed to, the deaths of the 21 people, the fast-food chain might have suffered enormously in the ensuing crisis.

However, the deaths were caused when a deranged individual, James Huberty, who was in no way connected with McDonald's, went on a shooting rampage and opened fire on the restaurant's innocent patrons.

McDonald's might have become as much a victim as those who had been shot, but McDonald's did not die. While there was a temporary but noticeable drop in the chain's national sales as a result of the murders, it is not inaccurate to point to the firm's very high, positive public image as a major contributing factor in eradicating the tragedy from the public's memory.

A lesser establishment, one without so much image credit at the bank of public opinion, might not have weathered the crisis.

Think about the extent to which your company's public image and/or your personal reputation would be damaged in the event of your potential crisis. Score from 0 (no damage) to 10 (severe damage).

QUESTION #5

Finally, and to some most important, in the event of your potential crisis, to what extent would your company's (or division's or whatever) bottom line be damaged?

It is possible to endure a crisis that, despite its other adverse effects, does not particularly injure the company's profits, profit margin, profit potential, return on investment, return on equity, lines of credit, and so on.

Remember, however, that when you are assessing predamage damage control, do not think simply in terms of "hard dollars"—those figures that are easy to calculate onto or off of a bottom line. The damage control done by cost accountants, mentioned earlier, is typically estimated only in "hard dollars."

But to be as accurate as possible, you also should factor in "soft dollars"—such real but harder-to-measure costs as decreased productivity, low employee morale, increased absenteeism, stress, worker unrest, increased workers' compensation claims, unemployment insurance claims, continual negative public opinion and bad press, erosion of community support, and so on.

Consult with public relations, labor relations, and human resources/personnel professionals—even outside consultants—for guidance in putting together your estimates. It is important to do this because too often certain management decisions may be made based on the oversimplified reasoning that "our insurance will cover those losses if they happen."

The insurance may cover the hard-dollar losses but not the soft-dollar damages, which may be even more costly.

The insurance may cover the loss of life caused by your company's gross negligence; but your policy will not cover you against the losses you will sustain if the news media or the government begins a series of exposés or investigations into your company.

So, hard and soft dollars together: what is your opinion of your own potential crisis? Score, as before, from 0 (no cost) to 10 (crippling cost), based on your assessment of the extent to which your potential crisis would damage your bottom line.

Now total your five scores (with a possible maximum of 50) and divide that sum by 5 to arrive at the Crisis Impact Value of your potential crisis.

Then plot your Crisis Impact Value on a vertical scale from 0 to 10 (see Figure 4).

You now have a quantitative number, a Crisis Impact Value, that forecasts how much impact on you or on your business a potential crisis will have. You now have a numerical, more analytical, response to the question that started this chapter: "What is the worst thing that could happen?"

And after answering the question by coming up with a potential crisis, you now have a scale against which to (a) measure the crisis; (b) compare it to other crises; and (c) chart its upward or downward movement.

If, for an example, you have forecasted a situation with a Crisis Impact Value of 8.5, your goal can be to bring the potential Crisis Impact Value down to a "livable" number. Perhaps you scored 10 on the "interference with normal business operations" question. Search for alternative ways to conduct business *before* the crisis hits.

In other words, if you forecast that the crisis will present danger, then search for ways to create opportunity.

Figure 4. Crisis Impact Scale.

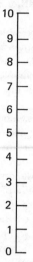

Score from 0 (lowest) to 10 (highest) the extent to which a potential crisis would:

1. Escalate in intensity.
2. Fall under close media or government scrutiny.
3. Interfere with the normal operations of business.
4. Jeopardize a positive public image.
5. Damage a company's bottom line.

Total all five scores, divide by 5, then plot your answer on the vertical Crisis Impact Scale.

Don't be reactive; be proactive. Take the initiative toward achievement. Find out which danger signs are causing your Crisis Impact Value (CIV) to be forecasted high. Then proactively seek alternative opportunities to eliminate or circumvent the danger.

As important as it is to assess the impact a potential crisis will have, it is equally important to gauge the probability that it will occur.

A 9.5 CIV situation that has a one-in-a-million chance of happening should obviously not receive as much intense attention as a 7.0 CIV situation that could happen tomorrow. Nor should it be ignored, however.

Therefore, the second step in forecasting is to couple the Crisis Impact Value with the Probability Factor.

Try to quantify such colorful phrases as "once in a blue moon," "a snowball's chance in hell," and "a pretty sure bet."

Using a numerical scale, try to be subjectively realistic within your own parameters of confidence, and determine whether there is a 10 percent chance that your potential crisis will occur. A 50 percent chance? A 70 percent chance?

Since the best predictor of future events is past events, it would make a good deal of sense to start estimating probability factors by seeing how frequently your *type* of crisis has occurred in the past—in your own division or company, in a competing company, or even in similar types of industries under broad headings such as "manufacturing," "agricultural," and so on.

By the same token, if there is substantial precedent for the sort of potential crisis you are concerned about, you can get a fairly good handle not only on the estimated probability of occurrence but on the cost of the crisis as well. This will then make your Crisis Impact Value and your Probability Factor that much more reliable.

As an example, General Motors is launching a new car company, Saturn. While the first car has yet to roll off the assembly line, it is still a safe assumption that senior management in Saturn's new Spring Hill, Tennessee, plant will be able to estimate the probability of a recall occurring on the basis of the past history of recalls incurred by other automobile manufacturers or GM divisions.

Interestingly, though, the *cost* of a Saturn recall would be disproportionately *higher* than, say, the cost of recalling a Chevrolet Camaro.

The reason has to do with soft dollars, not hard dollars.

The Camaro has a long track record behind it. Its reputation has been made. A recall will hurt, but it probably will not ruin the division or the parent company.

But if the first year's crop of Saturns is recalled, the manufacturer may have trouble planting the seeds for a new season. The car may suffer a terminal flat tire on the hazardous highway of public opinion.

So, by using past events to forecast future events, it *is* possible to make an educated estimate of the probability of occurrence.

Do not despair if you find that you are having trouble picking a Probability Factor. There is a good chance that you have never been asked to make the kinds of assumptions you are being asked to make now.

Remember: it takes courage to make assumptions. This may be why large corporations, such as Texaco, have high-level managers whose jobs consist in making assumptions. Not everyone can do it; not everyone has the courage to make assumptions.

This exercise forces you to make an assumption, a guess, a stab. And even if your assumption is off by 10 percent or 25 percent, you will be better off than having made *no* assumption in the first place.

So, on a scale of 0 percent (an absolute impossibility) to 100 percent (a dead certainty), make an assumption: what is the probability that your crisis will occur?

Then, on the horizontal Probability Factor Scale, which now intersects the Crisis Impact Value Scale at midpoint (see Figure 5), plot your probability percentage.

Using the intersection of the two axes as the dividing line, determine whether your potential crisis has a high or low Crisis Impact Value, above or below the horizontal line.

Next, do the same for the Probability Factor. Is it high or low, to the right or left of where the vertical line crosses?

Always referring to the Crisis Impact Value first, your potential crisis is now ranked either:

High/High
High/Low
Low/High
Low/Low

Figure 5. Crisis-Plotting Grid.

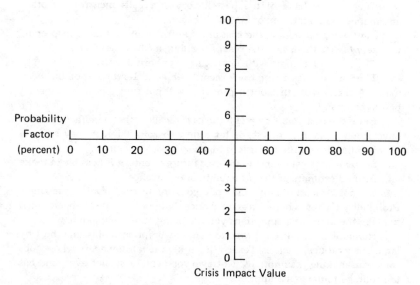

Plot your Crisis Impact Value on the vertical scale from 0 to 10. Plot your Probability Factor on the horizontal scale from 0 percent (an absolute impossibility) to 100 percent (a dead certainty).

And each of these directional designations corresponds to a colored zone on a Crisis Barometer (see Figure 6).

> High/High = Red Zone
> High/Low = Amber Zone
> Low/High = Gray Zone
> Low/Low = Green Zone

By plotting on both the vertical (Crisis Impact Value) scale and the horizontal (Probability Factor) scale, you have forecasted with probably more accuracy than ever before how big the crisis bang will be and what the likelihood is that it ever will erupt.

You even know what color your crisis will be.

What we have yet to consider is whether or not it is possible and/or wise to intervene.

In Malin's sensitive strategic work for Texaco, he showed how a particularly critical pricing decision may be made on the basis of an

Figure 6. Crisis Barometer.

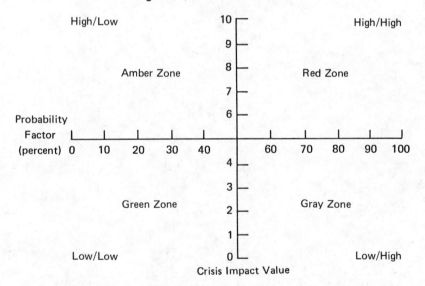

If you find that you have plotted your potential crisis into a danger zone, such as the Red Zone, with a high Crisis Impact Value and a high Probability Factor, your task as a crisis manager is to search vigilantly for alternative ways to plot yourself out of danger—*and into opportunity*—before the crisis strikes.

assumption about the future rate of inflation. But at a certain point down the road, Texaco's managers will re-evaluate that decision if prices rise faster than inflation.

Texaco will then have to consider what alternatives are available to it and what the costs will be.

It is possible to intervene in any number of crises if you can bear the costs. And determining the cost of intervention will help you to decide whether or not to do anything.

It is determining these new costs—what is known as "numbers crunching"—that Malin refers to as "a shorthand way of presenting a whole new way of thinking."[14]

That, in fact, is the best way to describe what this entire book is about: introducing you to a whole new way of thinking.

6

Crisis Intervention

Even if you're on the right track, you'll get run over if you just sit there.

—Will Rogers

For some people, just knowing where they fit on a crisis barometer may be sufficient for their peace of mind. They would view the process just described in Chapter 5 as a peek into a crystal ball.

But gazing into that orb permits the viewer only to observe what destiny might have in store for him or her.

Proper crisis management has the added advantage of allowing the participant to achieve more *control* over his or her destiny by suggesting certain proactive behaviors.

If you have plotted a crisis into the Red Zone, your immediate goal should be to explore every conceivable way to get yourself out of it.

See what steps you can take proactively to reduce your Crisis Impact Value to a more palatable number.

Ascertain, as well, whether there is anything that you can do to reduce in significant measure your Probability Factor.

These steps are known as determining the Degree of Influence you can exert over a potential crisis to turn the potential danger into potential opportunity.

You may examine each of the five variables to see if you have a Degree of Influence over any of them individually or if you may be in a position to exert a Degree of Influence over the potential crisis as a whole.

However it is done, you first should see if anything *can* be done to alter the currently forecasted event.

Assuming that you have arrived at a positive Degree of Influence response, or series of responses, you must next calculate the Cost of Intervention for each one.

What will it cost to intervene *pro*actively (before the crisis hits), and what will it cost to intervene *re*actively (after the crisis has hit)? And what costs can you afford to live with?

What will the crisis cost (Question #5: damage to the bottom line) with *no* action, *no* intervention at all?

Is it cost-efficient to intervene proactively?

Would it make more financial sense to do nothing?

Would intervention alter any of your responses to determining the Crisis Impact Value?

Perhaps, depending on circumstances, you may conclude that it is too costly to intervene *today,* based on your current assessment of the situation and your best assumption of probable savings versus estimated losses. However, the exercises alone will make you more prepared and vigilant for sudden situational shifts. You may conclude (as Texaco does): "I can't do anything today, but if X happens, then I'll be in a position to intervene."

Determining the Cost of Intervention—and, therefore, the economic wisdom of intervening or not—will undoubtedly force you to examine the earlier question #5 (damage to bottom line) more closely.

In calculating any costs and benefits, the same admonition as before applies: do not overlook "soft" dollars.

A "Big Bang" crisis—one in which there is typically a high Crisis Impact Value but a somewhat lower Probability Factor—will also be characterized by a large soft-dollar ingredient, high visibility, publicity, and external inquiries.

The soft-dollar impact on a "Big Bang" crisis might be exemplified by Procter & Gamble's Rely tampon crisis.

The cost to the company in hard dollars was more than $75 million for the withdrawal of the product, plus added hard-dollar costs for special advertising to inform women about the risks of toxic shock syndrome.

But for several months, the public was unsure of Procter & Gamble's responsibility, culpability, honesty, or involvement in a cover-up. The FDA made a concerted effort to keep up a barrage of bad media stories about P&G, the company's sales slumped slightly, and its stock dropped seven points. Productivity throughout the company may have decreased when the stories spread or when workers in Rely plants were laid off, and so on.

All of this is a representation of soft dollars. (The Procter & Gamble crisis is covered in depth later on.)

Typically in a "Big Bang" crisis—where the news of the crisis is surprising or frightening—the more that people and the media talk about it, the more soft dollars will flow out of your pocket.

Conversely, in a "Dripping Water" crisis—characteristically a crisis that has a high Probability Factor but low Crisis Impact Value—hard dollars play a larger role than soft: *some* visibility is possible, *some* publicity may result, but front-page exposés are unlikely. And if there is to be an inquiry, it will tend to be an internal one.

And if you keep in mind that soft dollars also represent the good will that is otherwise so difficult to measure, you will observe that even when the Cost of Intervention is approximately the same as doing nothing and allowing the crisis to occur, there are times when the soft-dollar *benefits* of intervention may be so large that it would be foolhardy not to act proactively.

EXAMPLE

Assume you are the CEO of a manufacturing company with several antiquated, unprofitable plants located in small towns in the industrial Northeastern United States. Economic conditions demand that you close one of these plants. And, for our purposes, assume that this is your only choice, short of allowing the entire company to fail because you did not take the necessary step in closing the one plant.

Furthermore (and for the sake of simplicity whole numbers will be used here), assume that your monthly overhead at the targeted plant is $1 million and that you have decided to close the plant at the end of six months. In other words, revenues aside, you have made the decision to expend an additional $6 million before the plant is closed. And you plan to announce the plant closing in five months—one full month before the plant is shuttered and its 500 employees are out of work.

Since the past is the best determinant of what may happen in the future, and you have had to close other plants in the past, you have valid reason to expect that the following sequence of events will unfold:

• At the end of the fifth month, your company announces the regrettable, but necessary, decision to close the plant in one month.

• Unions cry foul, workers protest, and families of workers (especially the toddlers, because of the great visual impact they make on television) picket in front of the plant.

• If you live in the same town, you can expect the same treatment in front of your home. (They will find out where you live.)

• Government officials (mayors, councilmen, councilwomen, and so on) call emergency meetings to see if they can come up with a plan to entice you to change your mind.

• The news media, after carrying the announcement of the closing as hard news, begin to run feature stories on how the closing will affect the workers, the community, the tax base, and so on.

• The evening news, with depressing regularity, will feature an interview with a soon-to-be-displaced worker and his wife and kids—all sitting together on their living room couch—trying to explain what the closing means to them and all the things they will have to do without. (You will not, however, see the media interview any displaced worker who has landed another job closer to home with better pay, better conditions, and so on.)

• You will expect to see at least one or two interviews with someone who is only three months shy of having a vested pension.

• The union holds a news conference to charge that you really have no plans to close the plant; your announcement was a smoke screen. What you really want is (a) to break the union; (b) to force the workers to agree to wage concessions; (c) to reduce the work force by 50 percent and replace those workers with robots; or (d) all of the above. However, none of this is true.

• Government officials will hold a news conference to announce the tax concessions they will make if you will stay.

• You are burned in effigy at a rally outside the plant.

• Newspapers run feature stories or exposés on you, your company, and all of the times your company had been cited over the years by any regulatory agency. They compare this plant with your other operations and always ask why *this* plant was singled out for closing.

• Eventually the month ends, the plant closes (with more media coverage), and you and your company—for a solid month—have been castigated, vilified, defamed, cursed, and had the legitimacy of your birth questioned by an endless stream of men, women, children, and politicians.

Maybe you even feel bad.

But remember; this hasn't happened—*yet*. It is just what your crisis management planning has told you to expect.

You have plotted the potential crisis with the forecasting model, and the Crisis Barometer is pointing to the Red Zone.

Your crisis also indicates a large expenditure of soft dollars: lots of nasty public opinion, bad press, anger, exposés, investigations, lost productivity, decreased morale in your other plants ("Will we be next?"), higher workers' comp claims, and so on.

You have determined that this predicted chain of events is unacceptable.

You determine that you *can* have a Degree of Influence. You *can* keep the plant open, but the cost in hard dollars is also unacceptable (which is why you decided to close the plant in the first place). In other words, the cost of this particular method of intervention is too high.

You search for alternative intervention scenarios; you try to move out of the Red Zone. You know what the outcome *has* to be (the plant closing), so you examine ways to turn the precrisis situation (the prodrome) into either an opportunity (a plus) or, at minimum, a nonnegative (a neutral).

You come up with two possible alternatives. The first defuses the incredibly strong negativism of the nonintervention scenario (the one just described) and creates, at best, a nonnegative.

ALTERNATIVE #1

As before, you decide that the plant must be closed in six months. But instead of announcing the closing in the fifth month—with just one month's notice—you announce it soon after the decision is made, in the *first* month.

But you announce that the plant will close in *one* month (which is the second month of your six-month plan).

All of the howls of protest described above begin on schedule. Except that you meet with the unions, government officials, everyone, in a series of marathon meetings.

After these meetings, you announce that, while economic realities preclude any consideration of keeping the plant open, the unions and the government and community leaders have convinced you to keep the plant open for six full months in order to give the workers ample time to make adjustments, seek other employment, and so on.

The union appears to have "come through" for its workers.

The elected officials look good to their constituents.

You are still a louse to many, but at least you're a louse with a heart. And you have closed the plant in six months—just the way you wanted to.

Cost of Intervention: approximately the same as the cost of nonintervention—$6 million, the $1 million monthly overhead times six months.

ALTERNATIVE #2

This alternative is slightly more complicated, but it creates a strong positive *from the beginning*. It never allows the negative ball to begin rolling.

First, behind closed doors, you brief union and government officials, telling them in effect that you have no choice but to close the plant but that—with their help—you are prepared to do everything humanly possible to see that the workers do not suffer. You then announce in the first month that you will be forced to close the plant in five months.

But in your announcement—which perhaps can even be made jointly by management, labor, and government—you say that after consulting with union and government officials, your company has decided to spend $1 million to help each and every displaced worker find other work.

This assistance will include such programs as on-site job/career counseling, job retraining, job skills evaluation, résumé-writing services, family counseling, and sessions with a psychologist to help cope with the stress of possible unemployment. Union representatives will be on hand daily to provide information about what other companies may be looking for skilled union labor. A government representative will be on hand to help cut bureaucratic red tape with unemployment forms, food stamps, and so on, if any worker requires these services.

After the announcement, the media cover the rest of the story from a human interest perspective, showing what a caring company can do to help displaced workers.

The unions look good to their workers; government officials look helpful to their constituents.

While people may never erect a statue of you, no one is burning you in effigy either. You are not a louse. You are a compassionate executive running a company that cares about its employees.

It was too bad that the plant had to go, but was there any more that you could have done to help the workers?

Cost of Intervention: approximately the same as the cost of nonintervention—$6 million, the $1 million monthly overhead times *five* months. The $1 million that you spent on out-placement services, and so on (if in fact you did spend that much), was the $1 million that you had originally budgeted for the overhead in the *sixth* and final month.

ANALYSIS AND CAVEATS

First, neither alternative is being recommended as a universal course of action.

Rather, the opinion expressed here is simply that negative events such as plant closings happen every day, and many business decision makers view these events merely as "bad news," or "unfortunate facts of life." They don't see the situations as potential crises—as turning points, as opportunities to turn a guaranteed negative into a possible positive. (Or a nonnegative, which, considering the alternative, is positive by comparison.)

Alternatives #1 and #2—and there are others, certainly—illustrate how it is possible to take a specific event, view it as a potential crisis, calculate the Crisis Impact Value and the Probability Factor (both very high), estimate the Degree of Influence and the Cost of Intervention, and arrive at an alternative that creates a positive from a negative, opportunity from danger.

Those who might argue that the alternatives are dishonest and manipulative are forgetting the workers. They are forgetting that the original nonintervention model gave all workers one month's notice. Period.

Alternative #1 gave the workers six months' notice. Does it matter so much how it came about? Ask the displaced workers in the unemployment line whether they'd rather have one month's notice to try to find another job or an additional six months of paychecks to be able to feed and clothe their families and make plans for the future.

Alternative #2 gave them five months' notice plus some very valuable assistance in job retraining, and so on. One of the reasons the plant was closed was because it was antiquated. For some of the workers, the job retraining could have been a beneficial turning point in *their* lives.

The closing is, in fact, a turning point for all of the plant workers—not just for the company. And with any turning point, any crisis, the more time you have to plan, the better are your chances for success.

In effective crisis management, you should consider that you have only two crises to consider: long-fused crises (sometimes called anticipated crises) or short-fused crises (unanticipated).

The hypothetical plant closing just analyzed is a long-fused crisis, with plenty of time to consider the crisis, the Crisis Impact Value, the Cost of Intervention, and so on.

You might assume that the only crisis you can plan for is a long-fused, anticipatory one. However, as we are about to discuss, with proper crisis management planning it doesn't matter what type of crisis occurs. You can—and will—be ready.

7

Crisis Management Plans

Make no little plans; they have no magic to stir men's blood.

—*Daniel Hudson Burnham*

Every business, large or small, public or private, should have a crisis management plan. Every division of every company, industrial or service business, should also have a crisis management plan. There are no exceptions, merely differences of degree.

Bear in mind that whatever your position within a company, you are not the only person affected by a crisis. In fact, if you are the CEO or are in a position to manage, or influence the management of, a crisis, then consider yourself fortunate. If things go badly, at least you had a shot at controlling your own destiny.

Remember that the outcome of a crisis affects the lives and the jobs of innocent people—people who are totally dependent on the skills of management to see them and their families through the crisis, to enable them to continue to put bread on their tables.

The ripple effect of a crisis affects support industries, too. Auto crises affect steel, rubber, and glass industries. Any major crisis can hit hard at community services such as restaurants, shops, schools, hospitals, and so on.

With all of these people counting on you, there is no room for complacency and no excuse for a lack of adequate planning.

In short, there is simply no valid reason why *any* manager should not know where the flashlights are kept.

Flashlights?

If you have ever been caught in a sudden power outage, you know that the first thing you need is some form of illumination to show you the way to the circuit breakers or the fuse box. Assume that you first need to find the flashlight in your home.

In the first moments of the power failure, a few possible causes of the darkness—and solutions for restoring power—run through your mind. None of these possible causes is very serious. But you realize that you cannot discover the cause (and certainly cannot achieve a solution) without *first* finding the flashlight.

It doesn't matter if the cause of the problem is a blown fuse or a tripped circuit. You're powerless to replenish the power without first getting a flashlight, which will help you to locate the cause of the problem.

Perhaps the real problem is an overloaded electrical outlet. Possibly, but first you've got to find the flashlight.

Could there be a downed power line somewhere? Again, you have to find that flashlight first.

You know you have one; you just can't remember where you put it last.

And it is time-consuming, frustrating, and highly stressful to try to find it in the dark.

Think of a crisis abstractly, for a moment, as a power outage. If you plan for this potential crisis during the day, when the lights are working and the sun is shining, one of the first things you may do is calmly locate the flashlights. In fact, if you live in an area that experiences frequent and violent storms—hurricanes on the East Coast or tornadoes in the Midwest—you may already know where the flashlights (or other forms of emergency illumination) are kept. That's because you've had plenty of time to anticipate and plan for this long-fused crisis.

The problems in managing these crises seem to occur when they become sudden, unexpected, unanticipated, short-fused crises. It is during these times when people are apt to get hurt running around in the dark because they cannot locate their flashlights.

In assembling a crisis management plan for your business, all you are really doing is locating your own versions of the flashlights well in advance of the actual crisis, when all is calm and things are running smoothly.

When the crisis hits, whether it is long- or short-fused, you will need certain things to manage it. Planning ahead for what—and whom—you will need saves you valuable time in the heat of the crisis, when you would otherwise have to (a) decide what you need and (b) then find it.

An effective crisis management plan presets certain key decisions on the *mechanical* portions of the crisis—those aspects that rarely vary—and leaves you free to manage the *content* portion of the crisis with your hands unfettered.

Another way to look at this is as contingency planning, or conditional thinking. You have to learn to ask "what-if" questions—and make assumptions about the questions *and* the answers.

"What if such and such happened? Then I would do thus and thus," and so on.

This contingency planning is what many forward-thinking companies are spending much careful time in developing. It's called a comprehensive crisis management plan.

It is a manual, a blueprint, a road map out of dangerous woods. It covers everything from A to Z on how to manage *types* of crises.

By planning for types of crises by crisis category, the comprehensive crisis management plan deals with the *mechanics* of the crisis in order to save precious time for the crisis management team, which will have to deal with the *content* of the crisis.

Here is an example.

If you were the publisher of a newspaper and you thought about the *sorts* of crises that would have a high Crisis Impact Value, you might state that the inability to operate your presses, and therefore to publish your paper on time, would be a severe crisis that would affect you adversely.

Try not to concern yourself just now with *why* your presses might be inoperable; just know that they will be inoperable.

When a hemorrhaging patient is rushed into the emergency room of a hospital with a gunshot wound, the doctor's first goal is to stop the acute bleeding, not to ask who shot the patient or what the argument was about. Asking why the victim was shot will not contribute to his or her immediate well-being.

In the acute stage of a crisis, "why" is a luxury question. Address "why" during the chronic phase of the crisis—as everyone else will. When the crisis hits, you must instead ask: *what* plans have you made? *how* will you implement them? *when? where* is the flashlight?

When the Los Angeles *Herald Examiner* suffered a sudden power failure a few years ago and was unable to publish at its own plant on time, it used the presses of the Los Angeles *Times* in order to get the paper out.

The *Herald Examiner,* at least in this instance, knew where the flashlights were kept. The flashlight, in that case, was the Los Angeles *Times,* and more specifically the name and home telephone number of the person(s) at the *Times* authorized to grant such an emergency request.

If another crisis hits the *Herald Examiner* next week—not necessarily another power failure, but some other inability to operate its presses—someone on the staff knows what to do.

No matter what your *actual* crisis, long- or short-fused, if it fits a certain preplanned-for *type* of crisis, you will be ready to act.

But there *are* times when you must ask *why* in order to know how to respond. Sometimes you must delve into a second level of intelligence before being able to respond, before knowing *how* to respond properly.

If you are a manufacturer of consumer goods, a crisis that might affect you would be your inability to get your goods to market.

Why you can't get them to market, in this instance, is important in the acute phase only to see which of two or three "can't-get-goods-to-market" crisis categories you have planned for.

Is it because of transportation problems? Have the teamsters gone out on strike? If so, what contingency plans have you made? Or has someone sabotaged all of your tractor-trailers? In one instance you need drivers (or an alternative means of transportation), and in the other you have drivers but no vehicles.

Another "can't-get-goods-to-market" crisis may involve the product itself. Has someone tampered with it? Has some research lab or government agency suddenly announced that your product (or all products like yours) are flammable (babies' pajamas) or carcinogenic (sugar substitutes) or possibly lethal (tampons)?

In the "can't-print-the-newspaper" crisis, the category itself is the crisis. But "can't-get-the-goods-to-market" is not actually the crisis; it is the result of the real crisis, which, as shown above, may be any one of a number of possible crises.

Before you assemble a crisis management plan, you must first assemble the crisis management team or teams.

Every crisis demands a crisis management team to run the plays, which may be called by the CEO or by some technical authority. But the team must huddle on a regular basis to review the game plans.

And one of the first things the crisis management plan should do is to name all of the team members. Different types of crises may require different types of team members.

There should be a central core to each crisis management team, but a technical crisis requires technical people; a financial crisis requires financial people; and so on. Depending on the type of business, a central core of permanent crisis management team members might include either the CEO or someone from senior management; the chief financial officer; the chief internal communicator (such as the head of your public relations or corporate communications department); the chief external communicator (the head of your outside public relations consulting firm); and perhaps the head of your legal department.

One of the first tasks of the central core is to draw up a list of names to be added to the crisis management team, depending on the type of crisis at hand. This is done so that, when the crisis hits, no one has to sit around and wonder who ought to be called in. That decision has already been made. And it has been made at the best possible time: when everything at the company is operating smoothly and there is no crisis. No decisions are being forced or rushed because of the "heat of the moment."

In fact, what you are striving for in the crisis management plan is to make as many mundane, routine decisions as possible when everyone has a cool head. You want to remove as much guesswork as possible from the crisis. You simply want to know where the flashlights are before you need them.

One of the first assignments for the added members for each crisis management team should be to name replacements for themselves on the team if, for whatever reason, the first string is unavailable.

The next assignment is to devise the crisis management plan. This is a test of the team's own knowledge and abilities.

The central core presents to the added team members a list of possible types of crises and merely says: what do we need to do to solve these? The added team members, after seeing whether any other types of crises have been overlooked, then set out to provide for all possible broad-based contingencies. This contingency planning merely asks and answers its own "what-if" questions: "What would we need to know and do if X happened?"

As a highly recommended and beneficial part of a comprehensive crisis management planning program, many companies are hiring outside consultants and psychologists to stage realistic crisis-simulation workshops for managers. These workshops create actual crisis conditions and scenarios in order to evaluate how well a company and/or its crisis management teams might perform under actual crisis conditions.

(The Department of Defense, whose primary peacetime mission is to get ready for the crisis of war, undertakes simulation workshops on a regular basis. The Pentagon calls them "war games.")

But before trying out the crisis in a workshop situation, the crisis management team first has to get the crisis management plan on paper.

One planning question that must be resolved early is who will be the public spokesperson. A common mistake often made by unprepared companies under siege is to assume the CEO automatically should be the spokesperson. The responsibility of the crisis management team, and of the company as a whole, is to put forth the spokesperson who will best present, explain, and/or defend the company's position.

If that should happen to be the CEO, fine. But if you are confronted with a crisis involving *technical* information—such as the Hyatt Regency Hotel's Kansas City skyway collapse on July 18, 1981, in which 110 people were killed—who would be the better spokesperson: the CEO of the Hyatt Hotel chain, or a structural engineer who might be able to discuss the crisis in more *meaningful* terms? Obviously, the engineer. If Hyatt's CEO has a background in structural engineering, so much the better.

During the Three Mile Island crisis, there were two spokespersons for the administration: Governor Thornburgh and Harold Denton of the Nuclear Regulatory Commission. At press conferences, Thornburgh responded to questions pertaining to the health and welfare of the citizens; he deflected technical questions to Denton. The nontechnical spokespersons offered up by Met Ed, the TMI utility company, on the other hand, knew little, said nothing, and had virtually no credibility, because of their early mismanagement and minimizing of the crisis.

As the acute TMI crisis raged on, many of the news media with vast resources and manpower sent highly skilled technical writers to Harrisburg to ask probing questions, which, when answers were received, were translated into laymen's terms to the extent possible and communicated to the world. The television networks, the major daily newspapers, and the wire services sent in crews of 10, 15, 20 people or more to try to make sense of the situation.

Choosing the spokesperson(s) early on is vital. And remember that you may select more than one. If, for whatever reason, it is necessary to have the CEO out front, he or she shouldn't go alone into a press conference or interview if the questioning may get into technical matters. It is perfectly acceptable to do a Thornburgh-Denton dog-and-pony show.

While detailed planning is required to some degree, try to remember not to get lost in minutae. You would be wise to make a conscious effort to avoid this trap at all costs. Plan in the broadest possible terms, and get detailed when brush strokes don't cover enough of the canvas.

For example, regardless of the type of acute crisis, a *consequence* of the crisis may be that you do not want workers to show up for work the next morning, or for the next shift. If you operate only one shift and the decision to keep workers at home the next day is made while they are still on the job, an announcement over the loudspeaker will take care of the notification and explanation.

But if the crisis strikes after the workers have gone home, or during a second shift, how do you notify the first-shift workers not to show up for work—especially when their doing so may be hazardous?

Your crisis management plan may say that you (or someone) will telephone employees (if it's a workable number of people) or that you'll notify the radio stations to make announcements. This is too broad a brush stroke.

Someone must be assigned the tasks of obtaining current telephone numbers and making certain that the list stays current. If your plan is to telephone in a pyramid style (that is, each person called calls ten more people), what are your contingency plans if certain links in the telephone chain are missing?

If you are planning to use the news media to make announcements late at night or in the early morning, be aware that the telephone number you have for a radio station may be the main, daytime switchboard number. If you call that number after hours, you may get a recording telling you that the business hours are 9 A.M. to 5 P.M. and advising you to call again in the morning. This will not help you during a midnight crisis.

However, virtually every radio and television station has "night lines," or news lines, which will get you where you want to go—into the newsroom—provided you know the number (which usually is not listed in the telephone book or available through directory assistance). Again, you should get these numbers during the day, when there is no crisis, and record them in your crisis management plan manual.

(In many large metropolitan areas there are at least two other ways to reach radio and television stations at night. One is to call the wire services, which may carry the story and the announcement on one of their wires directly into all of the newsrooms at once. Many cities also have what are known as news services. These agencies do not report the news, but they alert the media to important stories. If either option is available to you, make certain you can reach these valuable resources—"flashlights"—after normal business hours.)

Regardless of the type of crisis and whether it is long- or short-fused, some basic questions must be asked—and answered—when assembling your crisis management plan. These include such seemingly obvious, but often overlooked, matters as:

- Who is responsible for notifying the employees?
- Who is the *backup?*
- Who is responsible for notifying the media?
- And who is the *backup?*
- Which local, state, or federal government agencies may need to be notified, and who will do so?
- Your switchboard operators are your first line of defense (or offense). What will they tell reporters or the public at large when they call? Who is responsible for briefing them? And do they need to be bilingual?*
- Do the switchboard operators known whom to contact within the

---

*An unbelievable and grossly insensitive crisis management oversight occurred during the tragic Jalisco cheese deaths in southern California in the late spring of 1985. The contaminated cheese, purchased mainly by Hispanics, caused more than 30 deaths. A widely publicized poison center hot line, under the auspices of the Los Angeles County Medical Association, was flooded with more than 4,000 calls in three days. But the hot line was staffed with only *English*-speaking nurses, and the phones were jammed with calls from concerned, confused, scared, and angry *Spanish*-speaking callers, who could not be helped. A spokesperson for this pre-existing poison-information hot line, which had nothing directly to do with the cheese company, explained that budgetary considerations preclude it from hiring bilingual nurses full-time. But even aside from the Hispanic nature of the Jalisco crisis, this ongoing poison center, with its published emergency hot-line number, services an area of southern California that has the largest concentration of Spanish-speaking people in the country.

company if they start to get many calls of a certain type, such as rumors about your product?
- Does your company have plans for a rumor-control hotline? Again, do hotline operators need to be bilingual?

One of the single most effective crisis communications tools wielded during the Three Mile Island crisis was the immediate ability to install a rumor-control hotline with a toll-free 800 telephone number. There were no prior preparations for this hotline, but fate was on the administration's side.

There existed at the time in the Pennsylvania Department of Commerce a little-known and infrequently used service known as the Ombudsman's Office, complete with an 800 telephone number and people who were used to talking to strangers on the telephone and answering their numerous and sometimes irate questions. Within hours of the onset of the acute phase of the TMI crisis, the number of the toll-free rumor-control hotline was flashed across the state as a place for people to call if they had questions or if they had heard rumors about TMI. The people handling the telephones were briefed and debriefed by the governor's press office on a regular basis.

If you foresee the need for a rumor-control hotline, and you do not have a toll-free number, you may want to order an 800 number today. You don't have to use it; just know that it is there in the event you do need it.

Procter & Gamble has an 800 number to handle customer-service calls for all its products. During the toxic shock syndrome crisis, which was linked to the company's Rely tampon, P&G used this number to take panic calls. It served the company well; but because the number was so widely used by P&G customers who were calling about other products, the number was not as effective as it could have been had it been a "dedicated" number, similar to the 800 number used in the Tylenol crisis.

And who are the personnel who will operate the rumor-control hotline? Have they been psychologically stress-tested so that you can be a little more confident of their ability to handle a constant flood of calls from anxiety-ridden, and perhaps abusive, strangers on the telephone? For that matter, can the crisis management team operate well under stress? How do you know?

These considerations represent only a few common denominators that companies may have to deal with during an acute crisis. This book does not pretend to tell fortunes, so it is left to you to put together a list of "flashlight" locations that best serve your particular company.

You also will want to make certain that there are *enough* flashlights.
Here's a case in point.
Dealing with California's 17 million licensed drivers and 20 million

registered vehicles could have posed a crisis for the state's Department of Motor Vehicles. Surprisingly, some would say miraculously, it didn't—until August 6, 1984.

Prior to that date, the DMV's 154 field offices transacted business with walk-in customers on a first-come, first-served basis. There were always complaints, always long lines, always long waits.

But no crises.

Until someone decided it would be more efficient to have the public schedule appointments in advance on the telephone.

The scheme—and the very limited pilot program—seemed to be simplicity itself. It was genius born out of frustration. It was also a crisis waiting to happen.

The scheme: No more walk-in traffic. The public would call for an appointment. Anyone who showed up without an appointment would be turned away with specific instructions to call for an appointment. There would be no more lines, no more chaos.

The pilot program: A 6-month test, conducted at 24 southern California field offices, seemed to please DMV officials in Sacramento. The problem with the pilot program was that customers who had any difficulty in scheduling an appointment could simply visit, in person, a neighboring field office that was not participating in the pilot study.

The crisis: But after the program went into effect *statewide* on that fateful August day, the DMV came face to face with an acute crisis: most of the major field offices in the most heavily populated areas of the state simply did not have enough telephones to allow the much-heralded appointment system to work. As a result, people were not able to call for appointments. They couldn't get through. Some harried DMV offices just took the telephones off the hook.

In the face of stiff fines from the police if caught driving with an expired registration, Californians jammed the DMV offices in larger droves than ever before. But they were turned away because they had no appointments.

The number of telephones that would be required was clearly grossly underestimated. The process of installing new telephones was slowed considerably because of confusion resulting from the still relatively recent breakup of AT&T and antiquated telephone equipment in many DMV offices.

Nor had anyone bothered to check to make sure that telephone operators and directories listed all of the DMV telephone numbers and that the numbers listed were accurate. There were sufficient errors here to cause a minicrisis in its own right.

And while all of this was going on, an active program was well under way to computerize the field offices in order to speed up transactions with

Sacramento. Speeding up the transactions only served to further tax and stress the increasingly angry DMV field worker.

In a Los Angeles *Times* article on the DMV crisis, reporter Peter H. King described a classic "Catch-22" situation:

> Some [DMV field] managers . . . recalled with irritation their difficulties convincing Sacramento that the new system was in trouble. They believed that their superiors suspected them of loafing, causing problems for what appeared to be an ideal system.
>
> [One year before the start-up of the new appointment system] managers received memos instructing them to place their "most knowledgeable and proficient people" on the new computers.
>
> Then, as the appointment system began, they received memos telling them to put their "most knowledgeable and proficient people" on the telephone banks.
>
> When it became clear that the "Start Here" windows [a reference to the old, walk-in system where people were directed from pillar to post, after first beginning at the "Start Here" sign] were needed to sort out the large number of clients arriving without appointments, instructions came down for the managers to put their "most knowledgeable and proficient people" at that start window.[15]

King reported that this phrase became a standing joke among DMV managers who bemoaned the fact that they ran out of "knowledgeable and proficient people" back in the first phase.

Six months after D (for "Delay" with a capital D) Day, with the crisis still in the acute phase, DMV Director George E. Meese (brother of U.S. Attorney General Edwin Meese, III) issued a new directive in the form of a flyer that presumably was to be pasted up on some wall. It read: "Everyone entering a DMV field office is to be served. Appointments are tools for better service. WE DO NOT EXIST to make appointments. The DMV exists to SERVE THE PUBLIC."[16]

As a footnote to this story, and as a consequence of inadequate crisis management contingency planning, there soon was a backlog of business estimated at some 200,000 transactions that resulted in an estimated loss to the state of some $16 million in uncollected revenues from vehicles fees.

Result: In the spring of 1985—nine months after the ill-fated appointment system was instituted—the DMV returned to the original walk-in system of first-come, first-served. And on December 27, 1985, Meese resigned, claiming that his departure had nothing to do with the DMV fiasco. California's governor promptly appointed him to another bureaucratic post.

Probably no industry in the world is as completely vulnerable to crises as the airline industry. Nor is there another industry so well prepared to locate "flashlights" in any part of the world, at any hour of the day or night.

Not a day goes by—nor does a second of any day—when an airline carrier is not at risk of an acute crisis—a crash, a midair collision, a hijacking, a terrorist bombing or threat, extortion, or even an enemy country shooting down a civilian plane. Airlines are on alert literally every time a plane rolls out of a hangar. The entire airline industry operates in a constant, never-ending prodromal crisis stage.

"We're always on call, always ready to respond," said Charles (Chuck) Novak, manager of corporate communications for United Airlines and, as such, one of the key members of United's permanent crisis management team.

"And *this*," Novak said, indicating a loose-leaf folder, "is our Bible."[17]

The red-covered United Airlines crisis management plan is more than an inch thick and is tailored for each and every field office. The subjects covered are approved at the home office in Chicago, but each manual is localized. Thus if a crane needs to be found, each manual will furnish the nearest location and 24-hour telephone numbers of crane operators.

This is an eclectic but crisis-honed list of where to find the flashlights. And it is constantly being updated. More than that, it is a manual detailing precisely what United's people in the field should do to handle a crisis in the field.

And one of the things they do is funnel vital information to the preselected group of eight crisis management team members seated around a square conference table in the "situation room" in Chicago.

This room, used exclusively for crises, has a telephone at each seat and a speaker phone in the center of the table. Interestingly, neither United's president nor its chairman of the board serves on the company's crisis management team. There are, however, permanent seats on the sidelines for them—and for representatives from AT&T and the unions—where they may observe all that takes place.

The person who calls the shots is from System Operations Control, and the other permanent seats at the conference table in the situation room are filled by Public Relations, Flight Operations, Flight Safety, Corporate Security, In-Flight Personnel, Marketing/Customer Service, Medical, and the FBI.

Notice that no names are used in this crisis management team, for it is not the individual but his or her position that determines who occupies which seat in the situation room. And during a long crisis, replacements will take over and relieve their departmental counterparts.

Depending on the type and duration of the crisis, others who may be called into the crisis management team would include Food Services, Personnel, Internal Communications, Financial, and possibly the State Department.

Each member of United's crisis management team has a copy of the crisis management plan manual, but remember that the manual—the plan—is merely a guideline or a blueprint for the *mechanics* of a crisis. All it does is remove as much guesswork as possible in order to free the crisis management team to deal with the actual *content* of the crisis.

The United Airlines example illustrates the vital importance not just of collecting the information (by someone in the field) but making certain the information is properly routed to the proper decision makers (those United executives huddled around a conference table in the situation room).

United Airlines knows it will have another crisis. It doesn't know what form the crisis will take, since it is not a fortune teller. But whatever form the crisis does take, United is ready to respond.* So, too, are other major carriers.

Novak pointed out that being ready to respond to a crisis today means a lot more than it did when commercial aviation was in its infancy.

In the old days, Novak recalled, when the airlines were still trying to convince people of the safety of their planes, they would paint the airline's name directly over the plane's door. That way, when a Pathé or any other newsreel or photographer captured a movie star or politician disembarking from a plane and waving the traditional arm from the top of the stairs, the name of the safely landed airline would be visible.

But in the event of a crash, Novak said, the first job of the guy in the field was to rush out to the crash scene with a bucket of white paint to obliterate the name of the airline before the photographers showed up.

That, said Novak, was the beginning of crisis management and one of the first things ever written down in a crisis management plan.

Another, even earlier, type of crisis management plan has been traced back to the bedroom of General Tam Dalyell, commander-in-chief of the royal forces in seventeenth-century Scotland. Dalyell wore riding boots that were square-toed and made to fit either foot. That way, the boots could be pulled on quickly in a sudden crisis without losing precious time.

Texaco's Clement Malin, recognizing that a crisis is always a fluid time, maintained that the seeds for a crisis in business today are plentiful:

> For a major multinational corporation such as Texaco, whose operating areas include many different cultures and economic/social/political situations, the important factor is adequate management procedures [in averting crisis situations]. Ongoing contingency evaluation, through which the company is aware of and in a position to rapidly evaluate the effects of potential developments, provides the company the best means of avoiding a major crisis. Management procedures must permit quick but considered decisions and implementation.[19]

---

*During the pilots' strike against United Airlines in 1985, Novak reported that—with only slight modifications—the crisis management plan, team, and situation room were used effectively. "A crisis," said Novak, "is a crisis."[18]

Do not allow yourself or your company to be lulled into a false sense of security simply because you have a crisis management plan. A crisis management plan will *never* solve your crisis. The plan is nothing more than a tool to enable *you* to solve the crisis.

However, the better your crisis management plan, the better your tools. And superior tools in the hands of a skilled artificer will go a long way toward ensuring opportunity instead of danger.

8

A Crisis Survey

Zeus does not bring all men's plans to fulfillment.

—*Homer,* The Iliad

How many companies besides Texaco and United Airlines plan for crises? How many feel that they may fall prey to a crisis? How many feel confident of their ability to handle a crisis?

In conjunction with this book, a confidential survey was taken of the nation's top chief executive officers of the *Fortune* 500. Some of the results were predictable; others were jarring.

A staggering 89 percent of those who responded agreed that "a crisis in business today is as inevitable as death and taxes," but fully 50 percent of the respondents admitted that they do not have a prepared crisis management plan.

Shockingly, whether a company had ever suffered a crisis in the past was no barometer to whether or not the company had a plan. The survey revealed that of those companies that reported having had a crisis in the past, 42 percent *still* do not have any sort of crisis management plan in the event another crisis hits.

But of significant importance to today's business leaders is the fact that those companies with a plan reported substantially shorter crisis durations (during the chronic crisis phase) than companies which had no plan when they were hit by a crisis. On the average, those corporations without a crisis management plan reported that aftereffects of the crisis (the chronic crisis phase) lasted about two and a half times longer than was reported by companies that did have a plan.

And yet, almost everybody (97 percent) felt either very confident or somewhat confident that they could respond well to a crisis.

These sorts of almost logic-defying responses on the parts of some of the world's most successful businesses and business leaders force one to question openly whether some of the shocking headline-grabbing crises reported in the media today might have been managed better, or even successfully averted, with a more vigilant crisis-preparedness attitude on the part of management.

In some instances, you can almost see the "it-can't-happen-here" syndrome at work. Psychologists refer to this simply, and accurately, as *denial*.

For example, another telling result revealed that whether or not a company had a crisis management plan was unrelated to the company's perception of the probability that it would be hit by a debilitating crisis. Of those companies that believed that a crisis had a greater than 50 percent likelihood of striking them, 38 percent said that they had no crisis management plan.

And, conversely, 36 percent of those who thought a crisis relatively unlikely to hit their company *did* have a plan.

In response to a question about the CEO's perceived likelihood of the company suffering a crisis within the next five years, the responses were about evenly divided: 55 percent believed there was a less than 50 percent chance of a crisis; 45 percent thought that there was a more than 50 percent chance.

Of the firms responding, three-fourths (74 percent) described or reported ever having experienced what they termed a serious crisis. (The actual number may have been higher than reported, because some respondents may not have been willing to report or describe a crisis.)

Overall, there was a general consensus among *all* respondents that their companies are at least somewhat vulnerable to the following types of crises:

- Industrial accidents
- Environmental problems
- Union problems/strikes
- Product recalls
- Investor relations
- Hostile takeovers
- Proxy fights
- Rumors/media leaks
- Government regulatory problems
- Acts of terrorism
- Embezzlement

Of the sample responding, 57 percent reported that a prodromal situation within the previous 12 months had had the potential to become an acute crisis. In that same group, 38 percent said the prodrome did in fact escalate into an acute crisis.

Of the crises reported by the *Fortune* 500 respondents:

- 72 percent escalated in intensity.
- 72 percent were subject to close media scrutiny.
- 32 percent were subject to close government scrutiny.
- 55 percent interfered with normal business operations.
- 52 percent damaged the company's bottom line.
- 35 percent damaged the company's public image.
- 70 percent of the CEOs responding were in their present positions at the time of the crisis. Of those, 14 percent thought that their own personal reputations had been damaged as well.

The median length of the acute crises reported was 8.5 weeks; a statistically shorter duration was reported by those companies that had a plan in place at the time of the crisis. The median length of the chronic crisis phase was eight months. But, as mentioned earlier, whether or not a company had a crisis management plan at the time of its crisis significantly determined the length of time the chronic crisis lasted: companies *without* a plan reported chronic phases on the order of two and a half times longer than those reported by companies *with* a plan.

Of those companies that reported a crisis and said that they did have a crisis management plan in effect at the time, all agreed that their plan worked at least adequately—and, for the majority, "very well."

Without knowing the criteria that the companies used to rate the success of their plans, it is impossible to comment on this last statistic, except to say that the plans appear to have given the CEOs a degree of confidence. In an acute crisis, the key to managing the fluid situation successfully is the ability to make good, vigilant decisions. Psychologically, just having confidence in yourself and your managers—the sort of confidence that a crisis management plan instills—will help you to make sound decisions in the height of stressful, crisis-induced situations.

Some respondents also reported that using their crisis management plan under fire gave them a golden opportunity to see how it worked. They were then able to refine it (if necessary) when they reached the crisis resolution stage.

Almost three-fourths (70 percent) reported that they have turned, or would turn, to outside help during a crisis. Such help included firms specializing in crisis management, law, investment banking, public relations, and/or media consulting.

It is encouraging to note that there appeared to be uniform agreement that one of the "best things" about having a crisis management plan is not just knowing where the "flashlights" are kept, but knowing as well who is in charge of the flashlights *and* the batteries.

Comments that the crisis management plan "eliminates confusion," "specifies what is needed," and "lets everyone know who is responsible for what" were common in the survey results.

And a question to any readers who may not now be in a position to implement or influence a crisis management plan, but who own stocks in companies: do the companies in which you are a shareholder have active and updated crisis management plans?

Once again, remember: the chronic crisis phase lasted two and a half times longer in companies that didn't have a crisis management plan in place when the crisis began. And while more than half (52 percent) of the companies responding—including those with *and* those without a plan— reported a direct and calculable crisis-caused damage to their profits, it is a fair assumption that the longer the chronic crisis phase, the deeper the damage.

You should contact senior management of companies in which you own shares, or companies in which you are considering purchasing shares, to see whether or not they have crisis management plans in place. Then govern yourself and your stock portfolio carefully.

Naturally, having a plan is no guarantee that a company will not have a crisis, or that it will continually pay dividends, or anything of the kind. But it may give you an indication of the sort of strategic thinking the management employs and, in fact, whether *you* consider it to be a well-managed company.

Remember that managing a crisis is much like playing a game of chess. The ten moves that you have mapped out in your head in advance may become totally irrelevant the moment your opponent makes a move.

As 17th-century Japanese philosopher Ihara Saikaku wrote in Book II of *The Millionaires' Gospel,* "There is always something to upset the most careful of human calculations."

But taking the time to plan for a crisis will most assuredly be time well spent in readying you to capitalize on the opportunity at the next turning point in your life or the life of your business or division.

And it will better enable you to perform three essential tasks required in any crisis.

Because whether you are prepared or not, whether you have planned or not, you must:

- Identify the crisis—*quickly.*
- Isolate the crisis—*quickly.*
- Manage the crisis—*quickly.*

9

Identifying the Crisis

They are ill discoverers that think there is no land when they can see nothing but sea.

—*Samuel Johnson*

Imagine you are walking down the street wearing a brand new, very expensive suit. You look great.

Suddenly, it begins to rain. No, it begins to *pour*. A torrential downpour. And you are getting soaked. Your immediate crisis—the immediate problem that needs to be resolved—is preventing any damage to your new suit. You've got to find shelter, and *fast*.

As you begin to duck inside a building, a vicious-looking dog, who is blocking your entrance, decides he doesn't like the way your suit fits around your right calf and proceeds to make alterations with his sharp teeth. Your original, immediate priority has suddenly vanished, replaced by another, as you rush backward into the storm and away from the culpable canine. You suddenly realize that you don't mind a little water on your suit, as long as you still *have* a suit, to say nothing of your fervent desire to have a leg to put into the suit pants.

But in your attempt to beat a hasty retreat, you inadvertently bump into and knock down a woman who had been rushing along the street to try to find a dry haven herself. You seem to have a *new* crisis on your hands, since the woman appears to have been momentarily knocked unconscious.

As you quickly revive her—aided in no small measure by the buckets of water in which you now find yourself immersed—you manage a small inner laugh at how crazed you were just moments ago at your big crisis of trying not to get your new suit wet. Now your thoughts are filled with relief that the woman is coming around, thanking whatever powers you believe in that your brute strength didn't kill her, and hoping you aren't sued for your thanks.

71

She sits up, but instead of thanking you for helping her, she looks around quickly, grabs you by the lapels of your once-handsome suit, and screams, "My baby! MY BABY! WHERE IS MY BABY!!??"

Then *you* look around toward the sound of honking horns and screeching tires on a slippery street, and you spy an unaccompanied baby carriage careening downhill, headed right for the center of a busy intersection.

Gentle reader, in the past few moments you have been bombarded with an assortment of both real and imagined crises, the likes of which it is hoped you never actually experience. During this time, certain urgent matters required your immediate attention until other, more urgent matters supplanted the immediacy of the previous concerns.

Until, finally, something happened that just could not possibly get any worse. And the outcome of which you could influence.

Forget the rain.

Forget the suit.

Forget the dog.

Forget the lady.

But get up and run your heart out and save the baby!

The *kid* is the crisis. Danger or opportunity. Life or death. Hero or heavy. It's up to *you*.

What you have done is separated the wheat from the chaff and properly identified the crisis. And while it is hoped that no one reading this had any difficulty identifying the real crisis in this case, you should know that in business—and in life in general—it is not always as easy to identify the real crisis. In fact, it is usually downright enigmatic.

In the summer of 1980, just a few short months after Mount St. Helens's first eruption in recent memory, and almost a year and a half after the world first heard the chilling words "Three Mile Island," Washington's Governor Dixie Lee Ray and Pennsylvania's Governor Dick Thornburgh met at the front of a jam-packed room in the Denver Hilton Hotel. It was the National Governors' Association's annual summer meeting, and while most of the NGA's subcommittee meetings were poorly attended, this special session played to a standing-room-only crowd.

Its purpose was to bring together two crisis-scarred veterans to talk about their respective crises.

Governor Ray began to wax eloquent about the devastation and destruction that this angry mountain, this act of God, had caused in her state. She talked of the eruption, the fire, the lava flows, the barren land. And then she began to describe the awesomeness of the gray, ash-filled skies that hung overhead for days, for weeks; that floated into neighboring states; that dropped softly like a flannel blanket—like a gray snowfall—over cities, towns, and villages; over houses, cars, people.

And when she was finished, Thornburgh turned to her and said, "Well, Dixie, at least you could *see* your crisis."[20]

There are a few gambits we will discuss that will help you identify what is a real crisis and what is not.

But the first thing you should know is why it is important to identify a crisis. There are two reasons:

Reason #1: Only by identifying the crisis will you be able to manage it.

Reason #2: After identifying a crisis, you will have a better idea of whether or not you can exert any degree of influence over the desired outcome. If not, perhaps you can put it out of your mind and worry about something over which you do have some control. Don't diffuse your energy.

You should accept almost as a universal truth that when a crisis strikes, it will be accompanied by a host of other diversionary problems. As a manager, your task is to identify the real crisis (or, more likely, the prodromal crisis).

This may be accomplished by applying to the situation at hand the litmus test discussed earlier:

1. Is there a good chance that this situation will, if left unattended, escalate in intensity?
2. Might this situation foster unwanted attention by outsiders, such as the news media or some regulatory agency?
3. Is it likely that the situation might interfere with normal business operations in some manner?
4. Could it make you look bad or cause people (the public at large, or investors) to lose confidence?
5. How is it going to affect your bottom line?

Using the scoring model to calculate the Crisis Impact Value and the Probability Factor, and then determining the possible Degree of Influence and the Cost of Intervention, you will have:

1. Identified the crisis.
2. Determined whether or not anything can or should be done about it now.

When Johnson & Johnson became a crisis victim of the Tylenol poisonings, there was a lunatic on the loose, running around placing cyanide-laced Tylenol capsules back on shelves in a small handful of supermarkets and drugstores in the Chicago area. Tragically, seven people died as a result. Johnson & Johnson received a well-publicized extortion demand. Copycat crimes began to spring up in isolated pockets around the country. The public was panicked; law enforcement agencies were stymied.

Question: What was the *real* crisis from Johnson & Johnson's perspective?

Answer: The future life of the Tylenol brand and of the subsidiary company, MacNeil Consumer Labs. Virtually nothing else mattered.

Please do not misinterpret the meaning of these words. This is not to suggest that Johnson & Johnson was unfeeling toward the families of the victims, or that it did not do whatever it could to aid the police and the FBI in trying to track down the madman, or that it did not, at a cost of $100 million, voluntarily recall all product packages off of shelves nationwide to calm the public's fears.

The company did all of this and more.

But, from a bottom-line point of view, the *only* crisis over which the firm had *any* control was the crisis of the life or death of its brand and its subsidiary.

Because of all of the other crises surrounding the Tylenol case, and the attendant massive media attention paid to the situation, the public understandably was afraid to purchase the product. The company simply had to accept that fact until it could regain the public's trust and confidence, which they now have done, as well as having regained the lion's share of the market.

Among the reasons why Johnson & Johnson emerged from the Tylenol crisis a better company, or at least a better-*perceived* company, was that the company properly identified the *real* crisis. Quickly.

There may be a tendency among some readers to be armchair quarterbacks.

It's late in the fourth quarter, your team has the ball, third down and long yardage, you're down by a touchdown, the quarterback takes the snap, drops back to pass, but the blitz is on.

Down in the end zone is one of your team's pass receivers. And he's all alone. He's waving his hands like mad, trying to be spotted by the quarterback.

The original play has long been broken up, and the quarterback is scrambling for his life.

And sitting in the comfort of your living room, perhaps having a little snack, is you. Your shoes are off, and your feet are up.

And you shout at the television set: "Throw it, throw it, dummy!"

But, alas, he doesn't throw it. He's sacked. And on the instant replay it becomes apparent ("Everyone has 20–20 hindsight through the retrospectoscope") that, just as you knew all along, a receiver was wide open in the end zone.

And you say, "What a bum! Why didn't he throw it to the guy? He was wide open!" And then you grab another handful of pretzels.

There are probably any number of times when the real quarterbacks would like to change places with the armchair variety. Being on the receiving end of a blitz is probably one of those times.

When you are suddenly confronted by four 300-pound oncoming linemen whose only mission in life is to crush your bones, it is understandable why a receiver was missed.

(Or, as another popular version of the saw goes, "When you are up to your ass in alligators, it's hard to remember that your original mission was to drain the swamp.")

If you have ever experienced a crisis—especially an unanticipated, short-fused crisis—you will have a much better appreciation for what quarterbacks go through on game days. A crisis can hit you—and your company—like a blitz.

And of the four gorillas chasing you, three will rip you apart. But only one will kill you.

All you have to do is decide which one is lethal. And you've got to decide fast.

Therefore, when it is pointed out that Johnson & Johnson successfully identified its crisis, it would be imprudent to be an armchair quarterback and scoff at what *you* consider to have been obvious.

The CEO of a well-known company (who, along with his firm, will remain anonymous) came to my firm as a crisis management client. There actually were several crises at his company, which is usually the case, and the company was unable to deal with any of them. All of the crises were real but none were life-threatening nor immediate. But often, in such situations, there is one pivotal crisis, and if you can identify it, the others may either resolve themselves or become more easily identifiable.

Some of the crises this company was experiencing included:

- New and highly aggressive competition from two sources in markets where it had no competition previously.
- Production problems in antiquated facilities.
- Warehousing and distribution problems.
- Severe management conflicts among three top key executives.
- And somewhat unusual financial problems.

Throughout its existence and skyrocketing growth, the firm had always done business with one bank, the Bank of America. The firm, according to the CEO, had always been a good banking customer and always paid its bills promptly—both to vendors and to the bank.

In order to solve some of the other "problems," the firm decided it needed to modernize and consolidate under one roof. It therefore borrowed about $25 million from the bank to construct new facilities. But, as is sometimes the case, the firm went over budget by about $3 million—and the bankers went bonkers.

B of A agreed to cover only about half of the overage, and the company was forced to make up the other half out of its operating capital. Furthermore, to compound matters, the company agreed to an "open book" policy with the bank. At about the same time, the firm hired a new financial officer who, in his insensitive zeal, produced an incorrect projection (it was unknowingly based on out-of-date figures) that showed that the company would fall way short of its annual projection and, in fact, wind up in the red for the first time. Because of the "open book" policy, which gave the bank complete access to all of the company's financial statements, the bank routinely received a copy of this report.

Naturally, as you might expect, merely telling the bank that the projection was in error convinced no one.

Then the loan was reviewed by the "boys downtown" in the problem loan department, who began to insist on outside auditors and outside consultants; they advised the client to relinquish equity in the firm to outside interests or venture capitalists, and so on. Now the company executives weren't even dealing with the bankers that had known them for years.

Because of the financial crunch *caused by the bank,* the firm then found itself paying vendors about 90 days late. All the while, all of the other problems/crises were escalating. The CEO and other managers were scurrying about trying to put out fires here and there, but others just sprang up elsewhere.

Working on the assumption that everything the CEO said was accurate (that is, prior to these crises, relations with the bank had been excellent; the balance sheet had been in good shape, with a healthy debt-to-equity ratio; projections had been met every year; payments to the bank were never missed or late; vendors were always paid on time; and so on), then *something* was very wrong somewhere. The bank should not have been putting the hammer down quite as hard as it was; one would assume that the bank would want to continue working with a good customer who just went a little over budget on a construction/modernization loan. There was a crisis that needed to be identified—*quickly.*

And the crisis, it turned out, was *in* the bank, not in the client's company.

In managing this client's crisis, all likely sources of the keystone crisis had been considered and, for one reason or another, discarded. As improbable as it seemed, the client's crisis was not being caused by his own company; it was *indirectly* being caused by a crisis at the bank.

Only a few months before any of the client's problems began, the Bank of America had suffered another in a series of crises—only this one was far more public and far more embarrassing.

It seemed that six of B of A's escrow officers had unwittingly gotten the bank involved in an alleged mortgage securities fraud that cost the bank $95 million and added more tarnish to its reputation.

These six got the bank involved as escrow agent on "property which was fraudulently inflated by the National Mortgage Equity Corporation," according to Ron Owens, B of A communications spokesperson in Los Angeles.[21] As a result, and in a highly public display of employer ire, the bank fired five of the officers and demoted the sixth.

And, Owens explained, the unforgiving bank filed suit against the six for gross negligence and mismanagement. The bank then filed a federal fraud and racketeering action against the National Mortgage Equity Corporation (NMEC); the law firm that, according to Owens, prepared the memo used to market the securities; and a company involved in trying to buy the properties. Total amount of the suits: $385 million.

In discussing the crisis management, or lack thereof, at B of A, Peter Magnani, a senior public relations officer and spokesperson at the bank's San Francisco headquarters, explained that to prevent this sort of occurrence, the bank had had adequate controls but that they hadn't been followed. Which, of course, makes "adequate controls" a contradictory phrase. There were controls, but they obviously were not adequate.

Magnani went on to say that there was "no way a bank escrow officer would allow that to happen again." He spoke freely of the bank's "tightening controls" and said that "the message has gone out internally from on high to all employees that we don't do business that way." He also said that he doubted that "any employee in the entire bank is not affected by this situation."[22]

In an interesting turnabout of the Bank of America's crisis, a Cincinnati shareholder then filed suit against B of A's top officers, charging *them* in a cover-up of the entire NMEC affair. The suit alleged that the terminated officers were ousted with large severance pay in order to ensure their silence and to protect such high-ranking bank officials as Chairman Leland Prussia and President Samuel Armacost, who also were charged with gross negligence and mismanagement. And just to show what other types of crises B of A has been facing of late, the shareholder suit also charged the bank with reckless lending policies, which led to some $60 million in bad loans to Paraguay, and complained that B of A's poor reputation was the reason federal regulators rejected the bank's application to open 13 limited-service branch banks outside its home state of California.[23]

And as if the Bank of America didn't have enough problems, just one week after the bank—the nation's largest, by the way—announced a loss of $338 million in the second quarter of 1985 (the second-largest quarterly deficit in U.S. banking history), it was slapped with two additional share-holder suits.

One suit, filed by a New York consulting firm against the bank's directors and officers, sought more than $100 million in an effort to recover a fraction of the bank's accumulated $1 billion in loan losses since early 1984. The other suit was a class action filed by a New York City housewife, on behalf of anyone who bought or sold BankAmerica securities during the 18-month period from February 1, 1984, to July 17, 1985. The attorney handling both cases charged the bank with lying and covering up the true financial picture of the bank and of its loan portfolio.[24]

But before getting too deeply immersed in the Bank of America's crises, let's go back to the client's crisis and see how the ripple effects of the bank's crises triggered his.

Not only did the bank have egg on its face when the NMEC affair was made public, but go back and reread Peter Magnani's description of what was going on inside the bank. There wasn't one B of A employee—in any capacity, he said—who was not somewhat shaken by the events. Some may have even had reason to be downright nervous.

How would *you* like to work for a company that fires employees for negligence and sues them for millions?*

We are not presuming anyone's guilt or innocence here; we are just asking how *you* would feel. If *you* were a commercial lending officer at the bank, and five of your colleagues had been publicly fired and sued by your boss in the midst of a crisis, mightn't you be just a bit overzealous in your banking relationships? Mightn't you be just a mite overreactive? Mightn't you consider it better to err on the side of caution in your dealings with even a good customer?

---

*The B of A explained that this suit had to be brought in order for its negligence coverage to be activated. But as a result of bringing suit, in April 1985 the bank's insurance carrier, Employers Insurance of Wausau, canceled the bank's Director's and Officer's Liability Insurance policy. D and O insurance protects directors and officers against negligence claims by shareholders. The bank promptly created its own insurance company in the Cayman Islands—just for its own liability coverage. Without adequate D and O coverage, as many public companies are today discovering, outside directors are resigning from boards to protect their own personal assets. For some companies, this is a crisis; for B of A, however, it was a ripple effect of the bank's bigger crisis. And when you are a deep-pocket company, you can smooth out minor annoyances such as a canceled insurance policy by starting your *own* insurance company. Naturally, if the bank doesn't turn its loan portfolio and losses around, its pockets will start to shrink. They may be deep, but they're not bottomless.

Our client got caught in this ripple effect of the bank's own crisis.

The crisis was identified for the client, who was further advised (and even aided, as well) to do business with another bank. And having accomplished that, all of his other small crises managed to be resolved easily.

By properly identifying the real crisis, there was, indeed, a happy ending.

But remember: identifying the crisis is only the first of the three steps.

P.S. You saved the baby. You're a hero. But you need a new suit. And an umbrella.

10

Isolating the Crisis

Don't let go of a lion in your grip; he will devour you.

—Jewish proverb

There is no question that a crisis is a disease and should be treated as such. Moreover, it should be viewed and regarded as a communicable disease.

And as any first-year medical student will tell you, communicable-disease patients should be quarantined, or put into isolation, to prevent the disease from spreading. Similarly, you do not want to allow your crisis to contaminate anything else.

It can be a fatal mistake to think that a crisis, if left unattended, will heal by itself. A crisis should be viewed as highly virulent—and should be treated accordingly.

But you cannot operate on it until it has been isolated.

In its report, and criticism, of what went wrong at Three Mile Island and why, the Kemeny Commission wrote:

[The control room at TMI] is seriously deficient under accident conditions. During the first few minutes of the accident, more than 100 alarms went off, and there was no system for suppressing the unimportant signals so that operators could concentrate on the significant alarms. Information was not presented in a clear and sufficiently understandable form.[25]

The critical information, meaning the crisis itself, was not isolated.

When Alan Hirschfield first identified the Columbia Pictures crisis as David Begelman, he (Hirschfield) failed to isolate the crisis. He attempted to deal with the crisis and still run the studio, but he was unable to perform either task well.

Hirschfield—a talented studio chief and more-than-qualified executive—was unable to tend to his normal duties on a normal basis. And all the while, the crisis was spreading quickly. The more it spread, the more time Hirschfield spent in trying to grapple with the situation; consequently, the less time he was able to spend tending to the healthy part of his "patient" (the studio). Eventually, of course, the crisis began to dominate most of his business and nonbusiness hours, to the detriment of his ability to manage the studio in an uninterrupted style.

What were Hirschfield's options after he identified the crisis and the potential trouble it could cause?

1. He could have delegated the task of dealing with the crisis to someone else, which would have freed him up to run the studio.
2. He could have delegated the task of running the studio to someone else for a short time, while he dealt with the crisis.

Either of those options would certainly have been preferable to what did happen, or more accurately, what did *not* happen.

It is often the case that, once a crisis is properly identified, it rages out of control simply because of a CEO who feels that he or she is indispensable to the everyday operations of the company. It is not known whether this is what happened in the Columbia Pictures crisis, but it may be one plausible explanation.

A CEO should not be indispensable to a company. If he or she is, that company has a prodromal situation on its hands and may not even know it. But be advised that in the survey of *Fortune* 500 companies mentioned earlier, two respondents specifically listed the untimely death of their respective CEOs as the largest crisis their companies suffered. The companies were unprepared for that contingency and suffered because, apparently, the departed CEOs had become—by accident or design—indispensable.

The reality is that nothing can or should take precedence over a crisis. *Either* all other duties and functions of the CEO should be delegated to others or simply dropped for the duration—*or* others in the company with decision-making capabilities (for example, the crisis management team) should be asked to drop their normal duties to deal with the crisis.

Clearly, and as will be covered in more detail later in the book, the successes of Johnson & Johnson in handling its Tylenol crisis, and Procter & Gamble's in handling its Rely tampon crisis, were largely due to the ability of those two companies to isolate both the crisis and the people dealing with it.

David E. Collins, vice chairman of Johnson & Johnson's executive committee and the man who was given the mandate by J&J chairman

James E. Burke to "take charge," explained that only a handful of J&J people were involved in the day-to-day management of the crisis, while by and large everyone else went about his or her normal business. "But everyone in the company—worldwide—was kept informed on a regular basis," Collins added.[26]

And while the company was in otherwise good hands, the Tylenol crisis management team focused on nothing else except the crisis.

Procter & Gamble typically operates on a strict "need-to-know" basis, so isolating a crisis management team which then proceeded to isolate the Rely crisis was, in a sense, P&G's standard operating procedure.

In a November 7, 1980, *Wall Street Journal* article by John A. Prestbo, the late P&G chairman Edward G. Harness was quoted as saying that "only a handful [of P&G executives] were detached from regular duty to work on the Rely situation,"[27] while anyone and everyone else was excluded intentionally.

But whether a crisis is handled by the CEO or turned over to someone else in authority to handle it, the crisis needs to be isolated to be able to manage it effectively.

The major deal that your company has been working on for so long and that is about to close is meaningless if the company goes belly-up in the quagmire of a crisis. Save the company today, and there will be other deals tomorrow.

You should allow no extraneous matters to interfere with what clearly is the most frightening of the three steps: managing the crisis.

11

Managing the Crisis

It is common sense to take a method and try it. If it fails, admit it frankly and try another. But above all, try something.

— *Franklin Delano Roosevelt*

Identifying and isolating a crisis without managing it is as effective as trying to halt a swan dive into shark-infested waters when two-thirds of the way through it. It is only a matter of time before you and the water meet head on.

In example after example in this book, you will observe that once the decision maker has identified and isolated the crisis, it becomes immensely easier to manage the crisis, since any misleading and possibly dangerous diversionary paths have been blocked off.

A decision maker who has failed to identify and isolate the crisis at hand may waste precious time meandering through perilous highways and byways filled with seemingly promising—but counterfeit—escape hatches. This occurs because the nonidentification of the crisis obviously prevents the decision maker from identifying a specific goal or objective that will eradicate the problem. Hence the serpentine wandering.

But once the crisis is identified and isolated, you will have a clearer idea of what actions you will need to take to rectify the problem. This is a basic tenet of medicine: you must diagnose the problem before you can treat it. Isolating the crisis will give you the single-mindedness required to manage it.

And in managing the crisis—which involves knowing how to make proper decisions—you will be less tempted to wander down gingerbread-house paths if you vigilantly ask whether the route you are considering will lead you closer to your strategic objective.

Asking and properly answering these questions will shut off revolving doors that lead to quick-fix, Band-Aid approaches rather than to permanent, major-surgery resolutions.

This does not, however, automatically mean that the decision maker is suddenly presented with the one perfect halo-enriched answer. Several options may still be open. But each option should be closer to meeting the objective than the other, discarded suggestions. It is up to the decision maker (the crisis management team) to decide which of the possible decisions still on the table will achieve the strategic objective of managing the crisis toward a successful resolution.

For in managing a crisis, you are managing decisions. The more adept you can become as a decision maker who has the ability to find opportunity where others routinely take detours, the more skill, success, and regard you will have as a crisis manager.

Of course, just blocking off treacherous diversionary routes does not guarantee that a crisis will be successfully managed. As the Japanese proverb goes, "To know and not to act is not to know at all."

Sometimes an individual fails to act because his or her feet become rooted in the cement of the "it-can't-happen-here" syndrome. This person practices a form of denial and refuses to accept what is happening. This sufferer is relatively easy to spot.

The really dangerous decision makers are those who fall prey to "analysis paralysis." These obsessive decision makers are dangerous because they give the impression that they are making decisions, but their obsessive nature prevents them from moving forward.

"Analysis paralysis" sufferers will, of course, make a decision but will not act on it. Rather, they will chew on it until it becomes distasteful. Then they will spit it out and start the decision-making process all over again.

"Analysis paralysis" can be fatal in a situation in which the manager obsessively overanalyzes the crisis until he or she is paralyzed by it and totally incapable of even attempting to manage it.

During the Iranian hostage crisis—one of this country's most embarrassing episodes—it became acutely and shamefully obvious that Jimmy Carter could not manage the crisis because he was suffering from analysis paralysis.

Obviously he had *identified* it as a crisis.*

Because of the so-called Rose Garden strategy—a blatantly obvious political ploy in which he almost never left the White House so he could "concentrate" on the crisis, but which was really a tactic employed to

---

*Of course, this was after numerous prodromes were either missed or ignored.

conveniently avoid Senator Edward Kennedy during the 1980 Democratic presidential primary campaign—Carter obviously had *isolated* the crisis.

All that remained was to manage the crisis—to deal with it, to resolve it, to make vigilant decisions.

According to accounts of the White House under siege, Carter did indeed meet with his advisers—his crisis management team—for hours and hours throughout the day. Decisions would be made. But after wrestling with the decision late at night—perhaps obsessively overanalyzing—Carter would announce the next morning that he had changed his mind. The decision would not be implemented. The decision would be scrapped or reanalyzed. Either way, the process would begin anew.

Eventually, some six months later, a plan was hammered out—a rescue plan. This plan (a) failed; (b) took eight innocent lives; and (c) prompted the resignation of then-Secretary of State Cyrus Vance, who had disapproved of the plan.

Fourteen months after the acute crisis began, Carter did eventually manage to resolve it, as some have stated, by losing the election to Ronald Reagan. At the *precise* moment Reagan took the oath of office, the Iranians released the hostages.

The actual degree to which Carter was obsessive may be open to debate. However, what the world observed was one demonstrably proactive response to the crisis (the aborted rescue attempt), followed by almost nine months of inertness.

In managing a crisis, the decision maker must not be locked into rigid, inflexible plans. Keep in mind, as noted earlier, that a crisis is a fluid process that requires a similarly fluid decision-making process.

Adopting a "bunker mentality"—which is what Carter did during the Iranian hostage crisis—is a common strategy trap that poor decision makers are prone to fall into. While it is critical to have reliable fact-gatherers feeding you information (another reason why you should have a crisis management team in place before the crisis), it is wrong to continue to hide behind them. Get the facts you want, the facts you need, and get them fast. Then start making decisions; start managing the crisis.

Military strategists have debated whether or not Carter's crisis management decisions were fluid enough. From a crisis management perspective—and from a military perspective—the unfortunate results speak for themselves.

The military strategists have an old adage with which they admonish themselves while making strategic preparations for battle: "Do not take counsel of your fears."

It is good advice for anyone preparing to do battle by managing a crisis.

12

After the Fall

Storms pass, but their driftwood remains.

—*Ancient proverb*

Being well prepared to manage a crisis is still no guarantee that, during the acute phase of the crisis, you won't have the uneasy feeling that you are not in control of the situation. Acute crises have a way of taking on a life of their own, and it may be impossible for anyone to be in complete control.

Your aim should be to exercise as much control as possible, stopping every once in a while to assess the situation by asking, "Am I doing all I can do; are we, as a company, doing all that we can do; do I feel confident about my decisions, about my ability to continue to manage this crisis?"

Such questions are not intended to plague you with self-doubt. Rather, they are meant as additional working tools for you to use during the chronic phase of the crisis.

Accept it as a given that, depending on the nature and magnitude of your crisis, you will be placed under a series of powerful microscopes by a variety of operators as soon as it appears safe for them to dive into the waters that were clearly shark-infested while you were swimming in them. Some of the "probers" may even take on the same characteristics of the sharks you thought you had just disposed of.

(Nowhere is this more apparent than in the world of corporate take-overs, in which some of the defensive mechanisms are even referred to as "shark repellents." Companies such as Phillips Petroleum, Walt Disney Studios, and Bendix Corporation learned the hard way that fighting off unwanted suitors—and thereby becoming weak due to the debilitating effects of the fight—only makes them more vulnerable to a new school of sharks. More on this increasingly common type of business crisis in Chapter 15.)

The sharks referred to here may take the form of investigative reporters or government agencies (federal, state, or local). Shark propellants may include inquiries/investigations, congressional hearings, political position papers, lawsuits, depositions, and so on and so on. While it may be true that no one loves you when you're down and out, you wouldn't know it from the level of interest a whole host of people suddenly start to show in you.

As soon as you get the first inkling of the nature of your acute crisis and can envision or even predict a protracted chronic phase, try to take necessary steps during the acute phase to be prepared to answer the question "why" during the chronic phase.

Remember, as discussed previously, that whereas the acute phase eventually ends, the chronic phase can be of indeterminate length or, in some instances, endless. Therefore, the more carefully you plan for the chronic phase *during* the acute phase, the better you'll be prepared to navigate through its rough waters.

How can you predict a long, drawn-out chronic phase? Depending on the nature of your crisis, if the crisis and/or the company fit certain profiles, you can make certain well-reasoned assumptions. Such *business* profiles would include:

- A public company.
- A highly visible/household-word company, whether public or private.
- A visible CEO or other senior executive—sort of a celebrity type, whose visibility may or may not have anything to do with the company (a William Agee-type, or a Mary Cunningham-type, or both).

Such *crisis* profiles would include any crisis that:

- Involves the loss of lives, especially in large numbers.
- *Almost* costs lives.
- Creates a panic.
- Demonstrates an industry weakness or trend.
- Is exposed by the media *(especially* if it makes good copy).
- Entails conspiracies, morals offenses, kickbacks, bribes, or swindles.

If you or your company fit the profile in the first list, or if the sort of crisis you experience fits the profile in the second list, you can expect that after the acute phase of the crisis has concluded, you will be in for a protracted chronic phase.

As mentioned earlier, "why" is a luxury question during the acute phase of a crisis. But during the chronic phase, "why" *is* the question.

Along with "how" and "what" and "when" and "where" and so on. *These* questions were first asked during the acute phase and are reprised here in the chronic phase.

You should be prepared for this onslaught. And if you can steel yourself to be prepared for it even while still in the midst of the acute crisis, you will be more in control of the chronic phase.

It is safe to assume that you will be asked time and again by many different categories of people (two such types might simply be labeled "friend" and "foe") to rehash the details of what happened. Specifically you will be asked: "What did you know, and when did you know it?" If you can envision these questions being asked, then plan in advance to answer.

In anticipation of the chronic phase, try to chronicle your acute crisis, either on your own or by assigning that function to someone else. Tape-record—overtly, always—planning sessions, crisis management team meetings, fact-gathering reports, and so on. Write down or dictate into a tape recorder your thoughts, feelings, reasons for making decisions, and so on. Ask other people to do the same. Consider having a photographer and/or video camera operator on hand at all times.

In other words, you want to freeze a particular point in time—a point in time that you will be asked to live and relive and recount, perhaps for years. If you have a credible and accurate record from which to quote, it will make it easier to get through the chronic phase and will help to speed up the chronic phase itself.

Having records will also aid you if you find yourself in an uncomfortable position during an acute crisis—where you are advocating one course of action in the face of stiff opposition. Eventually you may be asked about your position.

The classic example of this type of scenario is that of John Dean, former legal counsel to Richard Nixon. During the Watergate hearings, Dean testified for days about his recollections of what transpired in the White House regarding the entire Watergate affair. Dean's testimony was unwavering, unshakable. And, in contrast to a parade of other senior White House functionaries who followed him to the witness table, Dean was believed.

If you take the time to duly record appropriate comments and events during a crisis, when you respond to "why," people will give your response more credence.

You will have demonstrated that you understood at the time the magnitude of the crisis as it occurred and that you memorialized in writing, or on tape, or on film as many of the proceedings as possible, anticipating that questions would be asked.

And you will have created your own opportunity by being prepared to respond authoritatively.

For your part, you should not spend too much time wondering why the investigations (articles, hearings, and so on) seem to be going on and on. There may be some up-and-coming investigator (reporter, prosecutor, politician, whatever) out to make a name for himself or herself at your expense. If there is no apparent malice, you may have to suffer ignominiously.

You may consult with your lawyers or public relations consultants to find out if you can pursue certain remedies, such as lawsuits or editorial briefings for the media, to put an end to your ordeal.

But, by and large, you may just have to tough it out. This is all the more reason for doing whatever is necessary during the acute phase to be prepared for the chronic phase.

Two other headaches to guard against are the almost inevitable attacks on your other corporate entities or subsidiaries and the invidious comparisons of subsequent crises to yours.

When a company suffers a megacrisis at one of its plants, as Union Carbide did in Bhopal, India, there is a natural tendency on the part of people (news media, community leaders, government officials) to point at other plants owned by that company (such as Union Carbide's plant in Institute, West Virginia) and put it under a similarly powerful microscope. Sometimes this attention is warranted; sometimes it is not. Nevertheless, the hue and cry can be anticipated. So, too, can the attacks on other types of facilities owned by the same parent corporation. Known as "guilt by association," extremely minor occurrences at any Union Carbide plant from now on will run a good chance of being mentioned by the media simply *because* they happen at a Union Carbide facility.

As long as this continues, you know the chronic phase of your crisis still is under way.

But the invidious comparisons—perhaps due to our insatiable appetite for superlatives—may continue long after the chronic phase, depending of course on the crisis. And it is typically the news media that are guilty of perpetuating the crisis in the public's mind.

The invidious comparison is the part of the news story that says, "The worst nuclear accident since Three Mile Island. . . ." Or, "The most widespread case of product tampering since the Tylenol poisonings. . . ." Or, "The most deaths from a chemical plant accident since Union Carbide's Bhopal disaster. . . ."

Those are the sorts of comparisons that make the corporate public relations people cringe. To their way of thinking, the media should stop dredging up ancient history.

But it is the nature of the media to "dredge up ancient history" when it enhances the story. And the sad and frightening truth is, the only thing that will make the media stop comparing chemical plant accidents to Union Carbide's is to have a *worse* accident to take its place.

Just because a crisis is not yours does not mean that you cannot find opportunity in it.

During the chronic phase of a crisis—someone else's crisis—while his or her bones are being picked apart, look around to see what mistakes were made and whether or not you are vulnerable to the same problems.

As someone once said, "The only thing better than profiting from your mistakes is profiting from someone else's."*

There is not a power plant in the country today that does not have some sort of crisis management plan in case of an "incident." But, how many of these plans were in existence *prior* to Three Mile Island? Few, if any.

Today, look at how many over-the-counter consumer drugs and other ingestible products come in "tamper-proof" containers, which feature warnings not to use the product and to return it to the store where it was purchased if a safety seal is broken. You can credit the Tylenol poisonings for this.

How many Americans today are more sensitive to putting their money into *federally* insured savings and loan associations (Federal Savings & Loan Insurance Corporation) or banks (Federal Deposit Insurance Corporation) instead of *privately* insured financial institutions? This is a direct result of the collapse and closing in March 1985 of Ohio's Home State Savings Bank, which precipitated a run on other state-chartered S&Ls that did not have adequate insurance to cover the panic withdrawals. (For more on this crisis, see Chapter 17.)

The point should be clear: although it may not be sporting to kick your opponent while he's down, if you can be felled by the same type of crisis that brought him to his knees, quickly find out where he was vulnerable and why, and govern yourself accordingly.

And if your competitor is vulnerable, are you, too? Are you legitimately vulnerable to a crisis because you are a chemical plant and because what happened to Union Carbide could happen to you? Or are you vulnerable because you are an over-the-counter analgesic manufacturer and when Tylenol suffered, people shied away from your product, too?

To guard against this sort of "guilt by association," you should view a competitor's crisis as a prodrome for your own company.

During this phase your own internal, brutally frank assessment must begin.

---

*Actually, this book is designed to show you how to profit from your achievements, which is even better!

This is *your* time and *your* turn to ask yourself and all other appropriate persons: what did you know, and when did you know it?

You should *now* ask "why" and not rest until you are satisfied with the answer.

Start—either on your own or by assigning a crisis evaluation team to the task—to review, assess, evaluate, rate, dissect exactly what happened, how it could have been prevented, and, if it happened again, what—if anything—you would do differently.

Examine your crisis management plan and your crisis management team closely. How did the plan work; how did the people on the team perform as individuals and as members of a team?

And who distinguished himself or herself? Who, in the face of a crisis, was able to rise to his or her own level of achievement, seizing opportunity instead of danger? Who deserves to be rewarded or promoted?

As a crisis is a battle, are medals for valor in order? Is anyone in line to be court-martialed?

If there was a failing somewhere, was it because of a component of the plan? Is it a problem that can be fixed?

Or could that so-called failing have been better handled by someone else? Why? What does that tell you about the individual who did not perform quite so well? Was he in over his head? Was there too much stress for him? Should he be removed from the crisis management team? Should he be reassigned within the company?

Be liberal in your praise but penurious in your criticism. Keep in mind that a crisis is extremely stressful for all concerned. While you hope that you have selected the most qualified people to serve on your crisis management team, you never know how someone is going to respond "under fire." Therefore, if someone "freezes," simply remove that individual, quietly, and send in a replacement.

This phase, then, should be viewed as a period of self-assessment, modification, fine-tuning, and even mid-course correction at all levels.

You may never have such another golden opportunity to evaluate how you, your company, your crisis management plan and crisis management team performed.

This period is like the week between games in professional football. Spend the time wisely to review the game films again and again, until you know everything that happened and how you can improve on it next time.

In football, next time comes the following week, come rain or come shine.

Your next time may not come so predictably. But, rain or shine, you should plan on your next crisis with at least the same inevitability.

13

Crisis Communications, Part I: Controlling the Message

Does anyone have any questions for my answers?

*—Henry Kissinger, at the opening
of a press conference*

We didn't always have radio and television.

We didn't always have 24-hour news.

We didn't always have telecommunications satellites orbiting in space.

We didn't always have instant communications.

But now we do have all of these modern marvels, and more are being added each day. The immediacy of our communications heightens the immediacy of our crises, and sometimes the communication itself becomes the news it is intended to cover. Television brought the Vietnam War into our living rooms every night. Walter Cronkite and the "CBS Evening News" put Menachem Begin and Anwar Sadat on a split-screen television image and, as a result, it appeared that television accomplished what Moses could not: it brought the Hebrews and the Egyptians together at a peace table.

If the media can communicate the news the instant it happens, crisis communications dictate that a company *must* be prepared to respond almost as fast. The inability to communicate your message skillfully during a crisis can prove fatal. And it would be a totally needless demise, a wrongful death.

In the section of its report entitled "The Public's Right to Public Information," some of the Kemeny Commission's findings were that:

• Neither Met Ed nor the Nuclear Regulatory Commission had specific plans for providing accident information to the public or to the news media.

• During the accident, official sources of information were often confused about or ignorant of the facts. News coverage often reflected this confusion and ignorance.

• Met Ed's handling of information during the first three days of the accident resulted in its loss of credibility as an information source, both with government officials and with the media. Part of the problem was that the utility company was slow to confirm "pessimistic" news about the accident.

• The quality of information provided to the public has a significant bearing on the capacity of people to respond to the accident, on their mental health, and on their willingness to accept guidance from responsible officials.

• During the first few days of the accident, Babcock & Wilcox, the desigers and builders of Three Mile Island, made a conscious decision *not* to comment on the accident, even when company officials believed that other sources were misinforming the public.*

Try to envision events in two categories: those over which you are probably not in total control, and those over which you are in much greater control. The former is the crisis itself, and the latter is your communication of the crisis to the outside world. And since it is your crisis, you at least have the ability to shape the public's initial (and perhaps total) perception of what has happened or is happening.

But, as with anything else, the time to begin is not when the crisis is upon you, but well before.

If you are the CEO of a company with an internal communicator† who does not have direct access to you, who does not have your confidence, who does not have authority, who does not serve in a senior management-level position, and who does not actively participate in all strategic planning sessions, then ask yourself *why*. If it's because that *particular individual* does not measure up to being an adviser to you, find yourself a replacement—immediately.

"The single most important thing for a communicator in a crisis is immediate access to authority," stated Lawrence G. Foster, Johnson &

---

*Author's Award for Ostrich of the Nuclear Age is awarded to Babcock & Wilcox.

†Different companies have different titles for this position, such as director or vice president of public relations, communications, corporate communications, public affairs, investor relations, community relations, and so on. For our purposes, the communicator appellation can and does refer to any of these many titles.

Johnson's corporate vice president for public relations and a pivotal player in the successful handling of the Tylenol crisis. He is a member of J&J's executive committee and reports directly to the chairman, James Burke. Foster continued:

> And the second most important thing for a communicator in a crisis is to have authority himself.
>
> I didn't have to go to anyone and discuss a "strategy" for handling the media; I had the authority to establish that policy, which in the Tylenol crisis was a policy of truthfulness and honesty.[28]

Unfortunately, communicators with Foster's degree of authority may be in the minority in American business. But there are any number of, one hopes, well-reasoned arguments for why that policy should change and why more companies should adopt the Johnson & Johnson model.

Outside the executive suite, most companies typically have two departments that command all-seeing vistas of the rest of the company. One is the personnel/human resources department; the other is the communications department. Of the two, though, the communications department, headed by your chief communicator, is in the advantageous position of processing incoming data from other departments with a broader application.

In other words, while the personnel department is concerned with personnel and personnel issues on a companywide basis, the communications department is concerned with how the outside world views what happens within the company and how those outside perceptions will affect other issues.

If your communicator regularly wanders the halls, visits other departments, and asks what's new there, does the company avail itself of the information he or she uncovers? When, as an example, the executive committee decides to close a plant for unshakable bottom-line reasons, is any thought given to how the story will "play in Peoria"? If you are about to *create* a crisis, isn't it only right that the communicator who at some point will be called on to explain and defend your actions to the media should be involved in the crisis management planning?

If you make your communicator part of the decision-making process, there is reason to expect that he or she will put forth suggestions of ways to "package" the "bad" news in the best possible light. In fact, this should be what your communicator does best.

This is not to suggest that you should adopt Machiavellian propaganda techniques; rather, you should simply present the truth in the most advantageous way. If there are indeed two sides to every story, no one says *you* have to tell both of them. Just help your communicator tell your side proactively, and let someone else tell the other side reactively.

If you are having trouble getting your message out—during a crisis or not—maybe there is something wrong with the message. Maybe the message needs to be reshaped. Or redirected. Or rethought. Maybe your communicator—had he or she been given the opportunity earlier—would have been able to show you where your thought process was off simply by saying, "That concept will be hard to sell to the media. It's too _____ [choose one: complicated, confusing, hard to swallow, or whatever]. If we try to put that message out as our rationale for doing x, we run the genuine risk of being _____ [again, take your pick: misunderstood, laughed at, ignored, ridiculed by our competitors, and so on]. However, if we were to do such and such, *then.* . . ."

An example discussed earlier in this book about different ways to close a plant—one way generating almost a guaranteed negative press, and another producing just the opposite effect—illustrates how important it is for your chief communicator to be elevated to a responsible position as adviser to the CEO and other senior management.

Another example of a potential crisis that was averted through conscientious public relations efforts involved the Commonwealth of Pennsylvania's awkward 6 percent sales tax and its beer-drinking voters.

Early in Thornburgh's administration, a proposal for a revised taxing structure that affected *how* and *where* the sales tax on beer was levied was put forth by the governor's own Office of Budget and Administration. It recommended—and everyone who saw the document approved—a plan to levy the 6 percent tax on beer at the *retail* level.

This would mean—and here comes the crisis—that every glass of beer a bartender previously sold for $1.00 would now cost $1.06. Think of how awkward that extra 6 cents would be. Consider, not only how annoying it would be for bartenders throughout the state, who would have to make change and make sure they had plenty of pennies on hand, but the nuisance to the patrons, too. Previously, they would plunk down a $5 bill and know that they could get five beers. Now, they'd get four beers and a mess of coins, not even a nice stack of shiny quarters. No; beer at the bar was about to jump to the "sore thumb" price of $1.*06*.

Adding the tax at the retail level would have meant additional revenue for the state. However, some sharp communicator[29] in the governor's press office* remembered what everyone else apparently forgot: beer drinkers

---

*So attuned is the Pennsylvania governor's press office to the sensitivities and vagaries of the electorate that, as a matter of routine, virtually anything destined to become public is routed past this office for final approval. This practice began in 1979, when Governor Thornburgh was chagrined to find that his signing of a "Gay Rights Week" proclamation brought the ire of members of his own party in and out of politics. The media had a field day with the resultant backlash. Thornburgh's embarrassment caused him (a) never to sign another gay rights proclamation and (b) to insist that *everything* be run past the press office before being released.

vote. And they might remember who was responsible for lousing up their good time at the neighborhood tap room.

Results: The tax was reapplied to the wholesale level, which meant less revenues for the state. And a genuine crisis was averted: prodrome direct to resolution, acute and chronic phases bypassed.

The time to begin crisis communications is when there is no crisis and when it is possible to create a reservoir of good will. Your communicator should be sure that your company is currently maintaining good relations with the media. Your company's credibility should be high, your company's management should be accessible to the media. Your communicator should arrange media briefings, interviews, plant tours, and so on.

There often is, and probably always will be, a natural adversarial relationship between the media and the subjects they cover. During times of crisis, when tempers may flare and deadlines loom, this adversarial relationship between the media and your company or your chief communicator may escalate. However, if during times of calm your communicator goes out of his or her way—in fact, your company goes out of its way—to improve this relationship even somewhat, it will make your communicator's job of conveying *credible* information to the media during a crisis much smoother.

Your chief communicator, or someone from the communications department, should be a member of every crisis management team. No matter how good your crisis management team is, no matter how complete your crisis management plan, if you cannot communicate your message during a crisis, you have failed. And failed needlessly.

One of the first things to be established is a crisis communications plan.

Refer back to the crisis management plan discussed in Chapter 7. Next to the listing of potential crises, put down on paper another category for each crisis, titled: "What sorts of things should we be prepared to say?"

For example, if you are a manufacturing plant and a potential crisis may be an industrial accident, you should have in your kit (more about the kit in a moment) all of the latest and most pertinent safety records of your plant as of a reasonably recent date. This information will enable you to quickly issue statements which say things like:

- Prior to today's mishap, our plant had not lost one man-hour of work due to accident in the last five years.
- We are a leader in the field in terms of safety, as demonstrated by the following citations from the Occupational Safety and Health Administration.
- The equipment that malfunctioned and caused the trouble was last serviced and certified for use one month ago.

If you are a chemical plant, and a potential crisis may be pollution or toxic waste, you should be prepared to report immediately on your plant's health and ecological record with the government, with such statements as:

- While this plant has been cited by the EPA for leaks, it has been cited only three times in the past six years, and the last time was two years ago.
- We have spent more than $X million in the past 12 months alone in improving our waste-removal system.
- Our level of compliance demonstrates our company's desire to be a good and environmentally sound neighbor.

Such messages are important to get out early in a crisis. You are not hiding the truth; you are presenting it in a *controlled, proactive* package. But how long would it take your company's communicator to gather such information and be prepared to issue such messages?

Here's another example.

At some point, someone in a high-level position in your company—or someone who used to occupy such a position—is going to die. (Which, in and of itself, may cause a crisis, as we have seen.) Whether this person dies a natural death or dies as the result of a company crisis, your communications department should be prepared to issue his or her official biography. There should be on file in the communications department official biographies of everyone in the company from a certain level up.

These bios, along with photographs and television slides, should be prepared as a matter of routine and not "in the event of death."

And the bios and all other information should be updated *regularly*.

This type of information—and this is just the tip of the iceberg—should be readily available during times of crises. And, most ideally, it should be prepared in the form of a crisis background kit that can be distributed to the media almost literally at a moment's notice. And if it has been updated regularly, it should never be so out of date as to be useless or make you seem as though you and your company don't know what you are doing.

You must be ready to respond. You must anticipate the media's questions by anticipating the type of crisis you may encounter.

If your plant runs the risk of explosion, one of the first things the media will want to know is when was the *last* explosion. (Remember the "dredging up ancient history" headache mentioned as part of the chronic phase of a crisis? Well, it begins now, in the acute crisis phase.)

By not having to waste precious time in tracking down this information, you unshackle yourself to manage the actual day-to-day, minute-to-minute aspects of crisis communications during the acute crisis. And it allows you to be *pro*active rather than *re*active.

What you are striving for is what you should always be striving for: to control and manage the message, control and manage the communications, control and manage the crisis. You want to issue the story or the statement *your* way, in the way that will tell the truth and make your company look best. You want to issue the most positive statements you can in a proactive way, rather than allowing yourself to be placed in a position to defend against negative, reactive questions from the media.

One of the most frustrating positions to be in is one in which the news media ignore all of the positive things you do and just report the negative. Your company employs 1,000 people, but because of a downturn in the economy you have to either lay off 200 people or close down entirely. You opt to stay open, but with a reduced work force.

The media icily report that you are laying off 200 people. They don't report your alternative option at all. But do they *know* the alternative?

Instead of reacting to the media's telephone calls—"Is it true that you are laying off 200 workers?"—your communicator should be expected to look for ways to turn negatives into positives—or, at minimum, at least to neutralize negatives. In a proactive stance in this situation, your company could report everything that was done to try to save the 200 positions and then regrettably conclude that laying off 200 workers was an action designed to *save the jobs of 800 other workers.*

If you are able to adopt proactive stances during a crisis, you will be in a better position to control the message.

When a short-fused crisis erupts, it is essential that facts are gathered immediately. While admittedly the initial report of the fact-gatherers may be sketchy, it will at least give a decision maker an idea of the scope and magnitude of the crisis. Knowing this information will tell the decision maker which crisis management team needs to be convened. (Assuming there is more than one.) The team, as part of its already established crisis communications plan, now has to decide *who* needs to be contacted, *how*, and *by whom.*

For example, if Chrysler Corporation found it necessary to recall one of its automobile models, it would probably notify customers via certified mail. But certified mail would take too long if the potential threat were more immediate, as when Johnson & Johnson needed to quickly alert its distribution points to remove Tylenol from retailers' shelves. It used electronic mail.

Sometimes, even Mailgrams are too slow. During Unocal's 1985 proxy fight with T. Boone Pickens, the company took out full-page ads in selected newspapers ("Because time is short . . ." the ad read), urging stockholders to vote by Datagram, also a service of Western Union. In this instance, the stockholder telephoned a toll-free (800) telephone number, and the vote was transmitted directly to a Telex machine located in Unocal's office. Elapsed time from telephone call to message received: approximately 30 minutes. And Unocal prepaid all charges.

In 1984 Americans transmitted approximately 976.4 billion messages[30] via:

- 600 billion telephone calls.
- 250 billion interoffice memos.
- 125 billion first-class letters.
- 1 billion telegrams, Telexes, or facsimiles.
- 250 million electronic mail messages.
- 125 million priority-mail, overnight-courier letters and packages.

The individual handling crisis communications must be familiar with these various methods of communicating and know which method to use when and with which public.

News conferences, news releases, interviews, teleconferencing, and so on should be viewed as ways to communicate to mass markets. While mass communications certainly can be vital, depending on the nature of the crisis, there are other groups that specifically require special communications:

- *Employees:* Even if they first hear of the crisis on the news, they should be notified at the very first opportunity—at most within 24 hours after the acute crisis breaks—of events as they stand and should be promised more information as soon as possible. (Assume that any correspondence to employees will somehow find its way to the media. Therefore, be honest, and be candid—but don't be careless with classified or confidential information.)

- *Customers.* You must reassure them that the situation is being handled and that their orders will not be delayed (or will be one week late, or whatever). But above all, you must reinforce their confidence in your company.

- *Investors.* Don't mislead them, but try to send them a message to the effect that their confidence in the management team is still well founded. Tell them what is going on, that it is (or soon should be) under control, and that they will receive regular communiqués until the acute crisis has passed.

- *Government/community leaders.* These communications, naturally, depend on the nature of the crisis and the potential for community turmoil, upheaval, or damage. Government and community leaders may also include law enforcement officials.

• *Insurance companies, lawyers.* Obvious reasons, when applicable.

• *Families of victims.* These people should be contacted in person, when possible, and by the highest-ranking company officer available.

Another way to communicate is by teleconferencing, which can take place between managers handling a crisis in one location and reporters in a host of other cities or between the CEO of the company under fire and his board of directors in other cities. Johnson & Johnson's November 11, 1982, teleconference, which announced the comeback of a repackaged Tylenol, was a nationwide satellite hook-up to reporters in some 30 cities. The mechanics of how to set up a teleconference link-up—like almost everything else we've been discussing—should be taken care of during periods of calm, not crisis.

Both United Airlines and its pilots' union set new standards of excellence in high-technology employee communications during the recent strike in mid-1985. Both groups used slick, highly sophisticated videotapes, video distribution, and pep-rally–type teleconferences to reach their respective audiences.

One additional method of communicating is through paid advertising. Do not discount this costly way of reaching your audience, especially if you want to:

• Demonstrate your compassion more graphically than you can through the news media.
• Convey an important message directly ("You can be sure that when we reopen our doors, which we were forced to close as a result of the tragic fire, we will be back bigger and better than ever").
• Communicate an 800 number. ("If you have any questions about our product, please call us toll free at. . . .")
• Announce that you're back in business.
• Or, as in the case of the McDonald's–San Ysidro massacre, *suspend* advertising so as not to appear insensitive.

A few additional points on crisis communications under fire:

• Spokespersons (who should have been preselected when the crisis management plan was assembled) *must at all times speak with one voice.*
• They must be easily and readily accessible to the media. Stonewalling will accomplish just the opposite of whatever positive messages you hope to convey and will make it appear you have something to hide.
• Your natural reluctance to communicate bad news will also make it

appear you have something to hide. This is why you have the background kits—to help couch bad news in a feather bed of positive background information. Just remember that whether you release the bad news or not, the media are going to get a good story with or without your help. Without your help, you may be viewed in the media's eyes as somehow culpable. With your help, you have a better opportunity to present the news *your* way, in a way that allows you to better control and manage the message. (Remember: have you laid off 200 workers, or have you saved 800 jobs?)

In an effort to find out how prepared American businesses are to communicate during a crisis, Western Union surveyed[31] internal directors of public relations or communications in the top 1,000 industrial and top 500 service companies as identified by *Fortune* magazine. There was a 27 percent response rate.

The survey revealed, on the basis of the responses, that only 53 percent of America's largest corporations have a plan that would enable them to communicate quickly and efficiently during times of crisis.

Not surprisingly, larger companies—those with revenues greater than $500 million—were more likely to have a communications plan and to have implemented it. In total, 48 percent of communicators responding said they had put the communications plan in effect.

Also, not surprisingly, firms with the largest risks of industrial and/or environmental accidents—as well as mining and petroleum exploration, utilities, and transportation companies—were more likely to have a crisis communications plan.

The three primary instances in which a company said it would be most likely to implement a crisis communications plan would be industrial accidents, environmental problems, and investor relations situations. Ranked in descending order, other instances were hostile takeovers, rumor suppression, strike notices, proxy fights, product recalls, and government regulatory problems.

The survey found that 41 percent of the companies established a crisis communications plan in response to a prior experience that indicated a need for one. Another 23 percent anticipate such a need.

And, while the overwhelming majority rated their plans effective, more than half indicated that they would make changes or modifications in their crisis communications plans.

As a final thought on the importance of controlling the message, as well as an appropriate lead-in to the second chapter on crisis communications (dealing with the media), consider this paragraph from a front-page *Wall Street Journal* article commenting on Mobil Oil's unsuccessful bid for Marathon Oil Company:

Marathon's success . . . may seem a bit surprising. Mobil's legions of experts may appear to have been splendidly equipped to fight a public relations battle, but Marathon's guerrilla campaign was highly effective. In fact, a careful reading of the judicial opinions in the court cases, combined with discussions with court officials, clearly indicates that Marathon's public relations campaign strongly influenced the court proceedings.[32]

14

Crisis Communications, Part II: Handling a Hostile Press

| Richard Nixon: | *Are you running for something?* |
| Dan Rather: | *No, sir, Mr. President, are you?* |

—Exchange at a March 19, 1974,
news conference in Houston, Texas[33]

Let's define our terms, and specifically, the term "hostile."

While it certainly is true that some reporters are just born hostile, others are driven to hostility by communicators or their bosses who give evasive answers, when they bother to give any answers or interviews at all. Still other reporters, particularly certain television reporters, practice what is known as confrontational journalism. Perhaps trying to make some kind of name for themselves, these reporters thrust microphones under someone's nose and try to catch their prey off guard on camera.

While there is a reality to the threat posed by the media, most reporters are decent folks, trying to do a tough job. And if treated fairly they will respond in kind. But during a crisis—when it is your crisis—you are going to feel as though they are hostile in the way that anyone who constantly presses you for something will be viewed as "hostile." So when we refer to "handling a hostile press," what we really mean is "dealing with the media during crises."

Part of the media's job in recent years has evolved into not just reporting the news to the public, but communicating the news from one person directly to another—relaying messages, as it were.

When the President of the United States announces that he is seeking a summit meeting with the head of the Soviet Union, the *official* word is transmitted in a sealed diplomatic pouch that travels via courier from the Oval Office to the State Department to the U.S. Embassy in Moscow and is then hand-delivered to the Kremlin by the U.S. Ambassador.

In actuality, however, as soon as the President makes the announcement, or releases the text of the letter, it is known by the Soviet Premier. The media—television, in particular—have become modern-day mail carriers, and we, the public, have been prying into other people's letters without ever steaming open the envelopes.

Communicating messages publicly in this electronic way is a responsibility that neither the message carriers nor the message senders should take lightly—certainly not with the world watching so intently.

This is a lesson that President Reagan—considered the "Great Communicator"—is relearning. Soon after his 1980 election, his public pronouncements against the Soviet Union were considered extremely harsh and downright threatening. He was advised by his staff to tone down his rhetoric, which he did. He then spent the next four years publicly taking the Soviets to task—in a more subdued but nevertheless effective manner—for refusing to return to the arms-negotiation talks in Geneva. This tactic was symbolically effective in the same way debating an empty chair is. The Soviets, at least in public, never really responded.

But then the Soviets filled the empty chair, in the person of Mikhail Gorbachev, a *young* (54 years old), personable, articulate, glib, charming leader with a youthful, stylish, and attractive wife—the British press compared the Gorbachevs to John and Jacqueline Kennedy. Gorbachev appears to be every bit the communicator Reagan is.

And the new Russian leader has indeed been communicating. He has been accessible and highly visible to the world news media since his ascension to the Politburo throne. His rare and headline-making September 9, 1985, interview with *Time* magazine displayed a candid and seemingly open Soviet Premier—with a sense of humor. Instead of constantly stonewalling all news, Tass (the official Soviet news agency) and *Pravda* (the official Soviet newspaper) have actually been *pro*actively releasing news and printing it, respectively.

This is certainly not to say that the U.S.S.R. suddenly has a free press. But changes have definitely been made and points scored in matching Reagan for communicating a message. In fact, in at least two instances, the Kremlin has succeeded in putting the White House on the defensive.

First, Reagan had been hoping to sit down with the Soviets for four years. At the funeral of Constantin Chernenko (Gobachev's predecessor, who died after only 13 months in power), Vice President George Bush hand-delivered a message from Reagan requesting a meeting with Gorbachev. But when Gorbachev quickly and *publicly* accepted and suggested an early "summit," the White House appeared to be caught off guard and said it was too soon for a full-blown "summit." The Soviets were seeking a summit meeting to coincide with a Gorbachev trip to address the United Nations, but the White House said that there was not enough time to prepare for such a "summit." A "meeting" would be fine, but not a "summit." The White House may be right; perhaps a lot of time *is* required to plan for a summit. *But* the media sent a strong message to the White House: "Why are you backing down? Isn't this what you've been after for four years?" (The summit was eventually held in Geneva in November 1985—about six months after Gorbachev took office.)

The second episode occurred when Gorbachev *publicly* announced a proposed mutual ban of medium-range nuclear missiles in Europe. The White House rejected the plan, saying the imbalance would still give the Russians an unfair advantage. Whether this is true or not—let's even assume that it is true—when was the last time you can recall the Soviets making such *public* pronouncements?

The Soviet Union apparently has decided to take a page from the capitalists' book of effective public relations. Don't be surprised if it should be revealed one day soon that Gorbachev has a press secretary, a communications director, and other "image makers" on the Kremlin dole.

These two brief stories illustrate that not only should you prepare for crisis communications, but you should guard against a crisis *caused* by poor communications. The Reagan White House has made its reputation on its creative ability to control its messages. The communications operation in the White House is a very well-oiled machine. If it can foul up, so can you.

There may be times when you just lose control of the message and the story gets out of hand. And Reagan's most colossal crisis of poor communications occurred in the spring of 1985, when the President announced that he would visit the Bitburg Cemetery during a European economic summit conference in West Germany. The purported purpose of the cemetery visit was to commemorate the fortieth anniversary of the end of World War II and to make a symbolic gesture of reconciliation with West Germany, a former enemy who is now a strong ally.

In the *initial* planning of the trip, Reagan adamantly refused even to consider visiting a concentration camp because it was too gruesome, too depressing. However, the Bitburg Cemetery contains the graves of 49 Waffen SS soldiers—members of Hitler's elite army of murderers. It was the SS that ran the concentration camps. To visit *that* cemetery—especially after refusing to visit a concentration camp—would make it appear that Reagan was honoring the Nazis, while ignoring the U.S. soldiers and other Allied forces who fought Nazism, as well as the 6 million Jews and 6 million others who were exterminated by the Nazis.

When the existence of the SS graves at Bitburg was made known and the implication of visiting the cemetery was made clear to Reagan, he could have canceled the visit to that cemetery. But he refused. He also refused (early on) to counterbalance the Bitburg stop with a visit to Dachau or Bergen-Belsen, two of the infamous German concentration camps.

It was a ludicrous position for any world leader to be in—a senseless stance born of sheer obstinacy and (as *The New Republic* said) "moral obtuseness." And considering Reagan's reputation for symbolic gestures, it was a particularly appalling move.

An occasion such as the fortieth anniversary of the end of World War II, according to *The New Republic,* "calls for ceremonies of remembrance and reconciliation. These are, by their nature, symbolic gestures. But the administration, obsessed with what the evening news will report, confuses symbolism with public relations."[34]

Oh, there was plenty of blame and/or excuses to go around *in the beginning:* Michael Deaver, Reagan's former White House deputy chief of staff and presidential image maker, didn't see the Nazi headstones because there was snow on the ground when he did the advance work for the cemetery visit; it rained hard the second time an advance team visited the graves, and the team decided not to get out of the car; James Baker, former chief of staff, and Donald Regan, former secretary of the Treasury, were busy swapping jobs while the trip was being planned, so their attention was diverted.

These excuses, however, attempted only to explain away *how* the error was made. But when the error was made public and the president *still* refused to change his plans, and *still* refused to add a concentration camp to the trip, all of the excuses went out the window. Reagan—once labeled the "Teflon President" because of his seemingly remarkable ability to walk through the middle of a pie-throwing fight in a white suit and emerge unscathed—suddenly had *everything* sticking to him.

Reagan's crisis was that his communications—what he was saying and what he was not saying—were causing the crisis to escalate.

Then on April 19, Elie Wiesel, Holocaust survivor, chronicler, and author, as well as Reagan's own appointee to head the new Holocaust Museum, was awarded a Congressional Gold Medal by the President at a White House ceremony. Wiesel, who had tried both publicly and privately to persuade Reagan to drop the visit, used this occasion to deliver directly to the President, and a worldwide audience via the media, one of the most moving pleas ever heard. Wiesel said, in part:

So may I speak to you, Mr. President, with respect and admiration, of the events that happened. . . . I am convinced as you have told us earlier when we spoke that you were not aware of the presence of SS graves in the Bitburg Cemetery. Of course you didn't know. But now we all know.

May I, Mr. President, if it's possible at all, implore you to do something else, to find a way, to find another way, another site.

That place, Mr. President, is not your place. Your place is with the victims of the SS.

The issue here is not politics, but good and evil, and we must never confuse them, for I have seen the SS at work, and I have seen their victims. They were my friends, they were my parents.[35]

Elie Wiesel's eloquence did not move the President to drop Bitburg, although Reagan did add a concentration camp to his itinerary. But it was too late: very few people accepted Reagan's gesture of visiting a concentration camp as genuine.

It was then reported extensively that Reagan had personally pleaded with West German chancellor Helmut Kohl to try to have Kohl cancel the trip. Kohl refused and insisted that Reagan come to the cemetery.

And Reagan's creation and subsequent bungling of the crisis caused the real reason he was going to West Germany in the first place (the economic summit) to be completely forgotten. For in stubbornly saying that he would not "cave in" to people who were trying to tell him what to do, President Reagan managed to:

- Send a message to the world that he would allow the Germans to tell him what to do, but not the Americans.
- Incur the wrath of virtually every U.S. veterans group.
- Give substantial ammunition to everyone (newspaper columnists, editorial writers, Jewish leaders, Congress, the Soviets, and so on) who wanted to denounce Reagan and his Bitburg visit.
- Make it appear that Reagan was more concerned for the feelings of the dead SS soldiers than for the living survivors of the Holocaust.

It was a colossal failure of crisis communications. And, as *The New Republic* said: "In the end, a president who lives by public relations will perish by public relations."[36]

During a crisis you have an important message to communicate. But *how* that message is communicated is sometimes as important as the message itself.

The same statement applies equally to how a message is *not* communicated. A case in point: the Unocal crisis.

T. Boone Pickens, the Texas oilman who heads Mesa Petroleum, launched a well-telegraphed, heavily anticipated takeover attempt of Unocal, the Union Oil Company of California. Pickens purchased 23.7 million shares of Unocal between October 22, 1984, and March 27, 1985. While Pickens is known for playing his cards close to the vest, the media had been expecting a takeover attempt for about six months and had reported it extensively, including prominent mention in the March 4, 1985, *Time* cover story on Pickens. The media had carried stories about acrimonious chance meetings between Pickens and Fred L. Hartley, Unocal's chairman. Unocal even filed suit against its own primary lending bank, Security Pacific National Bank, because it was participating in funding Pickens's maneuvers. So, when Pickens made his move on April 8, 1985, no one could have been surprised. But here's how the Los Angeles *Times* carried the story on the front page of the business section the next day:

Headline:	WAR OF WORDS ESCALATES IN UNOCAL BID
Subheadline:	Pickens Calls Hartley "Arrogant," Says Firm Neglects Stockholders
Paragraph #1:	Carried the essence of the story; Pickens had made his move; Pickens called Hartley "arrogant" and claimed that Unocal had neglected its shareholders.
Paragraph #2:	Very strong, to-the-point quote from Pickens: "I see Unocal as really a one-man band, which is Mr. Hartley. I would say he epitomizes . . . arrogance. . . ."
Paragraph #3:	Explained how many shares Pickens was trying to acquire and what he was offering shareholders.
Paragraph #4:	Pickens claimed Unocal was "undervalued," implying shareholders had not gotten what they deserved.
Paragraph #5:	Yet another strong quote from Pickens, explaining *why* he believed the company was undervalued—poor management.
Paragraph #6:	Still another bull's-eye quote from Pickens: Management did "not do enough for the stockholders. The only reason that the company's vulnerable is because the price of the stock is selling at a huge discount. . . ."
Paragraph #7:	"Hartley declined Monday to be interviewed."[37]

That's it. That's all Paragraph 7 said: *"Hartley declined Monday to be interviewed."* Nothing more. Meanwhile, Pickens was accessible to the media constantly, giving interviews and making good copy.

It makes one wonder how the *Times* could have referred to the confrontation as a "war of words." It also makes one wonder why Union Oil, why Hartley, would give the "enemy camp" free, unchallenged access to the media and—especially since Unocal is a Los Angeles–based company—to the Los Angeles *Times*.

While the article continued on much longer than the seven paragraphs mentioned here, there was no indication of why Hartley had declined to be interviewed. What could he have been thinking of to permit Pickens to go on for an entire article, calling him arrogant and saying that the company was undervalued and poorly managed?

Hartley gave Pickens open, direct access and an opportunity to deliver a clear message to the Unocal stockholders: "You'll do better with me." Anything that Hartley could say after that opening volley—an opening volley for which he had had more than six months to prepare—would be reactive ("We are *not* poorly managed; we are *not* undervalued; I am *not* arrogant").

When Hartley did grant his first interview, it appeared in the Los Angeles *Times* on April 25—two and a half weeks after Pickens launched the tender offer and two and a half weeks after Hartley had given Pickens virtually uncensored reign in the media.

However, assuming that you *will* want to meet with the media, here are a few reasons why it's a good idea:

- There is more of a chance to be proactive rather than reactive.
- There is a better chance of controlling the message.
- There is a 100 percent greater chance of correcting misinformation than if you don't talk with the media.
- Not meeting with the media sometimes makes you look not in control of the situation and, well, arrogant.

The questions then become: *how* should you meet the press; *how* should you communicate your message? In media-heavy crises, there is a natural tendency to call a press conference. Be careful. While it is true that a picture is worth a thousand words, the real question is *which* thousand: chaos or calmness?

It takes a very skilled communicator—and here we are not necessarily referring only to the internal communicator, but to the person who will be on the receiving end of a barrage of media questions—to be able to control a press conference, especially a "hostile" one.

Press conferences don't get much more hostile than some of those that were held during the Three Mile Island crisis. The media were hostile largely because they weren't initially sure whom to believe and because their lives—and the lives of their families—were at stake, too. At one point very early on in the crisis, a frustrated William Kuhns, chairman of the board of GPU, recommended that newspapers located near nuclear power plants should hire reporters who are familiar with nuclear energy and physics. Saul Kohler, editor of the Harrisburg *Patriot* and *Evening News,* shot back: "All nuclear plants should hire people who are familiar with the truth!"[38]

And consider the following scene, from the Kemeny Commission's account of the accident, which took place on the morning of Friday, March 30, 1979, between Met Ed Vice President John Herbein and a very large, very anxious horde of reporters, photographers, and camera crews:

> Relations between reporters and Met Ed officials had deteriorated over several days. Many reporters suspected the company of providing them with erroneous information at best, or of outright lying. When John Herbein arrived at 11:00 A.M. Friday to brief reporters gathered at the American Legion Hall in Middletown, the situation worsened. The press corps knew that the radioactivity released earlier had been reported at 1,200 millirems per hour; Herbein did not. He opened his remarks by stating that the release had been measured at around 300 to 350 millirems per hour by aircraft flying over the Island. The question-and-answer period that followed focused on the radiation reading—"I hadn't heard the number 1,200," Herbein protested during the news conference—whether the release was controlled or uncontrolled, and the previous dumping of radioactive wastewater. At one point Herbein said, "I don't know why we need to . . . tell you each and every thing that we do specifically. . . ." It was that remark that essentially eliminated any credibility Herbein and Met Ed had left with the press.[39]

The next day, Jack Watson, President Carter's newly installed Chief of Staff,* telephoned Herman Dieckamp, president of Met Ed's parent company, to suggest that because all of the conflicting statements were increasing the public's anxiety, a new system of briefing the media and the public ought to be established. Agreement on the new system, in fact, had already been worked out in advance between the governor's office and the White House: NRC's Harold Denton would issue all technical statements on the status of the plant; the governor's office would be the sole source of comment on protective action and possible evacuation; and the White House would coordinate any comment on federal emergency relief efforts, if any. The utility had no role whatsoever in the dissemination of public information, that privilege having been lost along with its credibility.

From this point, any hostility—and it still existed, to be sure—was at least not totally the result of the dubious credibility of the spokespersons. Early on in the crisis, one of the first public pronouncements from the Thornburgh administration occurred at a near-midnight press conference

---

*Hamilton Jordan, who had been White House Chief of Staff, had recently stepped down to handle another crisis: Jimmy Carter's ill-fated re-election campaign.

in the Capitol Media Center, a small room designed to hold about 40 or 50 reporters and camera crews comfortably in classroom style.

The press conference, originally scheduled for a couple of hours earlier but postponed several times, was carried live. Therefore, anyone watching television or listening to the radio prior to the press conference already suspected something chaotic was going on because the time of the press conference kept being moved back.

At the event itself, there could have been as many as 200 reporters sardined into the cramped room, including a goodly overflow who commandeered any inch or two of space they could find on the stage.

Let's just gloss over how hostile the reporters were for having been kept waiting so long and skip right to their shouting as soon as the governor appeared, vying to be recognized by him. It was utter and absolute chaos and it appeared that way for all the world to see.

The next press conference was an abbreviated* affair in the governor's Reception Room, which was able to accommodate a much larger crowd. But it still appeared somewhat chaotic—albeit less so than the earlier debacle—due to the size of the crowd and the reporters' shouting and jumping up to be recognized.

But any damage that these conferences may have done was quickly corrected by a series of one-on-one interviews that were set up between the governor and the media. These interviews, held either in the governor's private office or in the spacious Reception Room, showed the world a governor who was calm and in control.

Executives at Johnson & Johnson may have learned from Thornburgh's lesson. From almost day one in the Tylenol crisis, they readily made themselves available to one-on-one interviews with the media and appeared on most of the morning talk shows and evening news programs. They quickly got control of the message, and the message they soon conveyed was: "We're victims, too. We're doing everything we can to cooperate with the authorities, but we do definitely know that the tampering was *not* done by an employee. When the product left the company, it was all right."

The executives patiently answered the same questions over and over again—questions that perhaps could have been asked and answered *once* at a press conference. But Johnson & Johnson quickly saw that it was in its own best interests to get control of the message, which it did in part by avoiding chaotic news conferences.

Contrast that action with the behavior of Union Carbide. The company

---

*One advantage a press conference has over an interview is that it is easier to end. If you're a guest on a television talk show and you don't like the questions, it's considered bad form to get up and walk off the set.

held several press conferences about the Bhopal disaster, and almost all of them conveyed the appearance of a reactive company, rather than a proactive one.

Whether you find yourself in a one-on-one interview or at a press conference, facing friendly media or hostile, *honesty* is of paramount importance.

Do not for a moment think that any of the communications techniques or verbal sparring skills described here are meant to be, or to promote, dishonesty or chicanery of any kind. Nothing could be farther from the truth.

Being dishonest or less than honest with the media will only escalate your crisis into proportions that will stagger you. (Ask Met Ed.) It will serve to destroy your present and future credibility with the media. It will undermine your efforts to bridge that adversarial-relationship gap described earlier.

In short, trying to be less than honest with the media, especially during a crisis, will screw you. And as some wise man once said so succinctly, "Never get into an argument with someone who buys ink by the barrelful."

However, you are not a Mike Wallace, nor are you expected to be. It would be safe to assume that Mike Wallace is much more comfortable and confident under the hot television lights than you are. So, before the interview or press conference even begins, *you* are at a disadvantage.

Honing your crisis communications skills is meant merely to add another arrow or two to your quiver. It will not, however, give you quite the same fire power as a hostile interviewer might have.

But in order to even things out a bit, many executives are turning to outside public relations or media consulting firms that, under simulated but realistic broadcast conditions, put the managers through real-life interviews. The interviews, which are videotaped, are then played back and analyzed. Such services assist people to become more comfortable when it is essential that they communicate with the public and the media.

As with other aspects of a crisis, there is as much opportunity as danger in dealing with the media. (And as much danger as opportunity. Playing Russian roulette with a loaded television camera can be very hazardous to your health.) At minimum, calling in outside consultants to teach you and your managers how to play in the media's arena will help defuse and maybe unload the camera to make it safe to handle. At best, however, you can hope to become a skilled and adept communicator—one who is able to take control of the camera and point it toward a more advantageous target.

And if your goal is to become a skilled communicator at interviews or press conferences, you may wish to begin getting a few pointers from some of the real pros— the politicians, especially the good communicators such as Ronald Reagan.*

And the first lesson is this: people tend more to remember the *answer*, not the question. Reporters cover Reagan's answers at a news conference— what he *said*, not what he was *asked*.

Why is this important to know? Because if you don't like the question that is asked, feel free to do what the President of the United States often does: change the question. Or, more precisely, give the answer you want to give, and don't pay too much attention to the question.

As an exercise, watch the next presidential news conference, and pay particular attention to the *questions*. See if the answers given really fit the questions asked. Another way to play this game would be to have someone tape-record the conference for you and then play you the *answers*. Then see if you can deduce the *questions* that were asked.

What is it that the President—like hundreds of other skilled politicians/communicators—is doing? He is often taking the question, reshaping it to his own particular liking, and giving the answer that he proactively wants to give.

There are certain pat phrases that are used to turn a question around, such as:

- "That's an interesting question, but before trying to answer that question, I feel the people need to know. . . . "
- "Of course, that's one way to look at it, but it may be helpful to first examine the situation this way. . . ."
- "Usually when I'm asked a question on that subject, people want to know. . . ."

But even though people tend to recall the answers instead of the questions, you will still want to avoid falling into the trap of answering a negatively worded question, whether you are in a news conference or a one-on-one interview.

Whenever you respond to a negative question, you are on the defensive, and you are being reactive. Conversely, a positively worded question allows you to be proactive, more in control, more able to communicate the message you want to communicate.

Be cautious of red-flag questions that begin:

- Isn't it true that . . . ?
- Aren't you really saying . . . ?

*It was Reagan who, soon after taking office in 1980, put a stop to the practice of reporters shouting out, "Mr. President, Mr. President!" and jumping out of their seats to get called on. Reagan deemed this practice too chaotic. Now reporters must raise their hands and wait to be called on by the President.

- How do you respond to . . . ?
- Are you aware of . . .?

Since you cannot simply ignore the question, before responding, turn the negatively worded question into a positively worded question of your choosing.

Remember the earlier example of laying off 200 people. Transform that question into a positive; be sure to mention that you are saving 800 jobs; be sure to mention all the things your company tried to do to save *all* the jobs; be sure to mention what you will be doing to help the workers and their families; be sure to mention that while you are not trying to sugar-coat the bad news, you do hope that a predicted upturn in the economy soon will enable you to bring some, if not all, of the workers back; and so on.

Whenever you answer a question, be sure to work your main message into the response. At all times, whether responding to a negative question or merely reshaping a question, always know what your most important point is, and lead with that. This is especially important for broadcast responses where the electronic media are looking for a good 30-second sound "bite."

Try to use graphic metaphorical imagery in making an important, statistical point. For example, don't *just* talk in terms of kilowatt hours; say, " . . . enough electricity to light up a city the size of Denver for a year." Don't *just* talk in unfathomable monetary terms, such as discussing the national debt in terms of hundreds of billions of dollars; say, " . . . a debt so large that if every man, woman, and child in the country paid $50,000, it still wouldn't retire the debt completely." If you want to get an important statistical point across, be sure your audience can relate to it ("taller than the Empire State Building," "from here to the moon," "twice around the equator").

Never utter the words "no comment." This is a contemptible phrase (as in having contempt for the public) and is an insult to you, your company, your company's employees, and the public. If you have nothing to say, say so and say why. ("That's the first I've heard about it. I'd like to check into it before responding.") If there is nothing you *can* say, say so and say why. ("As you know, that matter is currently in litigation, and while I certainly feel confident that we will win the suit, our lawyers have advised me not to discuss it.") But "no comment," like the nolo contendere defense in court, is virtually considered an admission of either wrongdoing, ignorance, or arrogance.

"Off the record" is another phrase you should be cautious of. In short, and especially during a crisis, assume that everything you say to the media is very much on the record. (Pat Buchanan, Ronald Reagan's communications director, once said to a reporter "No comment—and that's off the record.")[40]

There are some interviewees who practice the art of "stonewalling," which means many things to many people. Here, however, the word is used to describe someone who *constantly* stalls the media by saying neither yea nor nay; by neither confirming nor denying. Just remember, as stated earlier, that the media will get a good story with or without your help. With your help, you have a better chance of controlling the message. Without your help, the story that is finally aired or printed may be not only damaging to you or your company, but also inaccurate. Had you exercised some control over the story by controlling the message, at least you would have had a better chance of minimizing the damage.

"Fortunately, most corporate leaders have outgrown such notions of how to best serve their own interests," wrote John F. Lawrence, economic affairs editor of the Los Angeles *Times*, in a weekly column dealing with the credibility gap between media and business. The corporate leaders have "discovered that the best defense against a bad press and a critical public is a good and continuing offense."[41]

Elsewhere in the column, Lawrence agreed that "Stonewalling seldom keeps the bad news out" and makes this interesting observation on human behavior: "In a crisis, there are too many angry people looking for media exposure."

And speaking of anger, try not to lose your temper during an interview.

In broadcast interviews—in either a studio or perhaps your office—you may run across a few particularly tricky (you may want to substitute the word "hostile") reporters or interviewers. If you do your homework about the person who will be interviewing you, or the show's format, before sitting down to the interview, you at least will have a notion of what you're up against.

Some interviewers intentionally ask convoluted questions, or multiple questions in one breath, to try to confuse or fluster the interviewee. Be patient; let the interviewer finish; and then begin your response by saying, "You've asked several questions, which I'll be glad to answer. Let me begin with your main point. . . ." Then *you* determine what the main point is.

Don't allow an interviewer to put words into your mouth. If he or she says, "What you mean to say is such and such" (and assuming that that is *not* what you intended to say), respond by saying, "No; that is not what I said, nor what I meant to say. What I said was. . . . "

If an interviewer continually interrupts you, don't be thrown. The more he or she talks, the more time you have to hone your response further.

Honing a response, in fact, is one reason why politicians often begin to answer a question with a pat phrase: it gives them an extra beat or two to think before answering. Kennedy's "Let me say this about that," Nixon's "Let me be perfectly clear," Ferraro's "Let me suggest," and even Reagan's "Well, there you go again" are merely examples of how skilled politicians stall for a moment or two while forging a response.

Be especially sure to remember that when you are on the air during an interview or news conference, you certainly do not want to have "dead air" between the time a question is posed and the time you respond. Therefore, just as the politicians do, it is perfectly acceptable to have your own pat responses ready, if and when needed, just to kill a few seconds: "That's a good question . . ." or "I'm glad you asked me that . . ." or "Let me see if I understand your question . . ." and so on.

For the same reasons, you should not necessarily rush to condemn an interviewer who interrupts you.* Especially when you are on radio or television, you should never begin your response before the interviewer has fininshed asking the question. This gives you more time to prepare your response.

And while the question is being asked, avoid at all costs the temptation to pepper your own silence with "Uh-huhs." This, though somewhat acceptable in everyday conversation, is taboo during a *broadcast* interview. Your utterances of understanding during the question make it difficult for the listener to follow the dialogue.

But the main point to keep in mind is that by whatever means you finally use to answer the question, try to work yourself around to putting forth the controlled message. It is a safe bet that the morning papers will say, "Smith [that's you] said such and such"; and not "Smith said such and such, even though he was asked thus and thus."

It's what you say that counts. And in crisis communications, what you say and how you say it are essential tools to effective overall crisis management.

It is not altogether clear why there are (or *seem* to be) so many more crises nowadays than there used to be. Decades ago, fiascos like the "Teapot Dome" scandal were juicy enough to last for years. Today, however, it almost seems as though you can't open a newspaper or a newsmagazine or listen to radio or television without some *new* (real or imagined) crisis being exposed.

Is it because of the age in which we live that there are really that many more crises—that much more sloppiness, carelessness, callousness? Is it because "they just don't build things like they used to"?

Is it because of more government intervention, regulation, or over-

---

*If, however, an interviewer continually interrupts and does not give you any chance at all to respond, you should be firm in insisting that you be allowed to answer. Of course, this type of interviewing technique is probably the interviewer's style, and you should have known that before you agreed to go on the show. This is what is meant by doing your homework.

sight? In an age of deregulation, will the crises subside? They haven't so far.

Or, perhaps, do there only *seem* to be many more crises because there are so many news outlets—television stations, newspapers, 24-hour cable news channels, wire services, radio stations, and so on? Or maybe we live in a more transparent society—one in which our actions are more easily laid bare, in which Freedom of Information acts and "unidentified sources" make information gathering that much easier for the media.

Certainly numerous business crises have finally led the media to realize that business is *big* business. When a financial crisis (a takeover, merger, bankruptcy, strike, layoff, and so on) hits big business, the news often makes the front pages of the newspapers and the lead stories of the evening news. Multibillion-dollar hostile takeovers and boardroom scandals that rock the foundations of a free enterprise system are given much more prominence by the media than ever before.

And they make for *great* copy.

The March 25, 1985, *Business Week* cover story, which screamed "GENERAL DYNAMICS UNDER FIRE," detailed how General Dynamics Corporation—the nation's number-one defense contractor—and its chairman and CEO, David S. Lewis, were trying to defend themselves against a barrage of claims that they overcharged the government by $244 million and acted unethically in the firm's work for the armed forces. *Business Week* explained that while the attack was then "escalating into a wide-ranging, full-scale offensive,"[42] the crisis had actually begun in 1971.

One would be hard-pressed to uncover any sort of similar news coverage back in 1971. But the media today loudly blare the word "crisis" in the same breath as "General Dynamics." And rightly so, of course. After all, the company is—or was, at the time—under investigation by such august bodies as a federal grand jury in Connecticut, the U.S. Naval Investigative Service, the Securities and Exchange Commission, the Justice Department, the Defense Department, the Internal Revenue Service, the U.S. House of Representatives Armed Services Committee, the U.S. Senate Judiciary Subcommittee, and the Navy. All at the same time.*

---

*Ultimately the Navy took the unprecedented step of freezing its defense contracts, worth up to $1 billion, with General Dynamics. It also canceled two contracts totaling $22.5 million and fined General Dynamics $675,000 for giving gratuities to Admiral Hyman G. Rickover. Navy Secretary John F. Lehman, Jr., accusing the company of "maximizing profits without regard for the public trust,"[43] tried to bar the three highest-ranking company officers from doing business with the government. And in December 1985, the government indicted three General Dynamics officials, and one former company executive, alleging contract fraud. (The former executive, James M. Beggs, was serving as Administrator of NASA at the time of the indictment.) The government took further action by barring the defense contractor from obtaining any new contracts from any branch of the entire federal government until the criminal proceedings were resolved. General Dynamics thereby earned the dubious distinction of being the only defense contractor in U.S. history to be barred from receiving government contracts twice in the same year.

That fits pretty much anybody's definition of a crisis.

Of course, anyone who even glances at the news these days has to be aware that defense contractors other than General Dynamics find themselves under the same intense scrutiny. Not only do we hear of hundreds of millions of dollars in overcharging, but even Johnny Carson jokes about $650 toilet seats, $1,000 hammers, and so on. (The Pentagon announced that about $140 million in money owed to General Electric, another defense contractor, would not be paid due to suspected overcharging. GE later pleaded guilty to defrauding the government of $800,000 on a Minuteman missile project, and it suffered a $1 million fine on top of the required repayment.)

As discussed earlier, when a crisis hits one firm in an industry group, the industry as a whole, as well as the individual people who work in it, are subject to microscopic scrutiny, too. (Perhaps a sound rationale for industries to police themselves?)

This industrywide indictment could not have been made any clearer than it was by the results of a *Business Week*/Harris Poll survey, which demonstrated that on overwhelming majority (70 percent) of Americans think that all defense contractors overcharge and rip off the taxpayers and that they ought to be made to pay for it. In addition, 62 percent advocated contract cancellation, and 57 percent said that the culpable contractors should be barred from receiving additional contracts. And a majority of those surveyed also believed that any individuals found guilty of fraud should "go to jail, no matter how important they are."[44]

But this story has been going on for years. Certainly it is a story that has to be reported—and perhaps should have been reported earlier—but only now, it seems, has it reached megamedia proportions. Why has it escalated?

First, and one would hope foremost, is that it is indeed newsworthy.

But there is also a need to fill space with a good story, to dig harder than a competing reporter and to get the story first. *Time* doesn't want the same story on its cover as *Newsweek* has; *Business Week* would rather have an exclusive than share it with *Forbes*.

The word is "competition," and among the media it is fierce. And along with the fact that there are so very many media outlets, this must account for much of the seeming overabundance of crises in which we as observers find ourselves immersed every day. The business editor of the Los Angeles *Times,* Martin Baron, frankly states that he won't do a story (fast-breaking, hard-news stories excepted) if the subject has been covered in the New York *Times*—a newspaper whose home-base circulation is 3,000 miles from Los Angeles.[45]

Some claim that this competition actually creates the crises the media cover. If this is true, it is all the more reason for you to get control of your message quickly.

In an interesting analysis of this phenomenon, Peter J. Boyer, on the "CBS Morning News," tried to explain why so much media attention was being paid to the second trial of a heretofore little-known New York socialite named Claus von Bülow. The first trial, in which von Bülow was convicted of attempting to murder his wealthy wife by injecting her with insulin, was covered by the New York media, since von Bülow is from New York. But the *world* media are housed in New York; and seeing that the New York media were onto something, the competitiveness of the world media (or perhaps it was a slow news day, take your pick) resulted in national coverage of a decidedly nonnational event.

But, Boyer explained, since the national media covered the *first* trial, they felt compelled to cover the *second* trial, even while acknowledging it was not newsworthy. This broad coverage extended far beyond a mere mention or two in the national print media; von Bülow and his attorney made the rounds of national talk shows and morning news shows.

This competition has also caused crises for the media. Yes, even the fourth estate is subject to its own scrutiny and its own scandals. Not only have the media suffered the same crises as any other group of businesses (UPI's filing for Chapter 11 bankruptcy protection, Ted Turner's attempted takeover of CBS, Writers Guild strikes, pressmen's strikes, paper shortages, power failures, and so on), but in recent years the public has been treated to such media crises as:

• The Washington *Post*/Janet Cooke debacle, in which Ms. Cooke was awarded the 1981 Pulitzer Prize for Feature Writing for her story of a young black boy's drug addiction in Washington, D.C.—only to subsequently reveal that her story was a work of fiction, written because she had felt "pressured." The Washington *Post,* on April 15, 1981, resigned the Pulitzer Prize in disgrace.

• Ariel Sharon's $50 million libel suit against *Time.* Sharon did not win any money, but the court ruled that *Time* did libel him, did print inaccurate information, and did use questionable reporting techniques, even though, the court ruled, the magazine did none of this maliciously.

• General William Westmoreland's $120 million libel suit against CBS-TV news, Mike Wallace, *et al.* Westmoreland claimed that he had been slandered by a 1982 CBS documentary, "A Vietnam Deception: The Uncounted Enemy." The case was settled out of court just before it was to go to the jury. Both sides claimed victory.

• The *Wall Street Journal's* acutely embarrassing "insider trading" crisis. One of the newspaper's "Heard on the Street" reporters, R. Foster Winans, was accused in March 1984 (and eventually found guilty) of providing advance information about his news column to certain stock traders, who used this "inside" information to make a killing in the market.

• The infamous Pentagon Papers crisis in which the U.S. government brought suit against the New York *Times* to halt publication of the Pentagon Papers, which had been turned over to the *Times* by Daniel Ellsberg, a former Rand Corporation employee. The courts forced the newspaper to cease publication until, on appeal to the U.S. Supreme Court, the *Times* won the right to publish the Pentagon Papers. Even though this happened back in 1971, it is included here because it was one of the first instances when the media actually were involved in a crisis that they were also covering as a news story.

• Of course, probably the earliest recorded evidence of a media-inspired crisis was William Randolph Hearst's classic "yellow journalism" cable to an illustrator he had sent to Cuba to cover the then-nonexistent Spanish-American War. Receiving the illustrator's cable that there was no war to be found, Hearst wired back, "You supply the pictures; I'll supply the war."

But perhaps the biggest crisis of all, at least for newspapers, is the release in April 1985 of an American Society of Newspaper Editors–sponsored survey, which showed that 75 percent of the adults questioned doubt the credibility of newspapers.[46]

And a follow-up survey by the Associated Press Managing Editors Association in October 1985 revealed that two-thirds of journalists feel their own profession suffers from a "serious" credibility problem.[47]

Well, with bad news like that, maybe the media have a right to be hostile.

15

Managing Hostile
Takeovers

A billion here, a billion there; pretty soon we'll be talking about real money.

—The late Everett Dirksen, U.S. Senator

The amount of money that is thrown about during the course of a hostile takeover attempt boggles the imagination. Even if the bid is not hostile, the amount of money being tendered in an offer to purchase a business is equally astronomical. Just consider the $6.28 billion that General Electric Company agreed to pay for the friendly acquisition of RCA Corporation.

But since crises are more common in the hostile takeover arena rather than in the mere buying and selling of businesses, we will concentrate briefly on these takeovers and on the crisis management defense plans that certain companies employ to try to stave off an attack.

In a hostile takeover, one company (or individual, group of individuals, syndicate, or some other entity) tries to gain either absolute control (more than 50 percent) of a company or effective control (less than 50 percent but still enough to control the board of directors or to prevent anyone else from controlling more than 50 percent). A hostile takeover typically is accomplished by purchasing stock in the company that is being sought.

For a variety of reasons, this is virtually never a surprise move. Such reasons include:

• A buyer that acquires more than 5 percent of the outstanding shares of a company announces its intentions (for example, ousting of existing management, or reorganization) to the Securities and Exchange Commission.

• Individuals or those small groups that typically involve themselves in such takeover attempts are well known, and their activities are reported in depth in the media. A few of these individuals are T. Boone Pickens (mentioned earlier), Carl Icahn, Saul Steinberg, and Irwin Jacobs.

• The takeover targets are well known, too. In addition to Unocal, Pickens's Mesa group (specializing in oil companies) has made recent runs on such giants as Phillips Petroleum and Gulf Oil. Icahn, who has averaged a major corporate raid about twice a year since the late 1970s, also made a recent run at Phillips. He also tried a takeover of TWA (which was successful) and of the Virginia textile company Dan River. Steinberg, who *also* went after Phillips in association with Icahn, may be one of the few people in the world who managed to get Mickey Mouse mad at him by making an attempt to take over Walt Disney Productions in 1984. Previously he tried for Quaker State Oil Refining. Jacobs, who is on Mickey Mouse's hate list for the same reason as Steinberg, is not spoken of too kindly in the corporate back rooms of ITT, Pabst Brewing, and Kaiser Steel.

• The media love to cover these hostile takeover attempts. The personalities involved are so interesting, the companies are so public, the terminology is so colorful, and the stories open up and lay bare as never before the once-enigmatic and staid halls of American business and business people. In short, they make for great copy.

It should be pointed out, too, that (aside from TWA, as of this writing) none of the companies mentioned in the above paragraphs has been taken over by these corporate raiders. Instead, the activity and the media attention, as well as the speculation that the company *may* be taken over and, if so, that shareholders will benefit in the process, forces up the price of shares. Those who previously bought millions or billions of dollars' worth of shares in the attempted takeover are then able to sell their shares at a huge profit.

Often they are even paid a "bonus" by the firm they were trying to take over—a sort of compensation for their "expenses." This is known as "greenmail," and it has angered stockholders—after all, the more the company spends, the less its profits, and less profits mean less dividends. It also has prompted several congressional investigations, and there are any number of moves afoot to ban the practice of "greenmail" by legislating it out of existence.

So a takeover target not only faces a crisis as it goes through the attempted takeover process, but if it succumbs to "greenmail," it faces another crisis from its own shareholders.

There is also a certain animal known as an arbitrageur, who buys up stock in companies that are takeover targets, hoping to make a killing if and when those who are trying to take over the company manage to drive up the price of the shares. One notable "arb" is Ivan Boesky who, according to a *Time* profile on him, made about $50 million in risk arbitrage when

Texaco took over Getty Oil in 1984 and another $65 million when Chevron purchased Gulf Oil in the same year.

But it is precisely because these megabucks are floating around that the acute takeover crisis virtually cannot happen without a long and highly visible prodromal phase. And with such a long fuse, management should have plenty of time to implement its crisis management/takeover defense plans.

"Long before the war began, the counterattack was being plotted," began the lead of the Los Angeles *Times* article on Pickens's unsuccessful takeover attempt of Unocal.[48]

The prodromes of attempted takeovers of oil companies go back at least to 1981, when Conoco fought a takeover attempt by Seagram. In 1983, Unocal's general counsel wrote a contingency plan of antitakeover defenses. Although its crisis communications plan (as mentioned in the previous chapter) was nonexistent, its legal maneuvers broke new ground in takeover defenses.

In a surprise—both because of the attempt and because they were successful in the attempt—legal maneuver in Delaware (Unocal's state of incorporation), the company's lawyers managed to establish a precedent-setting, exclusionary end run that, simply put, permitted Unocal in essence to do business with any shareholders it selected and to avoid doing business with any others.

The landmark decision by the three-judge Delaware Supreme Court panel on May 17, 1985, said: "A hallmark of the business judgment rule is that a court will not substitute its judgment for that of the board [of directors of a company] if the latter's decision can be attributed to any rational purpose."[49]

So who won?

Well, the obvious answer, of course, is Unocal. Hartley's goal was to remain independent. (Hartley, who has a reputation for being stubborn, once described his fight with Pickens as "Mad dog bites man; man bites back; man with superior intellect defeats mad dog.") And if remaining independent at any cost was Hartley's strategic goal, then Unocal won.

But at what cost?

To recap the events very succinctly:

• Prior to the takeover attempt, Unocal's stock was trading at about $36 per share.

• Mesa, the Pickens group, which at the time owned 23.7 million shares of Unocal, called the stock undervalued and made a tender offer of $54 per share in an attempt to purchase an additional 64 million shares and gain a 50.1 percent stake in the company.

• Unocal, which originally thought $36 per share was fair, called

Pickens's $54 per share offer "grossly inadequate" and eventually offered to buy back 50 million of its shares at $72 per share—an enormous premium above the original "fair" price—*but,* it wanted to *exclude* Pickens from cashing in on the offer and, consequently, making a huge profit in the deal.

• This resulted in the Delaware lawsuit and that state's Supreme Court decision, just mentioned.

What was the cost?

Besides having the Unocal name smeared ("mismanaged") from one end of the country to the other, besides having Hartley's name smeared ("arrogant") from one end of the country to the other, besides a mountain of legal fees from one end of the country to the other (California to Delaware)—besides all of this, Unocal retained its independence by incurring an additional *$4.15 billion in debt* to its own balance sheet.

And what of Pickens? Well, by *his* estimate he figures that, when the dust settles, he and his partners may stand to make upward of $100 million. Some analysts scoff at this prediction and say he may lose that much. But to put it all into perspective, keep in mind that in just the past few years, Pickens and his Mesa group have made between five and six times that amount in attempted takeovers of other oil companies. They still appear to be in very healthy financial shape.

If, as the saying goes, money is just a way of keeping score, *you* decide who won.

Unocal seemed to have all of the elements of a good crisis management plan in place, except for one mistake made early on.

Believe it or not, it appears that Unocal did not properly identify its crisis. (Or, if it did, it did not manage the crisis properly.)

Since the prodromes were obvious to the company, the question becomes: prodromes of *what?* Did Unocal understand what the prodromes were saying? It obviously knew it was vulnerable to a takeover attempt, but the question is *what* made it vulnerable?

Was Unocal vulnerable simply because it is an oil company and raiders were going after oil companies? Or was it vulnerable because its stock was undervalued and raiders were going after *any* vulnerable company? Obviously raiders attack any company they perceive as vulnerable. If Unocal thought it was vulnerable, so did others.

To determine whether or not Unocal managed its crisis well, you have to question whether it could have retained its independence at a much lower cost *or whether it even tried.* Had Unocal been able to properly identify its real crisis, its general counsel should have *also* written a crisis management plan to address the vulnerability issue. The memo he did

write on takeover defenses—as good as that may have been—conceded that the company *was vulnerable* and *would always remain vulnerable.*

This was not effective crisis management; it was damage control.

And when the window of opportunity in a prodrome or in an acute crisis is missed, sometimes damage control is the best that can be hoped for.

Many takeover targets lose sight of their shareholders before and during the process. When you consider that in order to gain control of a company, someone has to get existing shareholders to tender their shares, then it should be apparent that crisis communications and investor relations are—or *should* be—inseparable. The shareholders are going to do whatever seems to be in their own enlightened self-interest. For some reason—analysis paralysis, perhaps—management often neglects to enlighten the shareholders until it comes time to beseech shareholders not to tender their shares to the "enemy" in panicky full-page ads in the *Wall Street Journal* and other appropriate newspapers. The "enemy," meanwhile, had been enlightening the shareholders all along by sending out news releases, giving interviews, appearing on radio and television shows, sending out mailings, and so on.

If your list of worst-case scenarios includes the words "hostile take-over," then part of your proactive crisis management plan should be to enlighten your shareholders on a *continuing* basis. Open a dialogue throughout the year, not just when it is time to send out the annual report. This sort of activity falls under the heading of "the best defense is a good offense." If you've been doing a good job managing the company, if profits have been up, if growth has been good, if future earnings seem promising, and if the shareholders know and believe this, you may, just by your pas' actions, be able to stave off someone who is seriously contemplating tryi' to take over your company.

Even if the takeover attempt does come, and you and a stranger to compete for the attention—and the votes—of your shareholde' may be in a better position to command their loyalty.

Under the heading of "the best defense is a good *defens* plethora of colorful terms and actions that are designed to sa' company or its executives.

Herewith a sampling:

• *The White Knight.* This is the opposite of a *host'* embattled company seeks another company to ride purchase it in a *friendly* takeover. This is usually acc financial terms than the "bad-guy" pursuer firm w' friendlier terms (or assurances) to keep the existin'

An example of this defense occurred when T. Boone Pickens made a hostile raid on Gulf Oil. Gulf fended off Pickens's hostile takeover attempt by selling itself under friendlier terms to Chevron.

• *The White Squire.* This maneuver is less than a White Knight, which can be thought of as doing victorious battle with the dragon and riding off with the erstwhile damsel in distress. The White Squire does battle with the dragon, too, but leaves the damsel—and her virtue—intact. In a White Squire defense, a friendly company purchases a large chunk of outstanding shares—not enough to take over the company that is under attack, but enough to dissuade a hostile company from continuing its onslaught, or stock purchase. A recent example: on April 3, 1984, Los Angeles–based Carter Hawley Hale (parent company of Neiman-Marcus, Bergdorf Goodman, and other retail chains) was threatened with a surprise $1.1 billion hostile takeover bid by The Limited, Inc., a smaller national retail chain of women's clothes, headquartered in Ohio. As part of its defense, Carter sold 1 million shares of a new issue of preferred stock for $300 million to General Cinema Corporation of Boston, which also received, among other things, a 37 percent voting stake within Carter Hawley Hale. General Cinema became the White Squire, and in August 1985 The Limited abandoned all attempts to snare its quarry.

• *The Shark Repellent.* Companies that attempt to acquire other companies in hostile takeovers are sometimes called sharks. And a Shark Repellent, as the name implies, is any measure a targeted company uses to fend off, or repel, a shark. These repellents sometimes include changing the state of incorporation to Delaware. A state rich in corporations, Delaware allows corporations to change by-laws more easily so that, for example, by-laws can be changed requiring 75 percent of the shareholders to approve a merger before it takes effect.

• *The Pac-Man Defense.* This is named for the video game in which, at certain points, the pursued turns around and tries to swallow its pursuer. ("You're going to acquire *me?* I'm going to acquire *you!*") In 1982 Bendix Corporation made a disastrous move to take over Martin Marietta, which proceeded to turn around and start buying large shares of Bendix stock. Martin Marietta's Pac-Man Defense was interrupted when Bendix was rescued by a White Knight called Allied Corporation, but only after United Technologies was unsuccessful in its rescue attempt. Actually, Bendix and Martin Marietta had done so much damage to each other that Allied essentially had to buy Bendix *and* Martin Marietta and then sell Martin Marietta back to itself.

• *The Scorched Earth.* A pursued company sometimes attempts to make itself as unattractive as possible in order to ward off a takeover bid. Occasionally self-destructive, this ploy often includes arranging for substantial loans to come due all at once if the firm is acquired. This may make a

pursuer change his or her tactic, but the loans will still have to be paid off (or otherwise dealt with) by the targeted company. Other times the company may sell off desirable assets in hopes the pursuer will give up the chase. Sometimes this entails selling off the very divisions that made the company attractive to the raider in the first place.

One precedent-setting Scorched Earth maneuver was Arco's decision in the spring of 1985 to buy back $4 billion of its own stock (and obviously incur $4 billion in new debt on its balance sheet); take a one-time write-off of $1.3 billion against its 1985 earnings; withdraw itself from the refining and petroleum business east of the Mississippi River; sell off its 1,350 service stations in the East; lay off (or force early retirement on) thousands of employees; sell all remaining noncoal mineral operations; and reduce oil exploration spending by some $250 million annually. All of these moves seem to be, at least in part, inspired by fears of a possible takeover. But what makes Arco's action precedent-setting is that, so far as anyone was able to determine, *no one had been attempting to take over Arco.* Arco apparently felt it was vulnerable (a prodrome) to a possible takeover and, for the first time in American business, a company burned its bridges (so to speak) and made itself less attractive to a raider without anyone being on its trail.

• *The Poison Pill.* This defense could easily ruin an unsuspecting pursuer, as well as the pursued. In the most basic form of this strategy, the targeted company gives its shareholders securities or warrants, which confer the right to buy additional shares of common or preferred stock either in the new company (if a takeover is successful) or in the existing company as a result of some triggering event (such as the acquisition of just 20 percent of the existing outstanding shares by a raider). This ploy raises the stakes so high that Alan Greenberg, chairman of the investment firm Bear, Stearns & Co., calls it the Atomic Bomb, since it has the capacity to destroy everyone but the pilot. Perhaps for that reason, more than a dozen public companies have used the Poison Pill defense, and perhaps as many as 300 others have the authority in their charters or by-laws to enact this defense without their shareholders' permission, according to Investor Responsibility Research Center, a nonprofit, Washington, D.C.–based research organization specializing in business policy issues.[50]

Unocal used a Poison Pill as one of its defenses in its fight against Pickens; Crown Zellerbach used such a defense in its battle with well-known shark and Anglo-French financier Sir James Goldsmith, who also encountered a Poison Pill when he made a half-hearted run at Colgate-Palmolive. Crown Zellerbach's Poison Pill was noteworthy because it marked the first time that this defense was tried, and failed. The Pill, enabling holders of certain rights to purchase two shares of the surviving company for the price of one, was to kick in when Sir James's holdings surpassed the 20 percent mark. However, he deftly avoided swallowing the

Pill when he withdrew his formal tender offer and merely began to acquire a majority interest through open-market stock purchases. It may be said that Sir James and Crown went eyeball-to-eyeball for eight months, and Crown blinked first. On July 25, 1985, with more than 50 percent of the stock in his possession, Sir James took control of Crown Zellerbach. He was named chairman and gained majority control of the 11-member board.

• What this author has termed *The Three Musketeers Defense* ("All for one, one for all"). This entails splitting significant portions of one company into several limited partnerships. Such partnerships typically involve natural resources companies, such as International Paper, Lear Petroleum, and Transco. Unocal, for example, in a takeover defense designed to appease its disgruntled stockholders, agreed to spin off about half of its domestic oil and gas reserves into a limited partnership.

• The also newly named *Exclusionary End Run,* or *Reverse Green-mail,* just cited in the Unocal case. This tactic, as mentioned previously, allows the management of a company to buy back its own shares at a premium price, while excluding the raiders from participating.

• *The Golden Parachute.* When all else fails, bail out. But be sure you bail out with a Golden Parachute to ensure a safe and soft landing. This defense, often a standard clause in contracts for top executives today, guarantees huge payments and other benefits if the executive is fired by new management as a result of a takeover.

How important are preplanned takeover defenses? They can literally spell the difference between life and death, or independence and takeover.

Researchers at the Investor Responsibility Research Center (IRRC) have found that a growing number of firms are adopting antitakeover charter amendments. As of October 1984, almost 200 of the Standard & Poor's 500 companies (twice the number as in 1982) had adopted such amendments as the "supermajority lock-in," which requires *80 percent* of the shareholders to agree to change existing company by-laws relating to length of time a member may serve on the board, staggered board expirations, and restrictions on the introduction of new items to the agenda of annual meetings.

But what is critical here is the evidence that takeover defenses of the charter amendment variety do help companies retain their independence. The IRRC surveyed 36 companies that adopted antitakeover charter amendments and that faced the threat of a hostile takeover between 1974 and 1979. The IRRC also surveyed 32 firms that were targeted for takeover during the same period but did *not* have any such charter amendments. While 39 percent of the charter-amendment group *did* survive their takeover attempts, *none* of the nonamendment firms was capable of repulsing its raiders.[51]

So far, we've considered the crisis only from the pursued's perspective. Does the pursuer face a crisis, too? Of course.

Remember that the definition of a crisis, a turning point, is any situation that runs the risk of:

1. Escalating in intensity.
2. Falling under close media or government scrutiny.
3. Interfering with the normal operations of a business.
4. Jeopardizing the positive public image of a company or its CEO.
5. Affecting a company's bottom line in *any* way.

The raiders have the advantage of knowing in advance which companies they want to target, how they will do it, and when. They are in control. They are creating their own opportunity, on their terms.

They also create something known as "junk financing," which has brought them and their tactics under fairly close government and media scrutiny. "Junk financing" involves lower-rated, high-yield debt, sometimes known as "junk bonds." These are so named because they receive extremely low (sometimes no) safety ratings by securities grading firms.

A typical example of "junk financing" occurs when a bidder wants to make a tender offer for a company. An investment banking firm raises the capital the bidder requires to make the offer by creating "junk bonds" that will be issued *only* if the bidder is successful in the takeover attempt. The banking firm, however, raises capital by securing pledges from investors to buy the bonds if the deal comes off. The bidder then has the capital needed to attempt to acquire the targeted company.

Critics claim that "junk financing" is nothing more than a form of "corporate incest," since the investors who are *buying* "junk bonds" are actually the *issuers* of those bonds. And, these observers warn, in a recession the entire financial contrivance could fall apart like a house of junk cards.

How fast is the "junk financing" market growing? Would you believe the "junk bond" market attracts an estimated $2 billion in new monies each *month?*

The leader in "junk bonds" is clearly the investment firm Drexel Burnham Lambert, which was so successful in raising funds for attempted takeovers (the firm once raised $1.5 billion within 48 hours) that when Walt Disney Productions finally managed to fight off Drexel Burnham client Saul Steinberg, part of the settlement was exacting a promise that the Drexel firm would not represent any potential Disney suitor for two years. In the Unocal settlement, Drexel is barred for three years, although Hartley wanted them out of his hair for 50 years.

In 1984 Drexel raised nearly $6 billion in "junk bond" financing, with 46 issues. The next closest competitor, Prudential-Bache, raised only $800 million, with 13 issues. In that year Drexel controlled 69 percent of the market.

But 1985 may be the year that Drexel Burnham Lambert really outdid itself. As the investment banking firm for Pickens's Unocal takeover attempt, it raised $3 billion within *one week*.

Things may be very different for all "junk bond" dealers in 1986 and beyond, though. On January 8, 1986, the Federal Reserve Board voted to severely restrict the use of "junk bonds" in future corporate takeover attempts. The ruling, issued in a 3-to-2 vote, prevents certain shell companies from financing more than 50 percent of a takeover attempt with "junk bonds." This means that more cash or other equity will be needed, which may result in fewer "junk bond" deals in the future. Whether this ruling will stand, or whether "junk bond" merchants will simply uncover loopholes in it, remains—at this writing—to be seen.

In case you are interested in who buys "junk bonds," Table 1 lists some 139 individuals and corporations who invested in Pickens's failed attempt to take over Unocal. And in case you have trouble following the players without a program, Minstar, Inc., which went in for $101 million, is Irwin Jacobs's Minneapolis firm; the Reliance Insurance Co., in for a cool $50 million, is Saul Steinberg's New York–based company; the Bank of British Columbia ($100 million) and First City Financial ($65 million) are both partially owned and controlled by Canada's wealthy Belzberg family; the McCrory Corporation's $60 million investment translates into Meshulam Riklis, who heads the New York conglomerate Rapid-American Corporation, of which McCrory's is a subsidiary.

But also on the list are insurance companies, pension plans, banks, cosmetic companies, and real estate developers.

Perhaps Nelson Bunker Hunt was right when he said, "A billion dollars isn't what it used to be."

Table 1. Investors in Proposed Takeover of Unocal.

Here is a list of the corporations and individuals who agreed to invest in a proposed takeover of Unocal by the T. Boone Pickens investor group:

Name	Millions of dollars	Name	Millions of dollars
AFG Industries.	15	Alliance Capital	
ARA Manufacturing of		Management.	20
Delaware	10	Amalgamated Sugar	
A.S.F. Inc.	12	Retirement Trust for	
Norman E. Alexander	20	Hourly Workers	2
Alinco.	10		

Name	Millions of dollars	Name	Millions of dollars
Amalgamated Sugar Retirement Trust for Non-Union Employees . . .	2	Great Harbor Investment. . .	35
American Lutheran Church .	10	Great Pacific Capital	10
American Security Bank . . .	20	Great Pacific Industries	20
Ampacet Corp.	5	Jerome L. Greene.	6
Anita Holdings	30	H. S. Corp.	5
Ashwood Investments.	12.53	Home Insurance	60
Athlone Industries	5	W. R. Huff Asset Management.	5
B.A.I.I. Plc	10	Hunter Lyon Inc.	30
Bambrit & Co.	10	Incon Associates	10
Bank of Bermuda.	3	Independent Southwest Services	8
Bank of British Columbia. . .	100	Institutional Partners	35
Bankers Life & Casualty . . .	20	Instrument Systems	10
Bayford Inc.	7.52	Jesup & Lamont Holding . . .	25
Bow River Capital	20	Kemper Investors Life Insurance	20
Bradford & Marzec	4	Kemper Reinsurance	5
C & L Financial	10	Keystone Master Pension Trust	6
Carlyle Investment.	25	Keystone Provident Life Insurance	20
Central Jersey Industries . . .	10	Lambert Brussels Financial .	15
Chanel Corp.	5	Lee National.	10
Cherbourg Holdings	45	Life Investors Management .	5
Chicago Assets Management	5	Lincoln American Fin Investment	50
Clarendon America Insurance	10	Lincoln National Investment Management.	20
Courtleigh Associates	22.53	Lorimar	30
Dryden & Co.	22.53	Lumbermans' Mutual Casualty	15
Economy Fire & Casualty . .	4	M. I. Ventures	5
Eileen Corp.	25	MSWB Corp.	25
Elk Grove Associates	22.5	MacAndrews & Forbes Group	10
Equity Holdings	6	MacAndrews & Forbes Holdings	10
Federal Kemper Life Assurance	6	Magten Asset Management .	85.1
Frederick W. Field	5	Ted Mann.	5
Financial Trustco Capital . . .	45	Marquez Co.	22.5
First City Financial	65	Maryland Casualty	6
First City Trust.	35	McCrory Corp.	60
First Investors Management and First Investors Asset Management.	22.5	Megra Partners	30
Fisher Brothers	50	Minstar Inc.	100.1
Five Arrows Ltd.	10	Mocatta Organization.	10
Foothill Group	15	Modern Woodmen of America	5
Forum Group	25		
General Defense Corp.	15		
Ginkenhaus & Co.	25		
Granite Finance	88		
Great American Industries . .	6		

Name	Millions of dollars	Name	Millions of dollars
Mutual First.............	25	Melvin Simon............	10
Mutual Security Life Insurance	10	Snowpea Corp............	2.5
Natio Valeurs	10	Solomon Asset Management...........	25
Nortek	10	Martin T. Sosnoff.........	10
Northeast Investors Trust...	3	Southferry Building Co.....	20
Northern Capital Management...........	20	Southmark Corp..........	25
Olympia & York Developments..........	50	Springs Hotel Corp........	12
Orion Capital	12	Steinhardt Partners	35
Panther Holdings.........	22	Sterling Software	5
Paragon Holdings.........	33	Sunshine Mining	20
Pico Financial............	10	Tigo Corp.	50
Presidential Life Insurance .	25	Trafalgar Holdings	45
Progressive Properties	30	Triangle Industries	25
Reimer & Kroger Associates	13.5	Tudor International	5
Reliance Insurance Co.	50	Tuscany Operating Corp. ...	10
Remington Investments	10	United Greenbush	15
Requite Ltd..............	20	United Houston Financial ..	50
Roland International	20	United Oil Producers	5
Royal Investment.........	10	United Shelters	50
Rozzi Inc................	45	Variable Annuity Life Insurance	24
Ruxley Inc...............	50	Volt Holding.............	10
SP Investors International ..	30	Washington Funding.......	10
S.S.C. No. 3 Corp.	50.1	Wilshire Corp.	20
Savoy Partners...........	15	Woodbern Corp...........	5
Schenley Industries	40	Worldwide Trading Services.	71.6
Shamrock Holdings	15	Sam Wyly...............	5
		Zenith National Insurance ..	5

16

Decision Making Under Crisis-Induced Stress

To be without stress entirely is to be dead.

—Hans Selye, M.D.

The bad news is: crises cause stress.

The good news is: (see bad news).

The reality is that stress—just like crises—has suffered from bad press; just as a crisis can be equally filled with opportunity and danger, so, too, can stress be both bad (as in unhealthy) or good (as in stimulating). (*Dis*tress comes from the Greek prefix meaning "bad"; *eu*stress from the Greek prefix for "good," as in "*eu*phoric.")

But the good news—the *really* good news—is that you can control stress and improve your level of decision-making achievement during a crisis. Remember that managing a crisis is managing your decisions.

First, it is necessary to understand that any crisis, whether it is a business crisis or a personal one, is highly stressful, although it is not so much the event that causes stress as it is a person's reaction to the event. You may perceive the danger in the crisis as being a threat to your psychological safety, to your position within the company, to your status, to your individuality, or even to your survival.

But at the same time—literally, at the *same* time—be cognizant of how you are aroused by the opportunity that is inherent in a crisis situation. Be aware that the crisis, the turning point, holds out to you the potential for achievement; for obtaining your personal or business goals; for receiving admiration from your peers and subordinates, and praise or promotion from your superiors; for facilitating self-enhancement and for moving up.

Now, understand that *both* sensations—the negative and the positive, the fear and the arousal—are caused by *stress.*

A crisis (and your response to it) induces stress and there is no way of getting around it.

Therefore, prepare to make the stress work for you. Decision making under crisis-induced stress requires, more than anything else, an awareness of what is going on—an attitude of vigilance.

It is important in crisis management planning and preparation almost to go into training to deal with stress so that in times of crisis you have the ability to function well—to make decisions effectively—so that the stress you are experiencing does not have disruptive effects on the quality of your thinking and decision-making capabilities. This is why a crisis management plan can reduce stress; just *knowing* that you have a plan can soothe your anxieties to a degree.

It is for this reason that you were asked earlier whether the people on your crisis management team, or even those on your switchboard, have the ability to operate well under stress. And then you were asked: "How do you know?"

Well, once again: how *do* you know if you, or those around you, can handle stress well?

Many forward-thinking companies today are turning to outside psychologists or management consultants to help their employees deal with stress. This is a superior idea, but do not confuse a few minutes of deep-breathing exercise with the ability to handle effective decision making in a crisis.

Deep breathing, which is a relaxation technique, is a good way to bring stress levels down during a crisis, but you do not want to become too laid-back. That would be counterproductive.

"In order to be effective under stress," said Dr. Harriet B. Braiker, a leading authority on the subject, "in order to heighten your own natural ability to achieve and make sound decisions during times of crises, the mind needs to be placed into a vigilant state."[52]

In vigilant decision making, which is what all crisis managers should strive for, the person painstakingly searches for all relevant information and then—in an unbiased way—assimilates information and carefully weighs alternative choices before making a decision.

Dr. Braiker—a clinical psychologist as well as director of The Praxis Training Group, a Los Angeles–based management consulting firm that counsels corporate and individual clients on stress management—explains that there are two opposite poles to the vigilant state. One extreme is too high an arousal level; the other is too low a level. *Neither* is right for a crisis.

Braiker gives credit to the work of Drs. Irving Janis and Leon Mann on understanding the importance of stress in decision making. In a UCLA-sponsored seminar on crisis management, Braiker explained that if a person's stress or anxiety level is too high, that person will be panicky and frantic about the problem; he or she will engage in desperate moves just to get out of the situation as quickly as possible.

But conversely, as illustrated in Figure 7, if stress, or anxiety, is *too low,* the person is just not up for the job, not aroused enough; he or she may not even care enough about the consequences. Being close to this level of passive relaxation is what many people try to achieve by deep breathing, but too much "deep breathing" may be counterproductive in a crisis.

If you are stressed or uptight about a particular situation, such as letting the urge for a cigarette pass or trying to calm down after a disturbing conversation, deep breathing may be just the ticket for what ails you. But, as you can see, a totally passive posture is the last thing you want to achieve if you are being looked on as a key decision maker in a crisis.

Figure 7. The Performance/Anxiety Curve.

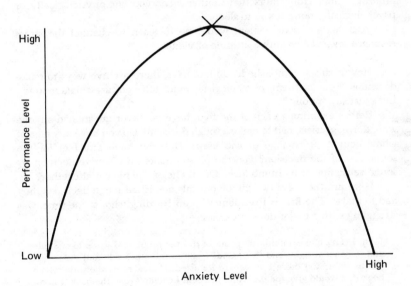

X marks the spot where *performance* and *anxiety* meet at their optimum levels. Moderate anxiety—for our purposes, stress or arousal—is ideal for achieving the required vigilant state and heightened performance. As anxiety increases beyond X, or decreases below X, performance begins to suffer.

As with the fine-tuning needle on your stereo receiver, you want to put your stress indicator needle right smack in the center on the "vigilant" setting, and not allow it to drift too far right or left, up or down.

Stress is a basic survival response.

All along, the point has been made that there is opportunity in a crisis. The opposite point has also been made: danger lurks, too.

And because of the threat of danger, certain innate animalistic responses of the body automatically take over to make us more aware of "things that go bump in the night." Stress is the response that puts you in that vigilant mode. And vigilance is exactly the mode you want to be in when you are in trouble.

In fact, in a genuine crisis situation, you would be acting inappropriately if you were not stressed.

The key to improving your achievement level and your effectiveness is learning to contain stress within levels of intensity that are not disruptive to your functioning. You want to keep the stress within moderate levels of arousal, manageable limits that neither wear you out physiologically or psychologically nor put you to sleep.

Your highest achievement would be to learn to channel the stress response toward a cognitive attitude of vigilance.

How is this accomplished? Under stress, there are five ways to make decisions. Four of them, psychologists would tell you, are "maladaptive." Let's just say "wrong."

Before examining each of the five, have you ever questioned anyone who, during a crisis, had to make a tough decision? Do you have any idea of what thought process he or she used? Did you have any feel for the soundness of the decision? Did the person make an effective decision by sound reasoning or by dumb luck? Or, did he or she blow it altogether?

Here are the ways two public officials described tough decisions they had to make. The first is President Warren Harding who, at the time, was struggling with a major domestic crisis:

> John, I can't make a damn thing out of this tax problem. I listen to one side and they seem right, and then, God! I talk to the other side and they seem just as right, and there I am where I started. I know somewhere there is a book that would give me the truth, but hell, I couldn't read the book. I know somewhere there is an economist who knows the truth, but I don't know where to find him and haven't the sense to know him and trust him when I did find him. God, what a job![53]

Whatever Harding decided, he probably was wrong.

But the toughest decisions, bar none, have to be those that involve life and death. During Three Mile Island, the possibility of an evacuation weighed heavily on the governor's mind. There were four possible outcomes:

1. Ordering an evacuation that was *not* needed.
2. *Not* ordering an evacuation that later would prove to have been needed.
3. Ordering an evacuation that *was* needed.
4. *Not* ordering an evacuation—and no evacuation was needed.

Because the nuclear reactor could prove highly volatile, the governor couldn't wait too long to order an evacuation, if that were the course he chose to follow. Possibilities #1, #2, and #3 would almost certainly result in death of some kind. And Thornburgh's advisers and cabinet were giving him just the same sort of conflicting counsel that President Harding had received.

Here's how Thornburgh described his decision making to the Kemeny Commission:

> There are known risks, I was told, in an evacuation. The movement of elderly persons, people in intensive care units, babies in incubators, the simple traffic on the highways that results from even the best of an orderly evacuation, are going to exert a toll in lives and injuries. Moreover, this type of evacuation had never been carried out before on the face of this earth, and it is an evacuation that was quite different in kind and quality than one undertaken in time of flood or hurricane or tornado. . . . When you talk about evacuating people within a 5-mile radius of the site of a nuclear reactor, you must recognize that that will have 10-mile consequences, 20-mile consequences, 100-mile consequences, as we heard during the course of this event. This is to say, it is an event that people are not able to see, to hear, to taste, to smell. . . .[54]

Thornburgh did not order an evacuation, and no evacuation was needed. In making that decision, he was weighing the known fatality and injury risks inherent in an evacuation against the more positive and encouraging assessment of Harold Denton, who felt that the dangerous hydrogen bubble *could* be contained. Another compelling reason not to evacuate was that the commonwealth's ability to effect such a massive movement of people safely was suspect.

VIGILANCE

Unlike the four maladaptive styles of decision making, vigilance is a style that is most assuredly adaptive. A decision maker objectively collects information, weighs it, searches for other possible options, and makes a well-reasoned decision.

The vigilant style uses stress in the most adaptive way to respond to crises in a manner that generally increases the probability that the decision maker will achieve a sound, high-quality decision, since the process that led him or her to the decision was a high-quality process.

Quality working tools yield quality results in the hands of a skilled artisan.

This is what you should be striving for: a vigilant manner that allows for adaptive, fluid responses to fluid crisis situations and that raises the probability of achieving high-quality, well-balanced, stable decisions that have the best chance of meeting your strategic objectives. Decisions arrived at through this vigilant method have the best chance of *not* being subject to overreactive setbacks, because the setbacks will have been anticipated.

Nor are these decisions obsessional in nature. You certainly consider alternatives, but not in an obsessional decision-making style (such as the mode Jimmy Carter operated in during the Iranian hostage crisis), which does not arrive at *any* decision at all.

And because decisions arrived at through vigilance are more directed, or focused on implementation (implementational problem solving), they are decisions in which the decision maker can have confidence.

This will avoid a very uncomfortable psychological state known as "postdecisional regret," sometimes called "buyer's remorse." You may be able to relate to this condition, either because you yourself have been a victim of it or because someone you know suffers from it. It is an uncomfortable situation in which you've just bought a car or a house (it's usually a "high-ticket" item, though not always) and you suddenly panic.

"Why did I do it?" you may wail. "I can't afford it. It's too big; it's too small. It's the wrong color, the wrong choice." And so on. You become enraged with yourself. You become enraged at the salesperson who sold it to you. And on and on and on.

And it often leads to an impulsive change to undo what you did before.

Postdecisional regret during a crisis can prove disastrous.

But if vigilance is what is desired, how is it that people who you assume—by personal knowledge, by company position, or by historical evidence—to be good, effective, competent decision makers sometimes seem to blow it? Suddenly during a crisis, when you need them the most, they are incapable of making good decisions.

Is it "analysis paralysis" or the "it-can't-happen-here" syndrome?

What is wrong is the decision-making process they are using. On close inspection, you may discover that many people respond to crisis-induced stress with maladaptive styles that often lead to poorly thought-out decisions, unstable decisions with high degrees of postdecisional regret, and vacillation.

Dr. Braiker believes that these otherwise good decision makers, understanding some of the pressures and conditions that characterize the crisis, such as time urgency or having vital interests at stake, suffer intensely high levels of stress that begin to compromise the quality of their decision making. Without proper preparation in the form of crisis decision-making training, these individuals may react so strongly to the intensity of the moment that one could almost understand, though not necessarily approve of, how they could fall into maladaptive coping strategies: making wrong decisions.

To understand more fully what vigilance *is*, understand the four things it is not.

UNCONFLICTED INERTIA, OR UNCONFLICTED ADHERENCE

The decision maker in this maladaptive coping mode decides to ignore any and all information about associated risks and instead opts simply to continue with whatever it is he or she is doing. One example of unconflicted inertia would be Richard Nixon's behavior during the early stages of Watergate.

The decision maker who uses this strategy is neither stupid nor ignorant. There is ample evidence to demonstrate his or her ability to make sound decisions. But, for whatever reason, the individual's vigilance antennae are not working during this crisis, and he or she has decided to ignore advice and associated risks and to adopt an inert laissez-faire coping style. The "analysis paralysis" or the "it-can't-happen-here" syndrome may be at work.

UNCONFLICTED CHANGE

In this instance, the decision maker maladaptively copes by following the *last* advice he or she hears. (*Part* of what was happening to President Harding was unconflicted change.) The decision maker follows what may be called the path of *last* resistance and typically does not make any contingency plans to handle setbacks. Why? Perhaps because it is just "easy" that way.

An example of unconflicted change might be Walter Mondale's decisions in the 1984 presidential election (first) to appoint Bert Lance to head his campaign and to replace Charles Manatt as head of the Democratic party; (second) *not* to have Lance replace Manatt because there was a loud hue and cry about Lance's past, although he would *still* run the campaign; and (third) to dump Lance altogether. All in the span of just a few days.

DEFENSIVE AVOIDANCE

This mode may be trickier to spot, because while the person who uses it avoids decision making by avoiding conflict and by procrastinating, he or she typically appears, in fact, to be making decisions. In reality, though, this person is evading the responsibility to make the decision, postulating shallow rationalizations for unsubstantiated and unsupportive alternatives, striving for the paths of least resistance and highest acceptance, but finding neither. It would not be beyond this decision maker either to twist the facts to suit his or her own rationale or to ignore certain correct information that, if considered, would negate and expose a wrong decision.

One example of defensive avoidance might be Met Ed's initial insistence that everything was all right at Three Mile Island and that there was nothing to worry about.

HYPERVIGILANCE

This is probably the worst coping strategy, and at times it may even be confused with vigilance.

In this maladaptive style, the decision maker is prone to make the biggest mistakes, the grossest errors, the costliest blunders. Arousal of the stress response is *too* great, and the decision maker, in a frenzy, frantically searches for a way out of this self-styled trap. Grasping at straws, he or she will select any alternative that seems to provide an easing of his dilemma, only to quickly abandon it in favor of another.

This is also part of what President Harding was doing. Two other, more contemporary examples might be Richard Nixon's actions during the *latter* stages of Watergate, and Jimmy Carter's conduct throughout much of the Iranian hostage crisis.

Hypervigilance is often characterized by a condition of panic or near-panic in certain disaster situations, such as fires, floods, or tornadoes, in which the victim of this maladaptive coping style may waste so much time simply agitating over the impending event in a state of panic or near-panic that he or she fails to use whatever time remains to find an escape route. This individual, like almost anyone in a panic situation, may typically have a rapid heart rate and shallow, rapid breathing. In fact, in *Selye's Guide to Stress Research,* Volume 3, Drs. Irving Janis, Peter Defares, and Paul

Grossman (the authors of the chapter "Hypervigilant Reactions to Threat") asserted that "many of the characteristic symptoms of hypervigilance may be directly traceable to hyperventilation."[55]

Because of their diffused attention (apparently alert to all dangers, but actually hypervigilant to too many potential threats) and reduced mental efficiency (characterized by a correspondingly high state of emotional arousal), hypervigilant individuals have difficulty discriminating among plausible, authentic, or realistic decisions and their faulty counterparts. People in a hypervigilant state will either follow the crowd or follow a leader, sometimes blindly.

In other words, in a panic-generating situation (such as a fire in a theater), a hypervigilant individual's first reaction is to do what everyone else is doing: to run for the same exit. However, if someone takes command and barks authoritative orders and is perceived as a leader, the hypervigilant person will do what he or she is told.

The full range of consequences and associated risks of alternative decisions is sometimes overlooked by the hypervigilant decision maker, because of emotional excitement, repetitive thinking, or what is termed cognitive constriction—literally, a narrowing of the thought capacities.

(And you thought "narrow-minded" was just a meaningless, pejorative phrase.)

These five coping strategies—vigilance and the four maladaptive styles—are the five basic decision-making processes that will come into play during times of stress—that is, in a crisis.

However, keep in mind, as Dr. Janis reminds us, that unconflicted inertia and unconflicted change occasionally can be adaptive and time-saving in making *minor* decisions. They will tend to lead to improper or defective decisions, though, when the stakes are high. Similarly, in certain rare and extreme cases, defensive avoidance and hypervigilance *may* become adaptive and useful, but it would not be wise to count on it—especially, as Janis states, if you want to improve your chances of averting serious losses.

And, although it may now be easier to see why these four decision-making strategies are defective, there is one caveat in order for vigilance: it may become maladaptive in life-or-death situations where *split-second decisions* are called for.

Who can argue with ranking the decision to drop the atomic bomb on Hiroshima and Nagasaki as one of the toughest decisions ever made? Talk about vigilant decision making!

It is well documented that President Harry Truman never suffered one iota of postdecisional regret about making that determination. In his *Plain*

Speaking, which was the result of a long series of interviews with Truman, Merle Miller wrote:

> But if there was one subject on which Mr. Truman was not going to have any second thoughts, it was the Bomb. If he's said it once, he's said it a hundred times, almost always in the same words. The Bomb had ended the war. If we had had to invade Japan, half a million soldiers on both sides would have been killed and a million more "would have been maimed for life." It was as simple as that, and Mr. Truman never lost any sleep over *that* decision.[56]

Elsewhere in the book, Miller wrote that Truman:

> ". . . asked his associates to tell him how long he had to decide whatever was to be decided, and when the deadline came, the decision had been made. And no regrets, no looking back, no wondering if-I-had-to-do-it-all-over-again, would I have? Dean Acheson [Truman's Secretary of State] wrote that Harry Truman was totally without what he called "that most enfeebling of emotions, regret."[57]

Assuming that whether or not to drop a bomb is *not* uppermost in your mind, and politics aside,* let's consider whom you would want as the head of *your* nation:

A: A leader (such as Harry Truman) who, on more than one occasion, has demonstrated the ability to collect data in an unbiased manner, weigh the pros and cons, and make a defensibly sound decision—in other words, a decision whose merits can be intelligently argued, whether you agree wholeheartedly or not.

B: A leader (such as Jimmy Carter) who, on more than one occasion, has given indications of maladaptive coping styles, flitting from pillar to post under the guise of collecting data and/or actual decision making; a leader who frequently displays symptoms of postdecisional regret.

C: A leader (such as Walter Mondale) who, on more than one occasion, has demonstrated a tendency to make the decisions that he feels others want him to make and often will rush headlong into a decision based on the last piece of information heard.

(The phrase "on more than one occasion" is important for the same reason true-false tests always consist of more than one question: just getting it right—or wrong—*once* is no indication of a person's ability; a coin flip could yield the same result. What you are seeking is a trend. By the same token, mentioning the names of three actual people is not to imply that all

---

*Politics aside, because while these men are all Democrats, the exercise could just as easily be done with Republicans, too.

of Truman's decisions were made along the lines of leader A, nor Carter's decisions along the lines of leader B, nor Mondale's along the lines of leader C. The names are used for illustrative purposes only to remove the question from the purely abstract. Having said all this, we can end the suspense, open the envelope, and announce the winner.)

The correct response is, of course, A. And if the nasty phrase "loaded question" begins to frame on your lips, let's examine why sometimes you *have* to look at the obvious to see what it is that you're otherwise missing.

If it is so obvious that A is the kind of leader needed to run the country, why do some people have trouble realizing that A is also the type who is needed and desired by senior management to run divisions, plants, corporate departments, and/or companies?

When your manager gives you an assignment, it is really a way of testing your authority or ability to problem-solve. If there were no "problem" involved, the superior would merely do it himself or herself.

Perhaps the problem is something you've done before, and done well, which is why you are being asked to replicate your past achievement. Maybe you are really being asked to seek alternative ways—*better* ways— to solve the problem.

Or perhaps it is something that you've never seen before, and neither has anyone else. What are you going to do with it?

Let's hope you are going to exercise vigilant decision-making techniques, so that after you have fact-gathered, after you have considered alternatives, after you have weighed everything in the balance, you will make a decision that *you* can live with, a decision you can defend.

When someone studies your response and asks, "Why?" you should not then panic and interpret that legitimate question as an attack on, or an encroachment of, your authority or your ability. Take it at face value. Someone just wants to know *why*.

You know why. You have already explored the alternatives, haven't you? Your decision was not made randomly or hastily. You feel confident in justifying and defending your position if called on to do so.

Learn vigilant decision making so that it becomes second nature to you. Learn this technique so that you can depend on it during a crisis, when your stress levels are high.

Some crisis situations are so volatile, so potentially explosive, that your stress levels get too far out of line. That's when it's time to call in outside help—which in and of itself is a vigilant decision.

If you are an individual suffering a personal crisis, call in a friend or a psychologist.

If you are in a company and are suffering from a business crisis, you may need to call in help, too. Such help can be either from within or from without the company hierarchy.

Help from within may include your in-house legal or accounting staff, your public relations or personnel departments, and so on. Outside help may include (perhaps in concert with those in-house sources just mentioned) legal and accounting assistance, public relations counseling, crisis management counseling, media experts, psychologists, police, government officials, and so on.

There is absolutely no stigma attached to asking for help. *Remember:* if you make a decision and you do not implement that decision, you have not made a decision at all.

And every company and crisis mentioned in this book has, at some level, called in help to assist with a crisis.

But why does the inevitable occurrence of stress in a crisis so very often reduce the quality of decision making? What makes it so hard to remain vigilant and "hold that technique" when the pressure is on? Why can you return every ball the ball machine hits to your side of the net, but when the ball machine is replaced by a real, live opponent, your tennis game falls apart? What is the psychological relationship between a crisis and the sort of cognitive distortion ("screwed-up thinking") or maladaptive coping ("wrong choices") that are being discussed?

First, the decision maker sometimes is immediately swamped by the recognition that everything in the crisis is "overdetermined"—that for any one effect there may be five causes, and for any one cause there may be five effects. The cognitive process begins to become almost hopelessly entangled, and the decision maker begins to realize his or her own cognitive limitations.

To compare this situation merely to being in a maze hardly does it justice. A better visual metaphor may be walking through a maze backward, wearing a blindfold, and juggling lighted sticks of dynamite. This condition is known as psychological overload.

Another psychological reason for poor-quality decisions is simply fear. It may be a fear that you—the decision maker—are in a lose/lose situation, meaning that even if you *can* figure out the least objectionable alternative, somebody is going to get hurt, somebody is going to lose, something bad will result.

You convince yourself that there is no good alternative, and you can fall victim to what psychologists call an avoidance/avoidance conflict. Just as the label implies, you avoid making *any* decisions.

Another real fear is the fear of losing self-esteem, the fear of being made to look foolish and of losing status if the decision is wrong. These fears raise psychological anxieties.

If you consider the premise that a crisis not only leads to stress but induces anxiety in the participants, including the decision maker, then you can better understand and appreciate why cognitive changes occur. When a crisis produces anxiety, the personality of the decision maker is mobilized to deal with anxiety the way he or she has always dealt with anxiety, with his or her standard psychological defense mechanisms. And as demonstrated earlier in this chapter, too high an anxiety level yields low performance.

Some psychologists take this even a step or two further. They claim that under the conditions just outlined, decision makers regress and move into more primitive styles of thinking and of coping. They become defensive, they become arbitrary. They may begin to make decisions based purely on what they refer to as their "gut reaction," rather than on a cerebral thought process.

Another cognitive error that is common in stressful crisis situations is something called polarized thinking, where everything is seen—*has* to be seen—in black or white terms. There is no room for gray issues.

But as quoted earlier, "Life is lived in the vast complexity of the gray."

In this instance, decision makers polarize their decisions by saying, "This is going to be either the best thing we have ever done or the worst"; "This is going to put us either on Easy Street or in the poor house"; and so forth.

Then thinking becomes egocentric: the decision maker starts to perceive how the crisis is affecting him or her personally. In reality, it is very difficult to detach yourself from an egocentric point of view during a crisis. It is very difficult to try to get people to understand and empathize with another person's point of view at such a time.

In the case of union strikes or walkouts, polarization and egocentric thinking and behavior are quite commonplace. It is for this reason, among others, that companies call in outside consultants (such as a labor lawyer) to negotiate on their behalf. In this way, managers isolate themselves from the crisis and don't get involved in name calling or other counterproductive activities during the more egocentric parts of the polarized negotiations; the people you call names in the heat of the moment are the ones you will have to go back to working with once the strike is settled.

When stress is extended—by days, weeks, or months—mental fatigue, characterized by preoccupation, rumination, and indecisiveness, can set in. A lack of, or inability to, sleep may also result in physical problems and burnout. The extent to which the symptoms occur is related almost directly to the duration and intensity of the crisis.

It is for this reason that United Airlines, as well as so many other companies that deal with crises on an almost "routine" basis, allow their people to work only for a limited number of hours during an actual crisis before calling in replacements. The "first string" people are sent home to sleep and recuperate; then they return refreshed for another shift.

When the stress level runs high, which happens during a crisis, decision makers may display something called premature closure. This is a characteristic of faulty decision making in each of the coping styles except, of course, vigilance.

As its name implies, premature closure is a condition in which the individual stops dealing with the crisis without identifying all of the alternatives and without seeking all the appropriate information or using these data to appraise the situation. This is a classic example of what was referred to earlier as cognitive constriction—a narrowing of the thought process, closing off the thought process early, prematurely.

It is as if you were to put a filter on the lens of your cognitive camera and view the crisis with significant parts of the whole story blocked, or filtered, out. And if you are a victim of negative stress, it is almost a certainty that you are operating with such distorting filters. You may be receiving unrealistic, inaccurate pictures of the situation.

For example, you may be subjecting yourself to a narrowing of the range of perceived alternatives, not allowing yourself to see that the situation is not polarized to black/white, either/or decisions. You may be overlooking the long-term consequences in favor of the immediate, short-range, get-me-out-of-the-frying-pan-*now* mentality—without considering that you may be jumping into the ever-hotter fire.

Still another cognitive constriction is inefficient searching for information. In many cases, the information is there all the time, but the decision maker's mind chooses not to process it—literally, not to receive it.

Not estimating the probability of a particular outcome properly is an additional type of cognitive constriction, as is a tendency to use oversimplified decision making that fails to take all of the available alternatives into account. Probably the worst example of this is someone who makes an important decision during a crisis by flipping a coin.

Under crisis-induced stress, decision makers may rely heavily on certain cognitive crutches that bring about less than efficient and less than totally effective decision making. Although the decisions made are minimally satisfying, they tend not to depend on optimizing criteria ("What do we have to do to get the best results?") and therefore do not constitute high-quality decisions.

This is really the difference between a decision maker who can simply survive a crisis and one who is capable of turning the crisis into an opportunity. This is what distinguishes the gliders from the achievers.

Beware the following types of decision makers, and their respective cognitive crutches:

• The decision maker who confines the alternative choices to only small incremental changes—sort of variations on a theme—when what are required are alternatives that represent major changes from the present course of action. Stated another way, do not use a Band-Aid approach to a crisis that may require major surgery; you will spend too much time changing the dressing, and no real healing will take place.

• The decision maker who is overly concerned about popularity and doing what he or she perceives as the popular thing to do. Politicians, who must be held accountable to their constituencies on a regular basis, are particularly prone to lean on this crutch and make these kinds of decisions.

• The decision maker who gives undue weight to historical analogies, relying on history alone. While it is important to look at historical examples, too much reliance on the past without taking the *present* situation into account can be a cognitive crutch.

• The decision maker who relies on only a general formula or plan—yes, even a crisis management plan—that fails to address the specific content of the issue at hand. The plan, like your decision, must be fluid in order to enable you to respond swiftly to the fluidity of a crisis. At all times you must be able to respond to the particular circumstances, the particular content, of the crisis if you want to be able to overcome debilitating stress and be able to make high-quality decisions.

It is important to keep in mind, as mentioned before, that it is not so much the actual crisis that causes stress as it is your *reaction* to the crisis. And there are several things you can do to respond well to the stress in order to promote vigilant decision making and reduce your use of defective coping strategies, cognitive errors, and crutches.

First, the crisis management plan will reduce much of the pressure of the situation. By telling you in advance where the flashlights are located, it at least moderates the number of questions you must process. It is clearly one of the best ways to counteract psychological overload, defensive avoidance, or even unconflicting inertia.

Second, avoid, if possible, making decisions in a vacuum. This is *not* to suggest that decisions be made by committee. Never! But critical decisions should be made in conjunction with a decision team. A decision team, for lack of a better phrase, is actually a reality-testing device.

Reality is a community affair. Reality is what a bunch of people think reality is, and there is no other way for you to check out if you're thinking straight if you don't check that out with somebody else. People who totally isolate themselves during a crisis (say, Nixon in the waning days of his Administration) tend to get carried away into hypervigilant positions that have no touch with reality. And their decisions reflect it.

Third, brainstorm. Again, this does not mean you should make decisions by committee. But after you have identified and then isolated the crisis, you are ready to begin systematic implementational problem solving, and brainstorming is the first step in this process. You can, if necessary, brainstorm alone, individually, in your own mind. Try to search vigilantly for all of the possible alternatives.

Even though in some crises there are enormous time pressures and emergency demands, it still is vital that you brainstorm. Exhaust every possible alternative until you are satisfied that there is nothing else to consider. Then, having come up with certain possible, perhaps even plausible, alternatives, think about what they look like. Often it is helpful to put things on paper, so you can see the possible choices.

Ben Franklin used to advocate merely drawing a line down the center of a sheet of paper, creating a cognitive balance sheet. On one side of the line, Franklin listed the positive sides to the question and the negatives were listed on the opposite side. He then tallied the score and made his decisions accordingly.

However, you may be far better off with something called a tree diagram (see Figure 8). This exercise in logic diagrams the possible outcomes of each of the alternatives you previously selected through brainstorming, reality testing, and so on. It requires you to take each alternative and try to envision all the possible consequences of that decision.

For example, if you were to select choice #1, what *might* happen? Well, A might happen, or B might happen.

If you choose A, what may happen? C, D, and E.

But if you opt for B, F or G may happen.

And what might happen as a result of C or D or E or F or G?

Carry this inquiry through about five steps, and see where you are. If it is hard for you to visualize, even with the help of a diagram, try it with a real problem of your own.

You should find diagramming a remarkably effective process for making almost any decision because it *guarantees an awareness of the consequences,* so you won't fall prey to a serious cognitive error if your decision results in a setback. You will have minimized the chances of getting blown out of the water and overreactive and anxious, because you will already have thought about the chances of this happening.

Moreover, what you are doing is a technique in which you can write down options in schematic form, thus exposing the mental maze of events, dead ends and all. In making decisions, it is always useful to have a means to translate mental abstractions into concrete, visible terms.

One other thing you can do to improve the quality of your vigilant decision making is to stage and participate in crisis-simulation workshops in order to "inoculate" yourself against stress. "Inoculation" is designed to desensitize you and build your resistance to stress by exposing you to simulated stress in role-playing exercises.

Crisis-simulation workshops have the added benefit of preparing management for dealing with an unexpected, short-fused crisis. If you can

Figure 8. Sample tree diagram for choice #1.

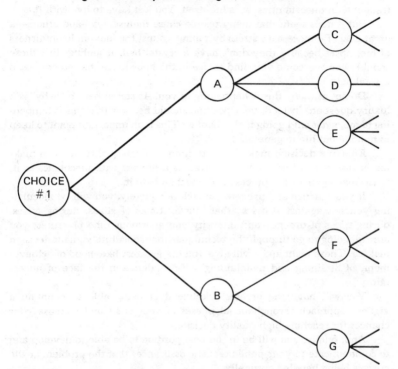

If the decision maker opts for choice #1, two things may happen, A or B. If A is implemented, C, D, or E may result. Implementing B may result in F or G. And so on. Using a tree diagram for decision making, especially during a period of crisis-induced stress, presents a clearer, more concrete, more vigilant picture of available alternatives and consequences.

prepare yourself—think of it as combat preparedness—you are less likely to be swamped by the intensity of stress when it hits you.

It is much like falling into quicksand, which is supposed to be a very intense, panic-ridden experience.

If you panic, you may not survive. But if you do not allow yourself to succumb to the intensity of the crisis—the actual fear of what has you entrapped—all you need do is calmly float on your back, move your hands slightly, and you will float to the edge of the perilous pond. But, again, this life-saving technique is possible only if you do not allow yourself to be swamped by the intensity of the event.

In the final analysis, all the preparation in the world for any crisis is fraught with uncertainties, as is life itself. You just have to live with that.

But it does seem that many people cause themselves—and others—a great deal of unnecessary stress by railing against the inevitable unfairness of life, upset because they don't have a crystal ball. If feelings like these should ever overcome you, find solace in the knowledge that no one has a crystal ball.

Do not ask *why* this is happening to you. As stated before, "why" is a luxury question. Instead, your position should be: *now* that this is happening to me, *what* am I going to do about it? This is an important point to keep in mind about life in general.

Effective decision making is a technique. High-quality decision making in the midst of crisis-induced stress is a process with mechanics to it. Crisis management is a process with mechanics to it.

If you practice and prepare yourself adequately, you will be inoculating yourself against stress so that, during times of stress, during crises, during times of urgency and intensity and enormous time pressures, you are still going to go through the techniques that constitute vigilant decision making. These techniques will give you the greatest likelihood of achievement, of attaining and maintaining self-confidence in the face of uncertainty.

You will have the greatest likelihood of being able to maintain a vigilant approach throughout all phases of your crisis and increase your chances for reaching high-quality decisions.

And, finally, you will be in the best position to be able to develop and to communicate to your public realistic assurances that the problem or the crisis is being handled optimally.

17

A Catastrophic Quartet

Experience is the name everyone gives to their mistakes.

—Oscar Wilde

In much the same vein as the armchair quarterback we discussed earlier, it is considerably easier to discuss crises in theory than in practice.

Ever since my own involvement in Three Mile Island, I have been constantly amazed by what passes for crisis management. A fairly well-known firm that claims to be an expert in crisis management—and which at the time it was introduced to me had never run into a real crisis—took the opportunity to show me a crisis management plan it used for clients.

In theory, the plan was fine. But in practice, it would not have been able to evacuate a kindergarten class during a fire drill. The plan's flaws were legion; but at the root of them all was that the plan was *all* theory; it was based on no actual practice, no experience.

All that you have read thus far, and all that you are about to read, is based on practice.

Certainly, the crises cited have all been familiar to you, and the snippets of crises used thus far have illustrated and demonstrated in practice—not in theory—how or why a particular point or two operated.

But in the case studies which follow, you will be able to trace four megacrises from beginning to end. And as you do, keep in mind what we have been discussing throughout. It will help you see more clearly which companies or individuals performed well in the face of a crisis, and which did not.

Ask yourself how *you* would have done had you been in their shoes. Would you have been able to spot the prodromes? Would you have been able to make vigilant decisions? Would you have been able to identify, isolate, and manage the crisis? Would you have distinguished yourself as a leader and as a decision maker?

Would you have turned danger into opportunity?

Remember, as with all of the crises situations and individuals mentioned in this book, at no time is culpability stated or implied, nor should any interpretation of such be inferred.

The information in this chapter—much of it from behind the scenes—was derived from a combination of personal face-to-face interviews with key participants, telephone interviews, correspondence, and in-depth media stories and analyses.

Now, let's see what *really* happens in a crisis. . . .

The Ohio Savings & Loan Crisis

Before trouble comes, obtain advice; after it comes, advice is useless.

—*Ibn Zabara*, Book of Delight

THE CRISIS IN BRIEF

The March 1, 1985, collapse of a Fort Lauderdale, Florida, securities trading firm called ESM Government Securities threatened to collapse Ohio's Home State Savings Bank, which had invested—and subsequently lost—some $100 million with ESM. Home State was one of 71 Ohio S&Ls whose depositors' funds were insured by the Ohio Deposit Guarantee Fund (ODGF)—a *private* insurance protection fund for state-chartered institutions that were not part of the *Federal* Savings & Loan Insurance Corporation (FSLIC). The ODGF did not have enough funds to cover the severe run on the bank, which, because of the media stories about the ESM collapse, was taking place at Home State and at other ODGF-insured S&Ls. As a result of the crisis, Ohio's governor closed all such banks for one week.

KEY PLAYERS IN BRIEF

- Richard F. Celeste, Governor of Ohio
- Marvin Warner, chairman of the Ohio Building Authority and former owner of Home State
- Ken Cox, newly named (two weeks before the crisis) director of the state Commerce Department
- Ray Sawyer, Governor Celeste's chief of staff
- Thomas Batties, interim head of the state Division of Savings & Loans
- David Schiebel, chairman and president of Home State
- Brian Usher, Governor Celeste's press secretary
- Rodgin Cohen, a New York lawyer

153

Governor Celeste maintains that the first he knew of any trouble with Home State came on March 6, in an early-morning telephone call from Marvin Warner, who was alerting him to a story in the Cincinnati *Enquirer.* The story was about the ESM collapse, and Warner—who had controlled Home State for more than three decades—undoubtedly knew what this meant for his former bank.

Giving Celeste the benefit of the doubt about when he first knew something was amiss, the question becomes: should he—or his staff—have suspected something earlier? Were there any prodromes to point to?

If the question is directed strictly to the collapse of one bank—Home State—the answer is a qualified and tentative no. Tentative because, on the *surface,* everything appeared to be fine; however, a strong argument can be made for what a thorough bank examination *should* have revealed.*

But—remember how important it is to identify the crisis—the *real* crisis in Ohio was not about Home State. It was, instead, about the future of the entire state savings and loan industry in Ohio and the inability of the ODGF to protect depositors, despite the window and door decals that proudly boasted fully guaranteed deposits at ODGF member institutions.

Why wasn't the collapse of Home State the real crisis for the governor? Because, sadly, it has become somewhat commonplace today for banks to fail and close for a short while, only to be taken over shortly afterward by a stronger financial institution. Certainly that is a crisis, but one bank's failure should not be able to shake the foundation of an entire banking insurance institution. The fact that one bank *could* shake that foundation, however, underscores the severity of the real crisis.

And as to the question of the real crisis itself, yes, it appears there *were* prodromes that the governor and/or his people should have spotted.

The most obvious prodrome was the collapse of Commonwealth Savings in Nebraska in 1983. The collapse of that *one* bank exposed Nebraska's private insurance firm as woefully underfunded; it was unable to bail out Commonwealth Savings. And in 1976, a similar crisis occurred in Mississippi, when the failure of one S&L caused a statewide crisis.

Remember how easy it should be to find opportunity in someone else's crisis. Apparently this lesson was lost on the good citizens of Ohio, or at least on those in charge.

If you were the governor of a state with a private insurance fund for state-chartered banks or S&Ls, wouldn't you think there was some golden opportunity here to recognize a prodrome and avert a crisis in your state?

On March 14, in fact, Celeste telephoned the governors of Massachu-

---

*In fact, the *Wall Street Journal* ultimately reported, in a piece by James Ring Adams entitled "How Ohio's Home State Beat the Examiners," that a bank examiner spotted the prodrome, and predicted the collapse, in October 1982—two and a half years earlier. But the warning went unheeded.[58]

setts and Maryland, which also have private insurance funds, to warn them to watch out for a similar problem in their states. It seems the message wasn't lost on Maryland's Governor Harry R. Hughes, whose swift legislative actions just two months later stemmed a potential crisis of almost identical origins.*

So what happened in Ohio? Did the fault lie partly in the fact that Ken Cox, the director of the Ohio Department of Commerce, under whose aegis the state Division of Savings & Loans is housed, had been on the job only two weeks?

Or did it lie in the fact that the head of the Division of Savings & Loans, Thomas Batties, was a young lawyer and only the interim division head?

Was it inexperience on their part, or wishful thinking on the part of the governor's chief of staff, Ray Sawyer, that prompted him to have Cox, on the afternoon of March 6, issue a premature statement: "I want to assure depositors that their assets are protected and there is no reason for concern. In spite of potential difficulties, Home State Savings is in sound financial condition and has a record of stability."

There is no evidence to suggest anything as ominous as a conspiracy to mislead the public, but remember the importance of accuracy and honesty in crisis communications. The statement issued apparently had no basis in fact. Issuing inaccurate statements—seriously inaccurate statements—is worse than stonewalling. The media will get a good story with or without your help. But if you are perceived as an unreliable source of information, *everything* you say will be suspect. (Just ask Met Ed for corroboration: the utility's credibility was so severely shattered during the Three Mile Island crisis that even today much of what it says is not believed by many of its customers.)

As things escalated, however, and the crisis began to assume enormous proportions, few people had the time or the inclination to throw Cox's words back at him or at the governor.

And speaking of the governor, how exactly did he do? Did he distinguish himself? Did he assume a decisive leadership role in the crisis and save the S&L industry? Was his decision to close the banks a good, well-reasoned, *vigilant* decision in the heat of the crisis, or did he panic in a hypervigilant mode and actually do more harm than good?

Did he identify the real crisis? Did he isolate it? Did he manage it well?

---

*In May 1985, after first imposing a $1,000 savings withdrawal cap at state S&Ls, Hughes signed legislation ordering all 102 state-chartered institutions to apply for federal deposit insurance by June 1, 1985, or face a takeover by the state. Additionally, a $100 million state bond issue was approved by the Maryland legislature to provide immediate, but temporary, assistance to S&Ls that could not quickly meet the stringent federal insurance coverage requirements.[59]

A daily log of the governor's activities for two weeks will shed some light on these and other pertinent questions. At the end of March 1985, as the acute crisis phase began to wane and evolve into the chronic phase, Governor Celeste agreed to be interviewed.

The interview (which took three and a half hours) appeared in the May 1985 issue of *Cincinnati* magazine, the result of the literary efforts of Adrienne Bosworth, Herb Cook, Jr., and Max Brown.

Using Governor Celeste's own words and account of the crisis from his perspective, let's examine how he did as a crisis manager.

But try to remember that we are looking at the *mechanics* of the crisis, not the content.

FRIDAY, MARCH 8

Although he had known about the ESM/Home State story for two days, Celeste said that this day, March 8, was the first day "that my schedule really started to get horsed around" as a result of the crisis. State examiners were poring over Home State's books, and negotiations were under way to try to sell Home State to First National Bank of Cincinnati. Because First National was a federally insured bank, had the sale gone through, deposits would have been safe and depositors would have had no cause for alarm.

Celeste took an active role in trying to encourage the sale. But there were problems.

First, according to Celeste's chief of staff, Ray Sawyer, First National wanted the state to kick in about $100 million to close the gap between the S&L's assets and its liabilities, and First National wanted what was left in the rapidly depleting insurance fund.

But Celeste didn't think he could persuade the legislature to approve such a measure, and he wanted to avoid any appearances that he was bailing out Marvin Warner—a friend, political ally, and fundraiser. Warner, whom Celeste had appointed as chairman of the Ohio Building Authority, had formerly owned Home State for 30 years.

This rationalization begs the question about Celeste's qualifications to manage this crisis.

Remember that in a crisis there may be occasions when you are too close to the situation to be able to be an effective manager. There are many times when it is necessary to bring in outsiders for just this reason.

If Celeste was concerned about the appearance of certain of his actions—such as using state money to bail out Warner—then a study of the governor's actions would reasonably ask if this concern clouded his judgment at any time and prompted him *not* to take a certain action. Did the depositors suffer because Celeste bent over backward to avoid any appearance of impropriety?

For example, Celeste's opinion on March 8 was that trouble would be avoided if Home State could be sold quickly.

His cognitive error here was to take a Band-Aid approach to problems that required major surgery: future of the ODGF, as well as a rapidly escalating erosion of public confidence and trust in the state banking system.

The sale to First National Bank did not go through. David Schiebel, Home State's chairman and president, announced that his bank's 33 branch offices would not open the next day.

SATURDAY, MARCH 9

Further action in attempting to effect a sale of Home State produced no results. Celeste bemoaned the fact that no one seemed to know the exact status of the S&L's financial condition, although the governor was told the asset-to-liability gap could be as much as $220 million.

Celeste went shopping with his daughter. This outing was preplanned and, although Celeste probably did not realize it at the time, was actually an extremely positive crisis management maneuver: come up for air every once in a while.

Crisis-induced stress can consume you, so be prepared to walk away from it from time to time. Get your mind on other things; take a break from the pressure cooker; take a walk; take a nap; go shopping with your teenage daughter. Remember the crisis management teams at places like United Airlines: in an attempt to minimize stress, members of the crisis management team are rotated every few hours.

SUNDAY, MARCH 10

What is most confusing about this day's actions are the governor's own words to explain why he spent virtually every minute of the day on the telephone or in meetings at the Governor's Mansion:

> I was trying to reach friends who knew something about insurance to find out
> if there was a way to buy private insurance, whether there was a way to take
> what was left of ODGF and get more insurance. . . .

Celeste reported calling an old friend from Cleveland, named Milt Wolf, who is described as a former ambassador to Austria. Celeste reached him for what Celeste called "a quickie lesson in finance."

And later Celeste called his father in Florida, who gave him the name of Arlo Smith, "a savings and loan guy in Cleveland fifteen years ago." Later the same day Celeste appointed this man conservator of Home State.

The behavior just described seems to be that of a hypervigilant decision maker.

In his efforts to do whatever he felt had to be done to stem the crisis, Celeste gave the appearance of running from pillar to post, which is understandable, given that he apparently was *not* getting necessary information from his staff. He was seeking answers *everywhere.*

But where *were* his full-time, on-staff Ohio banking and insurance experts?

Why was Celeste trying "to reach friends who knew something about insurance"? Why wasn't he trying to reach *state* insurance officials? (And if he *had* reached them, why was he looking elsewhere for information? Did he not trust or believe what his own officials had told him? If so, why? And if he had little confidence in his own officials, what did he plan to do about *that* crisis?)

Why, for example, would the governor of a state as large as Ohio, with all of its vast resources and talent, find it necessary to track down the former ambassador to Austria for a "quickie lesson in finance"?

And without casting any aspersions on the decision-making abilities of the senior Mr. Celeste, why did the governor of Ohio find it necessary to get the name of a possible conservator from his father in Florida when he had his own staff to turn to?

If you are managing a crisis and unconsciously find yourself constantly turning to questionable outside sources for information, it may be time to ask yourself consciously whether there is a problem with your internal staff. If you don't have confidence in them, then you should consider that realization a prodrome of a crisis and govern yourself accordingly.

And while the governor is to be commended for trying to manage the crisis, he is to be faulted to whatever extent he found himself immersed in details that should have been better left to subordinates. In short, was it the best use of the governor's time to spend "virtually every minute of the day" on the telephone "trying to reach friends who knew something about insurance . . ."?

On the positive side of that Sunday, Celeste did appoint Arlo Smith as conservator. It is presumed that someone checked to make certain that Smith's credentials were in order before the appointment was announced. Celeste's father's description of Smith as "a savings and loan guy in Cleveland fifteen years ago" is, by itself, hardly a strong qualification.

Later that night, the governor's press secretary, Brian Usher, managed to craft a statement announcing that Smith had been appointed, that Smith would attempt to sell Home State, that this was all designed to "provide the maximum possible protection to remaining depositors," and that Home State would be closed on Monday.

It was a good statement, but very poorly delivered. The crisis communications channels in the governor's press office were such that, in this age of instant communications, Usher spent most of the evening on the telephone, reading the statement to newspeople in Cincinnati one at a time. Consequently, the statement did little to allay depositors' fears, but at least it was somewhat productive.

Also on the positive side of crisis management, Celeste said he began making a checklist of things that had to be done. Good. Write it down; get organized. Become focused on the crisis. Isolate the crisis.

And the items on his checklist were positive, too: first was the conservator; second was dealing with the Federal Reserve Bank in Cleveland to get help on selling Home State; and third was legislation for a new insurance fund—the real crisis at last.

These are big-picture items, which befit someone in the governor's position. A good crisis manager must manage the entire crisis (rank-ordered, naturally) and not get bogged down in a pool of detailed quicksand.

By the end of the night, State Senator Richard Finan, chairman of the Senate Ways and Means Committee, was on his way to Columbus to begin drafting a new bill to address the shortage on the ODGF resources.

MONDAY, MARCH 11

The legislature was called into emergency session to try to create a new insurance fund. This was a strong, positive message in the midst of the crisis, especially since none of the Ohio banks that had been possible Home State buyers expressed any further interest.

Celeste again spent most of his day on the telephone, but it appears this time that he was speaking to people who were in a better position to contribute to his management of the crisis: members of the Ohio congressional delegation and officials of the Federal Reserve Bank.

From conversations with the Fed, Celeste learned that "there is not total panic at the other ODGF institutions, but there are little things making the Federal Reserve nervous . . ." —some substantial withdrawals from other state-chartered S&Ls.

On a constructive note, Celeste's chief of staff, Ray Sawyer, conversed with Federal Home Loan Bank chairman Edwin Gray about speeding up Federal Savings and Loan Insurance Corporation (FSLIC) applications.

While Sawyer was getting less than favorable news from Gray, Celeste was pursuing Paul Volcker, chairman of the Federal Reserve Board, who told Celeste to find someone "who had participated in workouts of failed banks."

This was good advice, but the list of names Celeste received (he makes a point of saying the names did not come from Volcker) were only names on a piece of paper. Celeste admitted he didn't know one name from another.

He did get through to the first name on the list—Rodgin Cohen, a New York lawyer—but Celeste confessed that he would have called the next person on the list if Cohen's line had been busy.

Without making any judgment calls on Mr. Cohen's qualifications, it seems odd that it would be necessary to find an out-of-state attorney. But more than geographic location, going down a list of unknown names the way Celeste did—or was prepared to do—does not seem to be the epitome of effective decision making. Was there *no one* for Celeste to ask to check on the qualifications of anyone on the list?

The stress of it all was getting to the governor when, at 11 P.M., he quit for the day, saying:

> I'm tired of all this. I've gone through these damn calls of people I've never met to deal with an issue I've never had to deal with before. I've got to get a break.

He had a beer with a friend—a positive step, for reasons noted before.

TUESDAY, MARCH 12

At Cohen's suggestion, Celeste spent the day trying to lure out-of-state banking interests to take over Home State. The governor talked directly to the chairman (or as close to that office as possible) of each bank: CEO to CEO. This is appropriate; this is where a governor's time is best spent: at the top, with other decision makers.

WEDNESDAY, MARCH 13

What should have been a good day—a real turning point for Celeste— got buried by the governor's own muddying of an important message.

The legislature approved a new $90 million insurance fund. (Actually, it was only $50 million, to be merged with the ODGF's already existing $40 million.) But at the press conference and bill-signing ceremony, a reporter, Tom Suddes of the Cleveland *Plain Dealer,* asked if Marvin Warner was going to remain as chairman of the Ohio Building Authority.

Remember that in crisis communications you want to *control* the message.

Instead of side-stepping the question, as he should have done, Celeste foolishly replied to a room full of reporters that Warner had called an hour ago and had resigned. Celeste had no idea of the impact of this announcement.

"I stepped on my own story," Celeste said. And he had. The story of the insurance fund was buried the next day; the big news was the Warner resignation. Also buried was a great message from Volcker, in which he called the appropriation for the fund "the most extraordinary step taken by a state to protect its own financial institutions."

The other bad news that day included:

- S&L executives from Cincinnati flew to Washington to appeal directly to the FSLIC and were turned down.
- There were long lines of depositors at two other S&L institutions, Molitor and Charter Oak.
- Two *federally* insured institutions, Provident Bank and Eagle Savings, refused to honor checks drawn on *any* ODGF-backed S&Ls.

And it appeared that even the new $90 million fund would not suffice.

THURSDAY, MARCH 14

All the bad news from the previous day—from Warner's resignation on down—dominated the news coverage. News of the $90 million was completely lost.

The crisis was escalating. It had gotten totally out of hand.

Hundreds of people were lining up outside the ODGF-backed S&Ls, and the devastating visual image was being captured by network news cameras. A radio talk show encouraged people to camp out in order to be first in line to get their money out when the bank opened in the morning.

Celeste again spent a good deal of time on the telephone—it was on this day that he called his counterparts in Massachusetts and Maryland—and then, knowing that he was facing a difficult decision, "started calling people who I thought could give me some reasonable, calm, cool, clearheaded advice." Until this time, he had consulted only with attorneys.

"One of my great frustrations in all this," Celeste said, was the "fundamental difference between lawyering and deciding. Lawyers will present more and more choices and try not to decide on any of them. In a situation like this you need people who are willing to decide. . . ."

He was, at last, seeking a vigilant decision maker.

Although the governor may be faulted for having taken a week to come to the conclusion he did, he must be commended, at the same time, for having at least acted on his conclusion.

He returned to his office in the evening and began calling the heads of ODGF-backed S&Ls at about 8:30 P.M. He discovered that more than $60 million had been withdrawn that day. The run on deposits was escalating.

FRIDAY, MARCH 15

The Ides of March greeted the governor with four possible decisions about the remaining S&Ls:

1. Allow them to remain open, but limit withdrawals to 35 percent of a depositor's funds.
2. Allow them to remain open, and permit the run to continue possibly unchecked.
3. Close only the weak S&Ls.
4. Close all of them.

The decision makers determined that the most politically appealing solution was #1: not closing any banks, but limiting withdrawals. However, in the early morning hours of March 15, it was decided that this was not a practical solution, since people would still be able to get to their money through automatic teller machines (ATMs) and by writing checks. So this idea—which might have contributed considerably to keeping the crisis more in check—was abandoned in favor of option #4: close them all.

But the fact is that option #1 *could* have been used, just as it was used in Maryland two months later, when Governor Hughes imposed a $1,000 limit on withdrawal of funds from troubled S&Ls in that state.

Celeste and his still-nonvigilant decision makers apparently gave too much weight to the *problem* of option #1, without giving enough weight to searching for alternative ways to achieve the desired option: keeping the S&Ls open.

This maladaptive coping style is a good argument for the tree diagram illustrated in Chapter 16, on decision making under crisis-induced stress. It is possible that a tree diagram, coupled with other vigilant decision-making techniques, would have revealed how easily automatic teller machines can be shut down and how the ability to write checks can be restricted or frozen if desired, making it necessary for a depositor to come into a bank in person to withdraw funds.

Later in the crisis, in fact, Celeste did sign legislation permitting withdrawals of up to $750 per month.

So the decision not to go with the first option was not well thought out.

On the actual question of whether or not to close all the state S&Ls, the governor reportedly went around the room, pointing to every person assembled there, and asked whether each one agreed or disagreed. No one disagreed, and the governor gave the order to close all the S&Ls.

On the positive side, this was an example of decision making in a community setting. But on the negative side, the decision was made at 5 A.M. The governor and his staff had been up all night long with no breaks. It is reasonable to question how sharp people's minds were at that hour.

Did some staff members vote the way they did because it was late, because they were tired, because others were voting that way? Was the decision not to go with option #1 also made at 5 A.M.? Were people too tired to see that there were ways option #1 could be made to work?

The governor had started making calls at 8:30 the previous night. Eight and a half hours later he declared the first bank holiday since FDR—albeit on a more modest scale.

Someone on the governor's staff began setting up a bank of telephone hot lines to handle what would total some 25,000 calls from angry and confused depositors by the end of the weekend. This was a very positive step in crisis communications: give a confused/hostile/inquiring public a reliable place to turn for credible information. Control the message, and stem the rumors.

SATURDAY, MARCH 16

Celeste's order to close the banks was due to expire on the morning of Monday, March 18. So he had, in effect, just the length of the weekend to get the banks reopened.

He first convened a meeting of Ohio's major commercial banks to try to get them to form a consortium to bail out the state-chartered S&Ls. They refused.

Someone began working on what they referred to as the "Mississippi Plan," whereby all S&Ls would have to apply for and be granted FSLIC coverage before being allowed to reopen. This was a modification of Mississippi's solution to its 1976 S&L crisis.

This also was the day the national press corps came to town.

Cincinnati magazine reported that when Celeste went to bed that night—actually early Sunday morning—he had had only about eight hours sleep in three days.

SUNDAY, MARCH 17

By the time an 8 P.M. meeting of the CEOs of the 71 closed S&Ls convened, Celeste was convinced that the only viable way to reopen the banks was with mandatory FSLIC coverage.

By all accounts, Celeste gave a masterful performance before what he had expected to be a hostile audience. He let it be known that the CEOs were there more because their own insurance fund had failed than because of *his* actions. He defended his decision to close the S&Ls to stem the run.

Now he had to decide whether to extend the closings or to allow some or all of the S&Ls to reopen. Celeste said that all but about a half-dozen asked to stay closed until they could receive federal insurance.

At 11 P.M., after flying back to Cincinnati because he had made a promise to be in Cincinnati every day until the crisis was over, Celeste announced that the S&Ls would be closed for two more days.

Celeste's obviously politically motivated pronouncement to be in Cincinnati every day until the crisis passed was foolish, or at best foolishly executed. Daily back-and-forth travel is exhausting and a crisis manager should at all times preserve his or her energies to ensure sharp faculties for vigilant decision making. Had Celeste *stayed* in Cincinnati, he would have reduced the travel tedium. However, this would have been inappropriate: his place was at the center of power, and the center of action, in the governor's office and close to the General Assembly. Celeste should have preserved his strength by staying where he belonged and where he could do the most good, traveling to Cincinnati only when necessary or appropriate. In other words, he should have been less concerned with voters and more concerned with depositors.

MONDAY, MARCH 18

Celeste flew back to Cincinnati again to meet with the Federal Home Loan Bank Board head, Charles Theimann.

A speedy passage of Senator Finan's hastily drawn bill requiring S&Ls to apply for federal coverage fell victim to partisan bickering in the opposition-controlled Senate. It had passed the House with a bipartisan 87–2 vote but went down to defeat twice in the Senate.

TUESDAY, MARCH 19

It was on this day that, according to *Cincinnati* magazine:

What had begun as a single S&L failure in Ohio had assumed international proportions. The dollar was plunging on international money markets. The price of gold jumped $30 an ounce. The world's financiers didn't quite understand what was going on in Ohio, but whatever it was made them jittery.

Celeste flew to Washington, where he received support from Ohio's congressional delegation, which was to be expected. After all, it was *their* constituency, too.

And he won assurances from Volcker and from FHLBB head Gray— whom Celeste had thought would be trouble—to assist in expediting federal insurance coverage and to pump in money at the appropriate time.

The one remaining stumbling block was the state Senate, which was still playing political football with Finan's bill. Celeste sent a no-nonsense message to Senate President Paul Gillmor (who may be Celeste's opponent in the next gubernatorial election) that if the Senate could not pass a bill that night, Celeste wanted to address a joint session of the General Assembly. The message was as subtle as a sledgehammer: Celeste was now prepared to lay the blame for the S&Ls *not* reopening on the doorstep of the opposition political party.

Celeste *finally* had control of the crisis.

WEDNESDAY, MARCH 20

The Senate unanimously passed a second House-backed bill, and Celeste signed it into law at 2:45 A.M. It required all ODGF-insured S&Ls to apply for federal insurance, to prove that they were financially strong enough to open and operate without it, to merge, or to be liquidated. The bill further permitted each depositor to withdraw up to $750 of his or her funds while the bank awaited FSLIC coverage.

It was not precisely the bill Celeste had wanted, but it would do.

And so ended the acute crisis.

THE AFTERMATH

Home State was sold two and a half months later to Ohio-based Hunter Savings Association. And the governor replaced Thomas Batties, who had been serving as interim head of the Commerce Department's S&L Division.

The chronic phase will last at least until November 1986, when

Celeste presumably will run for re-election. Then, the *real* decision makers will let him know whether or not he did the right thing in closing the banks.

Celeste thinks he did the right thing. Here's how he described his feelings to *Cincinnati* magazine.

> I think the measure of any of us is how we deal with that kind of crisis. Here was one whose implications went far beyond the State of Ohio, one where handling it wrong could have unpeeled the layers of an onion and laid bare the frailties of our economic and financial system. I think the fact that I acted when I did and as forcefully as I did was a source of great reassurance to those who know about those things. Now whether that's ever communicated to the average voter . . . is another matter. . . . I think the political fallout is partly dependent on whether the depositors really come out having been protected.

And, as just one tragic ripple effect of this crisis, although it was more of a shock wave when it happened, prominent Florida lawyer Stephen W. Arky, whose law firm represented ESM, committed suicide on July 22, 1985. Before shooting himself in the temple with a .35 caliber Colt, Arky left a note swearing his innocence of any wrongdoing.[60] Arky was Marvin Warner's son-in-law.

As a result of the Ohio and Maryland S&L crises, the Chicago-based U.S. League of Savings Institutions—the S&Ls' most powerful trade and lobbying group—announced plans to establish a national network of Regional Advisory Committees (RACs) designed to act swiftly to assist crippled financial institutions. The RACs would be able to step in to help manage the problem loans of any S&L in the event of a government takeover.[61]

On a broader scale, the aftermath of the Ohio and Maryland S&L crises is that there is now a growing nationwide trend for privately insured S&Ls to apply for FSLIC coverage, according to Edwin J. Gray, FHLBB chairman. Gray also maintains that his organization has detected no evidence that the recent Ohio and Maryland crises have affected any federally insured S&L. But he does express concern that the FSLIC system could be threatened by poor management and excessive risk taking by S&L managers.[62]

The FDIC (Federal Deposit Insurance Corporation), which insures banks, has an $18 billion fund. The FSLIC has a $6 billion insurance fund. Impressive and reassuring figures, certainly.

But the combined worth of banks and S&Ls, which these two funds insure, is approximately $3.5 *trillion,* give or take a few bucks.[63]

Just because the Fed insures deposits up to $100,000, is the system really safe?

Could Ohio and Maryland be national prodromes? Some S&L indus-

try leaders apparently fear so and, consequently, may be practicing sound crisis management.

In the fall of 1985, the Federal Home Loan Bank Board approved the formation of a new corporation, called the Federal Asset Disposition Association, which is designed to liquidate problem loans or failed S&Ls. FADA, as it is destined to be known, is actually a bail-out plan (read: crisis management plan) for the Federal Savings & Loan Insurance Corporation. It was recommended that FADA receive an initial capitalization of approximately $1.5 billion.

What is not known, though, is whether the funding is sufficient and/or in time.[64]

On May 31, 1985, seven financially ailing FDIC-insured banks were ordered closed by government regulators, thereby setting a 50-year record for the number of banks to close in a single day. Previously, the largest number of bank failures in one day since the 1934 creation of the FDIC had been six, in 1983.

The seven closings brought the total number of 1985 bank failures to 43—in the first five months of the year alone. (By December 31, the number nearly tripled to 120. The year before, the total number of bank failures had been 79.)[65] Of the seven banks, one each was in Oregon, Minnesota, and Arkansas.

And four were in Nebraska.

The Union Carbide Crisis

Where there is no vision, the people perish.

—*Book of Proverbs*

THE CRISIS IN BRIEF

In the early morning hours of December 3, 1984, while most of the impoverished residents of Bhopal's shantytowns slept, a Union Carbide pesticide plant in that Indian city experienced a fatal leak of the poison gas methyl isocyanate (MIC), which the plant produced. The accident resulted in the deaths of more than 2,000 people and serious injuries, including permanent blindness in many cases, to an estimated 200,000.*

KEY PLAYERS IN BRIEF

- Warren M. Anderson, Union Carbide's chairman and chief executive officer
- Jackson B. Browning, Union Carbide's director of health, safety, and environmental affairs

It was, as *Time* magazine called it, "a vast, dense fog of death that drifted toward Bhopal"[66] for almost an hour.

---

*Just one of the many tragedies surrounding the Union Carbide crisis is that no one ever will know exactly how many people were killed. Estimates have ranged from a low of 1,700 to a high of 4,500. The Indian government at one point put the number at 2,500, a figure disputed by Dr. Ramana Dhara, who put the figure at 4,000 based on the number of death shrouds that were purchased in the week following the accident. Precise figures are unavailable since, in some instances, entire families and neighborhoods were annihilated. Mass funeral pyres also made body counts difficult. It appears that blindness struck the young and the elderly most, as did permanent lung damage. Dr. James Milius, of the U.S. government's National Institute of Occupational Safety and Health, estimated that some 60,000 people would require long-term respiratory care. Debate continues on the number of stillbirths and miscarriages caused by MIC, and on the number of brain and nervous-system damage caused by low-level cyanide poisonings.

For our purposes, we will use the conservative figures cited above, which many others have adopted: 2,000 dead and 200,000 injured.

It was, as the New York *Times*'s definitive four-part series* on the entire disaster defined it, "the result of operating errors, design flaws, maintenance failures, and training deficiencies."[67]

It was (and let's hope always remains) the worst industrial disaster in human history.

Because of the violent manner in which MIC reacts with water, the fatal gas in the lungs of victims caused the equivalent of death by drowning. Hardest hit were infants and the very young, as well as the elderly, whose lungs were either too small or too frail to fight off the effects of the gas.

The fortunate victims died in their sleep.

Others ran through the streets in terror, some fearing the end of the world.

"Even more horrifying than the number of dead," said *Fortune* magazine, "was the appalling nature of their dying—crowds of men, women, and children scurrying madly in the dark, twitching and writhing like the insects for whom the poison was intended."[68]

Edward Van Den Ameele, Union Carbide's press relations manager and duty officer on the morning of December 3, 1984, was awakened at 4:30 A.M. by a reporter from CBS radio. The reporter was calling for a reaction to a news report from India that there were some deaths resulting from a Union Carbide pesticide plant in Bhopal.

Fortune said that as Van Den Ameele and the reporter talked, the continual incoming news reports raised the death figure from 75 to 200, and that by the time Van Den Ameele dressed and drove from his Connecticut home in the bedroom community of Ridgefield to the Union Carbide headquarters nestled on 674 wooded acres in Danbury, the death toll had escalated to 300. "And it just kept going up and up and up," he said. "It felt like I was in a continuous long-running nightmare—only I wasn't asleep."[69]

Without knowing too much more than has already been written on these few pages, without having spoken to Union Carbide officials in India, and without any idea of whether or not he would be permitted to visit the site, within 48 hours of the initial reports Warren Anderson told a crowded news conference in Danbury that he was going to India immediately to direct the investigation of the gas leak.

Much has been said in praise of Anderson's decision to go, calling the trip an expression of Anderson's and/or the conglomerate's humanity and concern.

*The New York *Times*, beginning on January 28, 1985, ran a special four-part series on the Bhopal disaster, written by Stuart Diamond and Robert Reinhold, which is highly recommended to any reader seeking a good, clear lay understanding of the technical causes of the accident.

But from a crisis management perspective, Warren Anderson's mad dash across the globe was ill conceived and poorly timed. It can be likened to sending Eisenhower to do reconnaissance at Normandy—you just *don't* send the general.

"It showed a lot of guts but not much intelligence," an unnamed official of a rival chemical company told *Fortune*.[70] There is a strong basis for that statement, unless the trip—as might be suggested—was nothing more than public relations posturing or, as Anderson himself later said, a measure designed to head off inevitable lawsuits.

But giving Anderson the benefit of the doubt that his journey was purely altruistic, let's consider where he went wrong as a *crisis manager*. And remember, once again, that it is strictly from the vista of a crisis manager that issue can be taken with Anderson's trip.

To begin with, there is no evidence to support the contention that Anderson made a vigilant decision in a time of crisis. If he had, chances are he would have realized the rash, foolhardy nature of the trip, since:

• He didn't have enough information to warrant the trip.
• He didn't know if he'd be able to visit the site.
• There is no evidence that he would have been able to accomplish anything had he gotten to the site.
• Communications with Bhopal were so poor (there were reportedly only two telephone lines, which hampered if not crippled plant-to-head-quarters communications—a source of frustration that helped prompt the trip in the first place) that the chances of his actually being able to *do* anything in Bhopal were greatly reduced. If he needed to issue orders to Danbury, his ability to do so would have been severely restricted.
• He ignored threats that he would be arrested—which he was—by the Indian government. He already knew that some of Union Carbide's Bhopal managers had been arrested. Anderson's arrest (actually house arrest, along with the people who accompanied him) on charges of negligence and corporate liability further diminished his ability to be an effective crisis manager for the several days he was incommunicado.
• And, finally, on the basis of his reactions (or overreactions) and decisions up to that point, how much more or less vigilant would his decisions have been had he gotten to Bhopal and witnessed the carnage all about? The conclusion is that if he were unable to make a vigilant decision while ensconced in the comfort and secure surroundings of his Danbury office, there is no reason to expect that he would have performed any better under fire when brought face to face with the devastation his company had caused.

So what could he or should he have done?

One of the first things a crisis manager needs is information: what is going on and what can be done about it?

Instead of taking himself *out* of the picture for almost a week—and the most critical week, too—Anderson should have set up a command post in Danbury consisting of crisis management team members.

He should have sent trusted emissaries—as many as necessary—to gather the facts *for* him and relay the facts *to* him and to the team members, who would have been in a better position to make effective, vigilant decisions.

A problem with communications? That could have been handled in at least three ways:

• Use the news media's existing communications channels. Union Carbide already was getting the bulk of its information from media reports, but the company could have negotiated a fast, emergency-basis arrangement with one or more media outlets for access to their communications channels, perhaps in exchange for an "exclusive" of some kind later on.

• Union Carbide was not alone in India. Many other American companies were and still are operating close by. Certainly a fast Anderson-initiated CEO-to-CEO (probably friend-to-friend, actually) telephone call in the States would have opened up additional lines of communication.

• And, given the vast global resources of a *Fortune* 500 company such as Union Carbide, especially in this age of instant satellite communications, it is well within the realm of possibilities that before a Connecticut-to-India corporate plane touched down on the other side of the world, a functional communications system between Danbury and Bhopal could have been up and operating.

A more sensible statement and approach on Anderson's part would have been a public statement that just as soon as he had a better idea of what was going on in India and that he was assured that everything that could be done in Danbury was being done, he would personally fly to Bhopal to head up an investigation into the cause of the tragedy—perhaps within 30 days or so.

While Union Carbide did send a small handful of technicians and medical personnel to Bhopal early on, a humanitarian gesture on Union Carbide's part could have been to send *planeloads* of Union Carbide personnel—volunteers from the corporate office as well as from other facilities—to help the citizens of Bhopal. Such a gesture would have accomplished much, much more than Anderson's ill-fated trip, both in terms of true humanitarian effort and in terms of public relations imagery.

Let's be clear about our terms. What happened *after* the disaster, from Anderson's trip on—what has been called "crisis management"—was nothing of the kind. It was *damage control*. And not a very good job of it, either.

The crisis had long since passed, as did the opportunity to manage it. The turning points were the innumerable prodromes that the company failed to recognize and/or act upon—prodromes such as the company's own internal report, which was discussed in Chapter 1. This was the report that warned of a possible "runaway reaction" and "catastrophic failure."

Or prodromes such as the 71 pre-Bhopal MIC leaks at the Institute, West Virginia, plant, plus the 107 leaks of the nerve gas phosgene.

Or prodromes such as the company's own 1982 safety report on the Bhopal plant, which said that safety problems within the plant represented "a higher potential for a serious accident or more serious consequences if an accident should occur."

The New York *Times,* said:

> That report "strongly" recommended, among other things, the installation of a larger system that would supplement or replace one of the plant's main safety devices, a water spray designed to contain a chemical leak. That change was never made, plant employees said, and [when the leak happened] the spray was not high enough to reach the escaping gas."[71]

The errors that Union Carbide made in attempting to control the damage generally can be lumped together under the headings of "contradictions," "inconsistencies," and, if you insist, just "poor crisis management and almost nonexistent crisis communications." But in order to support these allegations, it will be helpful to recap briefly a host of irregularities uncovered at the Bhopal plant.

Although the cause of the accident, according to the company and others, was that water got into a tank containing MIC and triggered the violent reaction and fatal gas leak, the responsibility for the cause ultimately will be decided through the judicial system. It is not our lot even to speculate on the responsibility for the accident.

But be that as it may, numerous irregularities prior to the disaster (and which led to or contributed to the accident, certainly) laid the foundation for the contradictions, inconsistencies, and so on, alluded to above— irregularities that, for the most part, were confirmed by Union Carbide on March 20, 1985—almost two full months after the New York *Times* revealed them, and almost four months after the accident itself.

To paraphrase the results of the *Times*'s exhaustive seven-week inquiry:

• When employees discovered the initial leak of MIC at 11:30 P.M. on December 2, the workers (including Shakil Qureshi, the MIC supervisor) decided to deal with it after the next tea break, which ended at 12:40 A.M. on December 3. The leak was detected in the usual way: employees' eyes started to water.

• One employee was quoted as saying that internal leaks never bothered them and were seldom investigated. Either the problem was repaired without further examination or it was ignored entirely.

• In June 1984, more than five months before the accident, a refrigeration unit designed to cool MIC and prevent just the sort of reaction that occurred, was shut down. This was a direct and blatant violation of company and plant procedures.

• Several employees interviewed by the *Times* reported that the leak began about two hours after a worker, whose training did not meet standards set by the plant, was directed by an inexperienced supervisor to wash out a pipe that had been sealed improperly. Knowing how violently MIC reacts with water, this procedure is prohibited by plant rules.

• In addition to the refrigeration unit being down, a vent gas scrubber and a flare tower—two vital "fail-safe" devices for preventing runaway reactions—were also out of commission. The scrubber had been down for maintenance since October 22, 1984, although the plant manual says it must be "continuously operated" until the plant is "free of toxic chemicals." The flare tower had been down for six days. According to technical experts, these two safety systems were built according to specifications drawn for Union Carbide's U.S.-based MIC plant in Institute, West Virginia—a plant that Union Carbide officials, in the early stages of the crisis, insisted was the "sister plant" and "model" for the one in Bhopal.

• A spare tank was supposed to be empty but was not. Contingency operating procedures called for the MIC in the problem tank to be moved to the empty spare, but workers said it was common practice to leave MIC in the spare tank, flying in the face of specific company rules to the contrary.

• MIC supervisor Qureshi labeled the instruments at the plant as unreliable and admitted ignoring the initial warning of the accident for that reason. He even ignored the gauge indicating that pressure in one of the three MIC tanks had risen fivefold within an hour.

• The Union Carbide plant in Bhopal does not have a computerized monitoring system, as its "sister plant" has. Instead, as mentioned, the workers used their eyes and noses to detect leaks, despite the company's technical manual directives to the absolute contrary: "Although the tear gas effects of the vapor are extremely unpleasant, this property cannot be used as a means to alert personnel."

• Due partly to budget cutbacks (the plant had been a steady money loser in recent years), training, experience, and educational requirements had been drastically reduced.

• A year earlier—presumably also because of budget considerations—the number of operators per shift had been cut in half, from twelve to six. The *Times* quoted Kamal K. Pareek, a chemical engineer who was the senior project engineer when the facility was built, as saying that "the plant cannot be run safely with six people."

• The warning system was woefully inadequate inside the plant and painfully absent outside the plant. The alarm that did sound inside the plant was similar or identical to others sounded for a variety of purposes as many as 20 times a week. Because one of those purposes was for a practice drill, employees hearing the alarm had no way of knowing if it was a drill or the real thing. There also was no public education, no safety tips at all for the residents of the area. Many of the residents, in fact, thought the plant produced *kheti ki dawai,* which is a Hindi phrase meaning "medicine for the crops." Thinking the plant's output was healthful, they had no reason to fear living in the shadows of the massive facility or breathing its noxious fumes.

Had *any* of the safety devices worked, the disaster could have been averted entirely, or at least delayed until the problem was corrected or the town evacuated. A senior Indian official at the plant said, for example, that had the refrigeration unit been working, it would have taken closer to two days to produce the MIC reaction that ultimately occurred in less than two hours. This would have afforded time for evacuations if, during that two-day period, the reaction could not have been brought under control.

Perhaps most tragic of all is the fact that an incredibly elementary procedure—placing a wet cloth over the face—could have saved countless lives. But no one had ever told the area residents of this simple life-saving technique.

Almost as soon as Anderson was kicked out of India and returned to the United States, his statements were far less sweeping than they had been, he was far less corporately parental in his statements about Bhopal, he was no longer embracing Bhopal into the corporate fold. He was, if anything, distancing himself from Union Carbide India, Ltd. (UCIL).

It seemed that there were not enough statute miles between Danbury and Bhopal to suit Anderson.

The speculation at the time was that Anderson had been too "giving" in his statements—and may have been buttonholed on his return by the lawyers who gave him an education about corporate liability. The press briefings ended for about a week.

The upshot was that Union Carbide began to appear foolish and to stonewall, when, for example, it refused to explain what the relationship was between Union Carbide Corporation and Union Carbide India, Ltd.

While it did become known rather quickly that Danbury owned a 50.9 percent share in UCIL, the parent corporation tried to downplay its majority interest and put forth a less than accurate story that Danbury had little or no control over the Bhopal operations—being especially careful to claim that safety issues were the concern of the local operators. It soon became known that Danbury not only had control over Bhopal's operation, but freely exercised that control.

Initial reports from Jackson B. Browning, Union Carbide's director of safety, health, and environmental affairs, that the Bhopal plant was identical to a "sister plant" in Institute, West Virginia—reportedly the plant after which the one in Bhopal had been modeled—were wrong, misleading to the worldwide public in general, and scarier than hell to many residents of Institute who feared a similar accident at the MIC plant there. And, as will be discussed, those fears were well founded.

(A statement by John Holtzman, a spokesperson for the Chemical Manufacturing Association—"The probability of the kind of accident that happened in India happening here [in the U.S.] is just not the same"[72]—was wishful, at best. *Any* probability should be considered too high. And a two-day post-Bhopal conference, attended by U.S. and Indian health and safety experts, concluded that Bhopal was *not* a freak accident but could occur in almost any high-risk industry *anywhere*.)

In a crisis, a spokesperson has to be knowledgeable and credible. Browning either was not knowledgeable or didn't bother to check his facts. Whichever, he quickly began losing credibility.

He maintained early on that the Bhopal facility had safety systems that were every bit as effective as the ones at the U.S. plant. Browning said:

> [the Bhopal plant was] designed and built by American nationals. As to the standards in effect in this country and those in effect in Bhopal, they are the same. We are confident that, to the best of our knowledge, our employees in India were in compliance with all laws, and we are satisfied with the facilities and the operation of them.[73]

If Browning truly was "satisfied" with the Bhopal plant and its operations, his standards were too low, as the irregularities cited before clearly would indicate.

In any situation—let alone a crisis situation—you can't make something so just because you say it's so. But time and again in the early stages, Union Carbide threw credibility to the wind as it made statements that were later proved incorrect, misleading, or downright false.

More than a week after the accident, Anderson and Browning still were insisting that the safety criteria at Bhopal and Institute were *identical*. Anderson said: "We put in India the same kind of facilities that we would put in [Institute], not just with this particular business line, but any business we're in."[74] As the irregularities began to surface and mount, Anderson had to retreat from that position.

One Union Carbide official, testifying at a congressional hearing before the House Subcommittee on Asian and Pacific Affairs, defended Union Carbide's uniformly high standard of safety for all plants regardless of locations, saying, "We're always concerned about our employees . . . we expect them to be as safe as any employees anywhere."[75]

The Bhopal plant, however, was inspected by the parent corporation only about every three years. As a result, while the parent company did eventually confirm that a serious chemical tank problem had been discovered in 1982, they admitted that it had no idea whether improvements or corrections ever had been made. The parent company only compounded the confusion it was creating when at one point it released *four* safety reports but did not make anyone available to interpret them.[76]

When Union Carbide did open its Institute plant to reporters, it quickly found itself on the defensive, answering questions about the *differences* between the two plants. The company apparently was unprepared for this barrage of questioning.

And when the predictable multibillion-dollar lawsuits began (the *Wall Street Journal* called it "the greatest ambulance chase in history"),[77] Union Carbide found itself being flogged in the media by attorneys from *both* sides, because of the company's potentially damaging statements about safety standards. (One of Carbide's own outside lawyers at one point said, "I don't call this a case, I call it a war.")[78]

And Anderson, who for more than a month refused to be interviewed, was taken to task by the *Journal* toward the end of 1984 for the "unevenness [that] has also marked Union Carbide's handling of the Bhopal disaster . . . the company has had to retreat from initial assertions that the Bhopal plant had essentially the same safety equipment" as the Institute plant.[79]

Everything just described occurred within 30 days of the disaster.

One month after the tragedy, Union Carbide announced that it had completed the first phase of its probe into the accident, but—incredibly!—said it had no findings yet to report.

The contradictions, inconsistencies, and back-pedaling became far more evident—and necessary—after a month's dust had settled and certain facts were brought to light by reporters, U.S. and Indian government officials, scientists, Union Carbide employees both here and abroad, chemical industry spokespersons, attorneys, and even some of the victims.

Some of the more enlightening revelations included:

• Warren Anderson, in a *Chemical Week* interview, admitted that he had traveled to India to head off lawsuits. (Anderson is a former attorney.) J. Walter Goetz, Union Carbide's director of corporate communications, refused to verify the accuracy of the interview, but the company neither denied it nor requested a retraction.[80]

• Congressman Henry Waxman revealed the existence of Carbide's damaging internal report warning of "runaway reactions" and "catastrophic failures."

• Jackson Browning acknowledged that he knew about the report but did not forward it to Bhopal. Several days later, Browning tried to downplay the significance of the report by referring to it as a hypothetical scenario. But what Browning failed to realize is that hypothetical scenarios are what "what-if contingency" planning is all about. If you address a situation while it is still in the "what-if" stage, you are practicing crisis management. If you wait until the hypothetical scenario becomes reality, you could be practicing damage control.

• But even so, Browning stated that several weeks *before* the Bhopal tragedy, the company did revise at least some of its operating procedures at the Institute plant specifically to prevent a runaway reaction there. In response to the question why these same changes had not been instituted in Bhopal, Browning said it was irrelevant because of the differences in the two plants. Up until this time, you will recall, Browning had been stating that the plants were basically identical.

• A news story revealed that Union Carbide decided not to install at its Institute plant a costly safety measure that was aimed at reducing "a real potential" of Bhopal-type water leak and reaction. Browning's response was that the company "could not justify the expense";[81] and despite what happened in India, he didn't think the West Virginia cooling system required any changes or modifications.

Three and a half months after the accident, Union Carbide held a press conference to announce *its* findings. At this press conference, the company launched a trial balloon hinting at the possibility of sabotage. But the balloon sank. Since that press conference, Union Carbide officials have tried several times to launch the balloon anew. But as of this writing— exactly one year after the Bhopal tragedy—the company has yet to produce one shred of evidence in support of a possible "deliberate act," as Anderson had suggested at the conference. And only hard evidence will lift that balloon.

The company, and its officers, which just a short while before had been praising the design and operation of the Bhopal plant, were now madly racing to put as much distance between Danbury and Bhopal as necessary. Ron Van Mynen, who headed up Carbide's seven-member investigative team, said his "colleagues were shocked by what they saw" at the plant. Anderson said the plant had been plagued by "a whole litany of nonstandard operating procedures, omissions, and commissions." Anderson also said that the Bhopal conditions were so inferior that the plant "shouldn't have been operating."[82]

It was at this press conference that Union Carbide "revealed" what had long been common knowledge: that the safety devices—which, as the company had long maintained, "failed" to operate—actually had been *inoperable:* the refrigeration unit, the flare tower, the scrubber, and the alarm system.

Also, at the same time, Anderson said that "safety is the responsibility of the people who operate our plants" and that "noncompliance with safety issues is a local issue." (Only a few months earlier, however, on his release from India, he said, "Somebody has to say that our safety standards in the U.S. are identical to those in India or Brazil or someplace else. Same equipment, same design, same everything."[83] But the New York *Times,* among others, took issue with Anderson's pass-the-rupee ploys and stated that Danbury did indeed have "the authority to exercise financial and technical control over its affiliate, Union Carbide India, Ltd., and the American parent often used that right, according to former officials of the Indian company and others with knowledge of the concern." All major decisions were cleared with Danbury, which "also had the right to intervene in day-to-day affairs if it concluded that safety might be affected."[84] While Anderson and other Danbury officials would have the public believe that all they did was collect the rent, UCIL officials disagree. "The line of communications was loud and clear," the *Times* quoted a former senior UCIL official as stating. "Any major safety, financial commitment or problem had to be cleared with Union Carbide Corporation."[85] And the senior project engineer during the construction of the MIC plant, Kamal K. Pareek, said, "Union Carbide Corporation had its finger on the pulse of the Bhopal plant all the time. They just didn't appreciate the information they were getting."[86]

Union Carbide's credibility was so severely damaged that Congressman Waxman stated publicly that the company was an unreliable source of information and that it had "come to the point where I don't think I can take Union Carbide's word for what's happened."[87] That sentiment was shared by the Indian government, which categorically rejected the Carbide report, labeling it "unjustifiable and unacceptable."[88]

In a statement presumably intended to build confidence, the company said it was going to triple the number of annual safety inspections but refused to disclose how many safety inspections had been held in the previous year. The question that never was answered was simply this: if Union Carbide did conduct safety inspections in Bhopal, how did conditions deteriorate so drastically that Anderson came out and said that the facility should not have been operating?

It later was disclosed that Bhopal used to pay Union Carbide a "technical service fee" to have the parent company conduct safety audits.

Fortune reported that "Carbide lacked a pre-existing corporate plan for coping with a catastrophe of this magnitude."[89] The company's actions in the months following the tragedy lent credence to *Fortune*'s statement. A company that made its reputation on a product called Eveready just wasn't ready when it should have been. It couldn't locate the flashlights.

"This was unthinkable until it happened," *Fortune* quoted an official from Monsanto, another big pesticide company, as saying.[90]

This statement is naive and wrong, and may just herald an industry attitude that spells potential trouble. Not only was what happened *thinkable;* it was even *forewarned.*

The Chemical Manufacturers Association—whose chairman, Edward C. Holmer, president of Exxon Chemical Company, said in 1981, "Risk management involves accepting 'cradle-to-grave' stewardship responsibility for the materials we manufacture," and "If a risk cannot be made acceptable, the project should be terminated or product sales discontinued"[91]—was asked specifically in connection with this book what steps the chemical industry had taken or what positions it had adopted to minimize the risk of another Union Carbide–Bhopal tragedy anywhere in the world.

"U.S. companies cannot rely on foreign infrastructure to enforce compliance with laws," responded Dr. Geraldine Cox, CMA's technical vice president and spokesperson for the industry. Suggesting that one major cause is the cultural differences between the United States and other countries abroad, Cox lamented, "How do you train and enforce good safety practices in a culture that does not place the same value on human lives as we do?"[92] She also produced a packet of information designed to show the industry's proactive stance on addressing the Union Carbide disaster. (Union Carbide is a CMA member.)

One of the booklets dealt with a program called CHEMTREC, which stands for Chemical Transportation Emergency Center.

On the first page of the booklet is a tale, perhaps apocryphal, perhaps authentic, about a tank-truck driver who discovered at a truck stop that the acid he was hauling had started to leak. "He ran to a telephone and called a 'hotline' at CHEMTREC," the booklet states, whereupon the CHEMTREC communicator gave him the following emergency instructions: "Erect a dike around the spill. . . ."

"Are you serious?" asked Texaco's General Manager for Strategic Planning Clement B. Malin, somewhat embarrassed. "It really says to 'erect a dike'?"

Assured that the Chemical Manufacturers Association, of which Texaco is a member, did indeed say to "erect a dike" in this tale, Malin protested: "With what? What tools does he have, what equipment, what instructions? How is he supposed to know *how* to erect a dike?"

Malin said that Texaco drivers are not equipped with dike-building materials, or the expertise to erect a dike. He also expressed the opinion that the first telephone call should be made to the local authorities—the fire department, the police. "You need people on the scene, not voices on the phone," he said. "Any information this 'hotline' could give the driver—such as information on what he's transporting, what fire retardants are most effective on it, etc.—should be put right on the driver's manifest."

Malin had two other interesting observations. First, on the question of

Carbide's position that safety is a local issue, Malin disagreed, describing Texaco's position as safety being "the parent corporation's responsibility. If you built the plant, you're as much responsible as the local operator for what happens." And, when told about Union Carbide's internal report warning of the possibility of a "runaway reaction," he said, "I find it hard to believe, given the very nature of our business, that they would not immediately address themselves to the potential crisis."[93]

In a special issue on Bhopal, in which editor Michael Heylin wrote that "Carbide as a worldwide corporate entity fouled up," *Chemical & Engineering News* discussed how the catastrophe had created a tremendous public relations concern for all chemical manufacturers. "The lay media have trumpeted the MIC leak as another 'Three Mile Island' and asked whether the chemical industry is 'the nuclear industry of the 1980s.' "

This respected technical journal went on to say, "Certainly, there was an understanding before Bhopal that public fears about toxic chemicals pose a threat to the growth of the chemical industry."[94]

And then, in a master stroke of irony, the publication quoted a speech that Warren Anderson delivered to the Chemical Industry Institute of Toxicology in March 1984:

> Public opinion about chemicals and the chemical industry is not likely to change very much if all we offer are public statements about our good intentions. What the public needs to see are the actions of an industry determined to operate responsibly and regain the public trust. We've learned how to detect the presence of substances in minuscule amounts. But we have not done very much to explain the implications for the public health and safety.[95]

To recap, what did Union Carbide do wrong in the Bhopal tragedy?

- It failed to identify its crisis.
- Having failed to identify its crisis, it was in no position to either isolate or manage it.
- It had no crisis management plan and reportedly still doesn't.
- It adopted a "bunker mentality."
- Its crisis communications were inadequate, misleading, and without credibility much of the time. It would not give information; it would not confirm, deny, or comment on "commonly accepted" information; it would not grant interviews.
- Its investigative team revealed findings that had been available in the media for months.
- The inconsistencies, inaccuracies, and retractions became the rule rather than the exception.

• Had the company practiced crisis management, it would have seen that the cost of intervention was far less than the cost of litigation.

On the subject of the cost of intervention—as well as on finding opportunity in a crisis—a small, little-known California-based computer company had its telephone ringing off the hook soon after the Bhopal tragedy.

Safer Emergency Systems, Inc., had had only moderate success in selling a computerized warning device that uses remote sensors and a data base of local weather information to monitor and track potentially hazardous chemical leaks at plants. This device also has the capability to warn local residents and automatically telephone appropriate authorities, hospitals, schools, and other institutions with a recorded warning message.

After Bhopal, many chemical companies have reportedly been taking a closer look at this system. It was also reported that Union Carbide not only was aware of the system, but prior to the Bhopal tragedy it had been considering purchasing the system for its Institute plant, "as part of an ongoing effort to review and upgrade safety," the *Wall Street Journal* quoted an unnamed Union Carbide spokesperson as saying.[96]

The cost—what might be termed the Cost of Intervention—was about $80,000. Installed.

If this book were fiction instead of fact, you might read the following brief footnote to the Union Carbide saga with unbelieving eyes, accusing the author of stretching your imagination to the limits. But as you undoubtedly already know, it is a sad fact—not fiction—that eight months and eight days after the worst industrial accident the world has ever known, Union Carbide's Institute, West Virginia, plant suffered a toxic gas leak that sent 135 area residents to hospitals for treatment. Fortunately, though, no one died.

This leak, on August 11, 1985, occurred despite the fact that the Institute plant—certainly, following Bhopal, one of the most well-tended, carefully manicured plants in the world—had been shut for five months immediately following the Bhopal disaster specifically to undergo an infusion of $5 million worth of safety improvements.

Even before the installation of the multimillion-dollar safety improvements, in December 1984 Warren Anderson testified before a U.S. congressional subcommittee that he couldn't imagine an accident like the one in Bhopal happening at the Institute plant,[97] and only a month later Jackson Browning defended the Institute plant, calling it "absolutely safe."[98]

However, in the wake of the multitudinous investigations into the cause of the Institute accident, it would appear that the beleaguered company did not spend anywhere near enough money (or time) to improve its crisis management procedures. For example, you can't install expensive improvements and then ignore them, or not train workers to use them, and assume you have done your crisis management homework.

This is not crisis management. What kind of management is it, then?

A lengthy piece by Michael A. Hiltzik that appeared in the Los Angeles *Times* shortly after the Institute leak suggested that Union Carbide instead has "aimless management." The Bhopal and Institute accidents, wrote Hiltzik:

> . . . represent far more than a public relations problem. Rather, they reflect the company's reputation for aimless management and its penchant for promising positive results and delivering mediocrity. In a prescient report on the company dated July 2 [1985], Paine Webber stock analyst Peter E. Butler argued, "poor management performances beget bad luck as well."[99]

A brief recap of the "bad luck" at Institute:

• Union Carbide initially—and certainly without really knowing—insisted that all safety systems worked perfectly and that proper, adequate, and timely warnings had been given to local officials and area residents. In truth, however, the company had to recant those words almost immediately. The leak occurred at 9:24 A.M. on a Sunday morning, but plant officials waited 20 minutes before notifying local officials and 36 minutes before sounding a public warning siren.

• For the better part of a week following the leak, Union Carbide didn't even know what type of gas had leaked—although it *thought* it did. The company reported that aldicarb oxime, which they were quick to label as merely a "minor eye and lung irritant," was the gas that had leaked. Five days later, it was revealed that methylene chloride comprised more than two-thirds of the gas that had leaked. Methylene chloride is a toxin that works on the nervous system. There were 23 different hazardous gases in all. The leaking mixture also included:

- 13 percent isobutyronitrile, a cyanide gas that is fatal in large doses. In smaller doses it causes dizziness, vomiting, and rapid breathing.
- 9 percent dimethyl disulfide, rated by Union Carbide as a hazardous respiratory and skin irritant.
- 7 percent methyl mercaptan, rated by federal job-safety officials as a nervous system depressant.
- 2 percent dimethyl sulfide, an animal carcinogen that, in large doses, causes respiratory, liver, and kidney damage.

Jackson Browning, however, maintained that there was no reason to expect any lasting health effects from the leak.

• When the plant reopened on May 3—five months to the day after the Bhopal disaster—one of the highly touted safety improvements was the addition of the computerized tracking and warning system developed by Safer Emergency Systems, Inc. The system was used during the Institute leak, but Union Carbide plant and corporate officials were initially at a loss to explain why the SAFER system, as it is called, did not properly respond when accessed. It quickly became embarrassingly obvious that the system did not respond "properly" because plant officials had never programmed the computer to monitor any of the gases that leaked.

• Gary Gelinas, president of Safer Emergency Systems, Inc., when interviewed for this book, explained that Union Carbide chose to program only three chemicals into the computer: phosgene, chlorine, and methyl isocyanate. Union Carbide had paid for an additional seven chemicals to be programmed, but at the time of the August 11 leak the plant had yet to give Safer the necessary data. However, none of the chemicals involved in the Institute leak were among the additional seven anyway. Gelinas, who said the system can handle virtually any number of chemicals, reported the cost of updating is only $500 per substance.

• Summarizing ever so briefly, the SAFER system must be accessed by a human being who has the task of telling the computer what gas has leaked. The computer then projects, via a computerized model, precisely where the gas plume will travel, based on the computer's programmed understanding of the chemical's properties, how those properties react in the atmosphere, current weather information, and a programmed knowledge of the local geography and topography. On the basis of the computer model, local residents can be warned to evacuate, if necessary. On August 11, 1985, an operator at the plant—thinking that aldicarb oxime had leaked out but knowing that the computer was *not* programmed for this chemical's properties—told the computer instead that MIC (of Bhopal infamy) had leaked. MIC is much lighter than aldicarb oxime, and the computer projected that the cloud would not drift, but would hover over the plant and soon dissipate into the atmosphere. But the gas that *did* leak, being heavier than MIC, did not dissipate. Its toxic tentacles swiftly spread through the Kanawha Valley (sometimes called "Chemical Valley"), reached the citizens of Institute, Dunbar, St. Albans, and Nitro, and sent 135 of them to hospitals for treatment. Gelinas described the erroneous accessing of SAFER as "garbage in, garbage out."[100]

• Four days after the leak, *still* believing that it was aldicarb oxime that had leaked—and as a way of defending the actions of the plant operator who told the computer that MIC had leaked because he knew the computer was not programmed for aldicarb oxime—a statement issued by Robert Oldford, president of Union Carbide's Agricultural Products Division, said, in part, "However, it should be noted that no sensors are available from SAFER that would detect the emission of aldicarb oxime."[101] A frustrated and exasperated Gelinas responded that SAFER has *nothing* to do with sensors and does *not* detect gas leaks at all. Once the computer is told, by a human being, which gas has leaked, the computerized SAFER system *tracks* the leak.

• Six Union Carbide workers also were injured in the leak. With the gas cloud so thick in the plant's control room that they had trouble seeing their hands before their burning eyes, they were unable to find a safe haven and could not even get to emergency breathing apparatus in the very next room. Instead, they huddled together on the floor of the control room, sharing the only two available breathing devices in the room. What panicked thoughts of Bhopal must have terrorized their minds!

On August 23 Union Carbide released its own internal report of what it termed a string of human and machine errors and flagrant and blatant violations of plant procedures. Specifically (and incredibly when you consider how vigilant you would expect the company to be following Bhopal) Union Carbide accepted full and complete blame and responsibility for failures and breakdowns in management, operations, and equipment directly under its control. Several of the more serious failures went either undetected or uncorrected for ten days prior to the Institute accident.

According to the Union Carbide report, more than 31 plant employees were at various times derelict in their duties, leading to such dangerous transgressions between August 1 and the August 11 accident as:

• Repeatedly ignoring and actually shutting off high-pressure alarms.
• Not repairing a high-temperature alarm that was out of service.
• Not repairing a level indicator in the storage tank, which leaked and was known to be broken.
• Never questioning the unit's computer, which had diligently—but silently—been recording the rising problem for days.

The New York *Times,* in reporting on the internal Carbide report, said:

> The company said the principal cause of the accident was steam that leaked through a faulty valve for 10 days, unbeknownst to plant workers, into a tank where its heat eventually caused an uncontrolled reaction of toxic chemicals. Contrary to plant procedures, the workers never checked the tank and associated equipment before using it to make sure it was running properly— which it was not. The staff then did not program its computer printer and terminals to display readings of the system's temperature, pressure, and other conditions, so the operator did not know a major problem was developing.

> In addition, the workers assumed the tank was empty because a pump being used to drain it had stopped a few days earlier. But the workers never verified

that assumption. Such a check would have been difficult in any case because the tank's level indicator was broken, the company said. In fact, the tank contained nearly 4,000 pounds of toxic material, most of which eventually got into the atmosphere.[102]

In what must be considered one of the great understatements since the industrial revolution, Laurence H. Dupuy, the assistant Institute plant manager, said, "It's not good operating procedure."[103]

Dupuy, who headed Union Carbide's internal investigation, told the *Wall Street Journal* that "if the steam had been detected, 'it could have been isolated' and the leak prevented."[104] (Readers of this book will recognize this as *identifying* the crisis, *isolating* the crisis, and *managing* the crisis.)

But in this "departure from normal procedure," Dupuy explained that workers shut off repeated high-pressure alarms over several days and merely raised the set point of the alarm (the "it-can't-happen-here" syndrome).

He said the workers did not recognize the real significance of the warning signals (known as prodromes).

Dupuy's boss, plant manager Hank Karawan, added that on August 1, an approximate two-to-one mixture of methylene chloride and aldicarb oxime was "temporarily" housed in an oxidation reactor, a tank used for chemical reactions. But for the next seven days a "steam jacket" was accidentally switched on, and the contents of the tank began to heat. Most of that mixture was pumped back into the reactor to produce the pesticide Temik,* but the workers inadvertently left 4,000 pounds, or 500 gallons, in the tank, cooking away to the boiling point—and disaster point—for another four days.[105]

It was the rising gas pressure that finally caused the leak.

Union Carbide was roundly criticized for creating a crisis communications vacuum following Bhopal. After Institute, almost the opposite was true: there was an abundance of crisis communications coming from plant officials, but most of the information was wrong, misleading, or startlingly insensitive:

• Early on, Dick Henderson, a Union Carbide spokesman, said, "We activated our computer tracking and it showed most of the material went back over the plant. . . . "[106] As previously noted, this was wrong because the plant had never properly programmed the computer.

---

*Temik, a common pesticide, figured prominently in the great watermelon scare of the summer of 1985, when contamination caused illnesses in 180 consumers in four Western states and Canada and the eventual destruction of much of California's watermelon crop.

• Henderson also was reported as saying that the emergency siren was sounded immediately, as soon as the leak occurred. "Most everyone stayed indoors and it's good to see that the system worked."[107] Most everyone did *not* stay indoors, the system did *not* work, and a door-to-door survey conducted by the staff of U.S. Congressman Robert E. Wise, Jr., whose Third Congressional District includes the Institute plant site, disclosed that of 254 people queried, only 40 knew of the alarm. In fact, Congressman Wise reported that 144 people learned of the leak by being exposed to it.

• Also, as to whether or not the system worked, part of the emergency plan, devised in the wake of Bhopal, called for a Union Carbide official to report to a command post at the plant. But, according to William White, the local emergency service and fire coordinator at Institute, no one ever came.[108]

• Even when still believing, and reporting, that it was aldicarb oxime (the "eye and lung irritant") that had leaked, the company's own internal classification rating system rated it a 4—the same rating given to MIC, the gas that leaked at Bhopal. In December 1984 Union Carbide presented to a congressional subcommittee a copy of a November 28, 1983, internal report that described chemicals with a rating of 4 as capable of causing cancer, birth defects, genetic damage, irreversible nervous system disorders, and other illnesses.[109]

• Trying to minimize the seriousness of the leak, but obviously insensitive to legitimate fears of a Bhopal-level catastrophy, Henderson was quoted as saying, "You don't close the whole operation because of a little hysteria over a little leak."[110]

• The Los Angeles *Times* quoted LeRahn Guthrie, a Union Carbide employee for more than a decade as well as the chief of the Institute Fire Department, as saying, "It was really pathetic the way Carbide handled it. If it had been a strong concentration of chloride or MIC, it would have killed everybody. And then they tell you to trust them."[111] Guthrie, by the way, was the person who ultimately sounded the alarm.

• Thadd Epps, another company spokesman, at one point defended aldicarb oxime as being only one-tenth as lethal as MIC.[112] (Author's query: would this be akin to being only one-tenth as pregnant?)

• Epps, also a master of the understatement, at another time admitted that the company had some serious fence mending to do with its neighbors. "We've spent a lot of time [since Bhopal] trying to reassure our neighbors that we run a safe plant. The incident can do nothing but shake their confidence."[113]

• And then, in an example of double speak, Epps was quoted in the *Wall Street Journal* as saying, "I would not automatically say that if aldicarb oxime were programmed into [the SAFER system computer] the result would have been better because it confirmed the visual [judgment]. But obviously the chemical should have been programmed in."[114]

Other problems to plague the company for some time include several lawsuits by area residents. As of this writing, these suits total more than $92 million. Also, as of this writing, several companies—most notably GAF—have been busy buying up large chunks of Union Carbide; but it is too soon to predict whether a hostile takeover attempt will succeed, or whether Union Carbide will be able to mount a successful takeover defense, such as buying back a majority of its own outstanding shares.

In addition, despite company assurances that no long-term health consequences would surface, West Virginia's Health Department announced that it would conduct a long-term health study of all 135 people who were treated at hospitals. And Ellen K. Silbergeld, a senior scientist with the Environmental Defense Fund, a public-interest research group, voiced the feelings of many in a New York *Times* op-ed piece, in which she wrote, "This time the lessons cannot be brushed aside with aspersions about the inefficiency, corruption and lack of technological sophistication of Third World workers and managers."[115]

The Environmental Protection Agency was, not surprisingly, sharply critical of Union Carbide.

Lee M. Thomas, EPA administrator, said, "There has been a credibility gap. I am very distressed over what has happened here [at the Institute] location. It is one where there had been an awful lot of time and attention spent, both off-site and on-site."[116]

Richard Horner, an EPA engineer who analyzed the Institute plant systems, said, "In emergency planning, I'd say we're in our infancy" but acknowledged that one possible benefit to the leak is that "people will quit chuckling up their sleeves" about emergency plans and actually get to work on them.[117]

But James Markis, the EPA's chief of emergency preparedness, may have put part of the problem into perspective when he cited community intimidation over the sheer number of potentially hazardous chemicals. "The locals say they don't know how to begin the task of emergency planning and the companies say they don't know how to approach the locals."[118]

However, as a first step toward addressing the problem, the EPA has called on the Chemical Manufacturers Association to begin compiling information on how to treat people who have been exposed to hazardous chemicals.

One can only hope that the Chemical Manufacturers Association doesn't begin its advice by saying, "First, erect a gas mask. . . ."

The careful reader will recall from Chapter 3, on the anatomy of a crisis, the dizzying illustration of what a crisis-filled time feels like: rarely do you experience the luxury of moving blissfully through the four stages of one crisis without a host of other prodromes and acute crises bombarding you from all sides.

Union Carbide has become literally and figuratively the textbook case.

Just two days after the leak at the Institute plant, there was *another* leak at the Union Carbide plant in South Charleston, West Virginia. That leak, a spill of about 1,000 gallons of chemicals, was relatively minor in comparison to the Institute incident. Only four area residents had to be treated for eye irritations and nausea.

And on August 26, at the *same* South Charleston plant—the one that had been cited by the EPA for 16 toxic spills in 1984—there was yet *another* spill: hydrochloric acid leaked. Fortunately, there were no injuries. But there *could* have been a tragedy of staggering proportions: more than 60,000 Chubby Checker fans were gathered to hear the rock 'n' roll legend and see him "twist" at an outdoor venue just a mile and a half upstream and upwind from the leak.

These two relatively minor occurrences made news throughout the world simply because they happened at Carbide facilities. Remember that one of the parameters of a crisis is the intensity of public, media, or government scrutiny to which a person or a company is subjected. For instance, during this period of crisis for Carbide in West Virginia, there were several other gas leaks and chemical spills throughout the country involving non-Carbide operations. Chances are that, unless you lived in or around one of those other areas, you were unaware of those accidents.

Remember, too, the discussion of the ripple effect of a crisis.

On August 28, 1985, as Warren Anderson announced a $100 million safety and environmental protection program, he also revealed that the company was eliminating 4,000 jobs (representing about 15 percent of the company's nonhourly U.S. work force) and taking a write-off of another $1 billion.

Those 4,000 workers sadly discovered the ripple effect of a crisis and of poor crisis management.

Soon after the accident in Bhopal, at about the time when the company's stock had dropped so low that Carbide had been devalued by more than $900 million and one lawsuit alone was for $15 billion, the New York *Times* did a small piece entitled "Crisis Management at Carbide," in

which it explained that the company was "trying to strike a difficult balance between the instincts of human compassion, the demands of public relations, and the dictates of corporate survival."[119]

Union Carbide certainly has failed at public relations, and it seems that whatever human compassion may actually have been genuinely present following Bhopal has long since given way to the dictates of legal considerations.

On corporate survival, however, the jury is still out.

The Procter & Gamble/ Rely Tampon Crisis

It is only when you are pursued that you become swift.

—*Kahlil Gibran*

THE CRISIS IN BRIEF

In September 1980, for the first time in its now almost 150 years of successful and reliable operation as a consumer goods company, Procter & Gamble withdrew a product from the marketplace in the midst of charges that the product might be lethal. P&G's successful Rely tampons were linked with a little-known—but sometimes fatal—disease called toxic shock syndrome. The decision to withdraw Rely, which cost P&G $75 million, was made despite the absence of conclusive evidence that Rely actually caused toxic shock syndrome.

KEY PLAYERS IN BRIEF

- The late Edward G. Harness, then chairman and chief executive officer, Procter & Gamble
- Owen B. Butler, then vice chairman, P&G
- John G. Smale, then president, P&G
- Thomas Laco, then executive vice president, P&G

Trivia question: Who is Procter & Gamble's largest competitor?
Answer: Procter & Gamble.

The company that started manufacturing Ivory soap (by accident)*

---

soap that floats does so because a careless worker, while concocting a new batch of
tingly left his mixing machine on while he went to lunch. The frothy result was air
the soap, which caused the soap to float. Customers liked it and demanded more.

back in 1879 also makes the Camay, Coast, Safeguard, and Zest brands of soap.

If you are unhappy with the company that manufactures Crest toothpaste and, in protest, decide to switch to the Gleem brand, forget it: P&G makes them both. The same is true for Prell and Head & Shoulders shampoos.

While Pampers and Luvs slug it out over your toddler's bottom, the real bottom line is that P&G profits from both brands. They have something to say about *your* bottom, too: Charmin and White Cloud toilet tissues.

And these are just the personal care products. If you looked at laundry and cleaning products, the list would include such household names and competing brands as Cheer, Dash, Duz, Era, Ivory Liquid, Ivory Snow, Oxydol, Tide, and on and on and on.*

And over the years, as P&G has invaded all of our under-the-sink hiding places in approximately 100 ways, no one has ever accused the company of rushing new products untested into the marketplace.

Procter & Gamble is the proverbial tortoise. The company has earned a well-deserved reputation for meticulous, exhaustive market research and test marketing before introducing a product. And "exhaustive" can be anywhere from 20 months to 20 years.

It is, for example, entirely possible that a research scientist fresh out of school could begin work on a new P&G project, only to have the research completed and the product introduced into the marketplace a generation later by his own son or daughter.

Once the product is ready for the marketplace, P&G's huge advertising budgets make sure the public is ready for the product. The P&G tortoise has been a consistent winner for almost 150 years.

But do not think that it is merely the power of its advertising budget that accounts for the company's success. Simply stated, Procter & Gamble is a name that people have long known and trusted.

Trusted, that is, until a Procter & Gamble product—Rely tampons—was suddenly and without warning linked to a number of deaths, attributed to a mysterious-sounding disease known as toxic shock syndrome (TSS). (This is not to suggest that Rely did cause TSS. In fact, there is a substantial and respectable body of evidence to the contrary.)

*Procter & Gamble entered 1985 as the nation's largest consumer products company, with annual sales of more than $13 billion. A midyear merger between R. J. Reynolds Industries and Nabisco Brands (a $4.9 billion deal) created a $19 billion conglomerate and a *new* largest U.S.-based consumer products company. Then, in the fall of 1985, another merger—the $5.75 billion friendly takeover of General Foods by Philip Morris—resulted in a new company with combined assets of $23 billion, and the *latest* largest U.S.-based consumer products company. But, on the basis of competing brands, P&G still is its own biggest competitor.

But again, the intent here is not to sit as judge and jury regarding the guilt or innocence of Procter & Gamble or Rely tampons. Rather, it is to examine how the company acted and reacted in the face of a serious crisis.

And specifically, the questions to be asked are:

- How could Procter & Gamble decide in one week to pull Rely off of the shelves—especially when you consider that the product, in one form or another, had been researched and tested for close to twenty years and marketed nationally for five and a half of those years?
- How could it even consider such a decision, when there was no concrete evidence that Rely did cause TSS?
- Did it act too soon?
- Did it react too late?
- And, in general, how did this giant of a company perform as a crisis manager?

It seems as if every crisis starts with a telephone call, and this one was no exception. But even before the Food and Drug Administration (FDA) contacted P&G in mid-September 1980, the Center for Disease Control (CDC) in Atlanta had contacted P&G and other tampon manufacturers on June 13, requesting data on tampon usage. The CDC at the time revealed no specific evidence linking tampon usage to TSS.

However, just six days later, on June 19, the CDC again contacted the manufacturers, this time inviting them to a two-day meeting on June 25–26. The findings of the CDC's initial investigation now indicated a statistical link between TSS and tampon usage. This statistical link did *not* identify any particular tampon brand—merely tampon usage generally.

This, though, was not the case in studies done separately by the state health departments of Wisconsin and Minnesota. These two studies indicated that there most definitely was a statistical link to Rely tampons.

At the time of the crisis, P&G's Rely had only 18 percent of the market share and was the third best-selling brand of tampons, behind Tampax and Playtex.

In this prodromal phase of the crisis, Procter & Gamble—in the lumbering ways of a giant—slowly began to collect its own information on tampon usage. In effect, P&G was duplicating its own extensive research. When P&G asked to examine the CDC's case studies, the CDC refused, citing the Privacy Act.

The information P&G did manage to collect from health departments, hospitals, and private physicians shed no new light on its findings. The company was still unconvinced that there was a connection between its product and TSS.

P&G therefore spent the summer of 1980 running its own laboratory tests with the TSS bacteria. The findings of its own internal microbiologists lent no support to the findings of the CDC or the two state health departments. P&G concluded that the superabsorbent material in Rely did not encourage the growth of the suspected TSS bacteria.

Procter & Gamble hoped that this would be the end of the matter.

But on September 15 the CDC released the results of its second study, and this time the news was particularly bad for P&G. Of the 42 TSS women studied, 71 percent had used Rely.

From the very moment this information was released, P&G found itself on the defensive, and the FDA was determined to see that the company stayed that way. Using the news media as its vehicle, the FDA made sure the public was constantly aware of TSS and Rely's involvement in the controversy.

According to a *Wall Street Journal* article soon after the recall, the FDA deliberately orchestrated the tide of bad press against P&G and Rely. It was part of the FDA's offensive strategy.

"Knowing P&G to be supersensitive to bad publicity about any of its products and concerned about its own responsibility to protect the public health," the *Journal* reported, "the FDA deliberately used the media as a weapon to drive Rely off the market."[120]

Rather than denying the use of such tactics, the then associate FDA commissioner for public affairs, Wayne L. Pines, bragged about it to the *Journal*'s reporters:

> Throughout the series of events, we made sure the press was notified so as to keep the story alive. We wanted to saturate the market with information on Rely. We deliberately delayed issuing press releases for a day to maximize the media impact. There was quite a concerted and deliberate effort to keep a steady flow of information before the public.[121]

These tactics would seem to be far better suited to an attack on a slumlord or a child pornographer. There is nothing (nothing public, anyway) in P&G's history to suggest that the company would not have cooperated with the FDA without the agency resorting to heavy-handed methods.

This having been said in defense of P&G, it should also be noted that the company did not properly take advantage of the rather lengthy prodrome of this crisis: almost three full months, from June to September.

Yes, as mentioned, there certainly were tests, but it does not appear that there had been any contingency planning on P&G's part. No one, it seems, from board chairman Harness down, or from anyone else up, sensed a need for contingency planning to question *what* the company would do *if* Rely was indeed culpable of TSS.

It was precisely because of this lack of planning that P&G apparently was caught off guard when the FDA telephoned the company on September 15. The FDA was looking for Harness or Butler or Smale, the chairman, vice chairman, and president, respectively. But in a set of circumstances the company usually doesn't allow to happen, *all* three of the top brass were out of town at the same time.

The call was routed to Thomas Laco, then executive vice president, who had been left minding the store.

Laco tracked down Harness, who, along with Butler, was in Seattle for some high-level discussions with officials of Procter & Gamble's Japanese subsidiary. The FDA wanted a meeting in Washington, D.C., the next day; there was no time to lose now.

And the company lost no time in acting.

While P&G may be faulted for not anticipating this acute crisis, once the crisis hit, the company became not the tortoise but the very hare in implementing some very tough crisis decisions.

Harness, who was "determined to fight for a brand, to keep an important brand from being hurt by insufficient data in the hands of bureaucracy,"[122] immediately appointed Laco to head up a crisis management team, which was assisted by several staff departments as needed. According to their mandate from Harness, they were to address themselves to "handling the Rely situation without disrupting the rest of the company."[123] This, as discussed previously, is known as isolating the crisis.

The crisis, of course, had been identified by the FDA. The agency was stating or implying that Rely caused toxic shock syndrome; the CDC stated or implied that TSS can be fatal. The public was hearing: *Rely kills!*

P&G's research did not support this claim, certainly; but neither did it absolutely refute it. "We wanted to prove our innocence," said vice chairman Butler, "but we couldn't get the data to do it."[124]

At stake in all of this was the company's good and trusted name.

The company ultimately decided, as you shall see, that the name and the trust were more important than the brand. Despite Harness's initial burst of maladaptive coping (unconflicted inertia)—vowing to "fight all the way" and to "fight for a brand"—other social responsibilities eventually took precedence.

Before moving on to examine how P&G managed the crisis, let's take a closer look at what steps the company took in isolating the crisis. As stated previously, but certainly worth repeating here, no crisis has ever really been successfully and effectively managed unless it has first been identified and isolated.

Laco quickly assembled a crisis management team of 13. It included the paper products division vice president (Rely had been housed in this division), a P&G staff physician, and various research and legal staffers.

Harness returned to Cincinnati headquarters the next day, September

16, to oversee the entire crisis, and Butler followed shortly to act as chief of staff in coordinating all of the movements and actions of the crisis management team. Smale ran the company.

All the others in the company—vice presidents, senior managers, middle managers, secretaries—were intentionally excluded from having anything to do with the Rely crisis.

Harness wanted to avoid having the company gather around the water cooler to gossip about Rely and not get any other work done, according to a *Wall Street Journal* report at the time. Here's how John Prestbo, the *Journal*'s Cleveland bureau chief at the time, described Harness's drive to isolate the Rely crisis:

> The assistant chief of the paper products division, who was put in charge of that operation while his boss worked on the task force, was told to worry about Bounty paper towels, Pampers diapers, Charmin toilet tissue—everything but Rely.
>
> "If I'd caught him inquiring into the Rely problem, I'd have nailed him good," Mr. Harness says.
>
> High-ranking officers of P&G's other divisions weren't told anything special about Rely; they learned of developments at the same time all employees did. At one point, a curious vice president sidled up to a public relations staffer to ask what was going on with Rely. He got no details.[125]

Isolating the crisis means *isolating the crisis.*

Having battened down the internal hatches, Laco and company shuttled to the Washington area the next day for a face-to-face meeting at the FDA's Bureau of Medical Devices in Silver Spring, Maryland, with a dozen FDA staffers and three from the CDC.

Ostensibly, the meeting had been hastily called "to exchange and review available data" on TSS. In reality, it was an opportunity for all of the parties involved to size up the others' case. In legal terms, this is known as discovery, where everybody lays his or her cards on the table.

The FDA's position was simple and straightforward: "Unless the company had a justification for keeping the product on the market," said Pines, "we would ask that the product be withdrawn immediately."[126]

P&G's positions were (a) that extensive TSS news coverage may have prejudiced the CDC's survey results; (b) to question some of the survey interviewing techniques; and (c) to challenge some of the actual data.

However, despite the fact that the company had had little time to prepare for the meeting, it did come with proposed warning labels that it was prepared, if necessary, to put on the Rely packages. The upshot was that the FDA gave P&G one week, and one week only, to review the CDC full findings and prepare a response.

The next week was critical for Procter & Gamble.

Unsure of the fate of Rely, the company halted production. "It seemed likely," explained Butler at the time, "that at the very least warning labels would be required on tampon packages, so we didn't want to keep filling more and more packages without labels."[127] P&G had about a one-month inventory supply at the time.

There are others, however, who discount this explanation, saying that the company merely saw the handwriting on the wall and decided to pull the plug on the product. Citing guilt by association and blemishes on its otherwise good name, P&G watchers at the time felt the company had no choice but to halt production.

"The fact that P&G was being tied to a bad product could have potentially been connected to the company's other products," the *Journal* quoted a financial industry analyst as saying. "They couldn't let one bad product pull down the company's whole name."[128]

But halting production was not the problem. The problem was that a St. Louis newspaper got wind of the production stoppage at P&G's Cape Girardeau, Missouri, plant and reported it to the world, leaving the public with the clear, indelible impression that P&G knew something it wasn't telling. This only served to intensify the pressure on the company and escalate the crisis further.

The decision to halt production "quietly" was made in the absence of any crisis communications counseling. This, as it turned out, was an error on P&G's part.

It was—and still is—the Procter & Gamble style of management that says if you are not really needed at a meeting, go back to work. The company has made a reputation for operating on a strict "need-to-know" basis. And so it was in the crisis management of the Rely crisis.

"The determining factor," wrote Prestbo in the *Journal,* "was whether the discussion involved public reaction or how to convey information to the public. But when the meetings centered on other matters, no PR person was included."[129]

In a crisis, a company should assume at *all* times that information will be made public. As stated earlier, there are too many angry people looking for media exposure in a crisis.

Therefore, even if you are absolutely positive that a decision you make in a crisis will *not* become public, have a qualified crisis communications expert present just in case.

Had P&G anticipated the negative publicity the production stoppage was to engender, the company might have been able to defuse the situation by taking the initiative and announcing the stoppage in preparation for the placement of warning labels.

But there were other problems besides this one. On September 19, a study performed by the Utah State Health Department reported another statistical link between TSS and Rely.

However, the crushing blow came during the weekend of September 19–22 when P&G's own scientists, as well as a previously recruited group of independent scientists, physicians, microbiologists, and epidemiologists, meeting at the Hilton O'Hare in Chicago, were unable to give Procter & Gamble executives the ammunition they so desperately needed to "fight for a brand."

The internal report was anemically thin. "Looking at the numbers in it," Butler recalled, "we couldn't tell if toxic shock was already a major disease, with reported cases just a bare indicator, or whether it was still a small-scale disease but was spreading rapidly."[130]

The external, independent advisory group pored over what meager information P&G had been able to compile, and they agreed that the results were inconclusive—that there was no direct evidence which would specifically link Rely to TSS any more than any other tampon.

However, with the sparse information and the lack of time—remember, the FDA had given P&G only a week to review the CDC findings—the independent group was unable to assure Procter & Gamble executives that the CDC's findings could be safely ignored.

In an admirable example of vigilant decision making in a crisis, the P&G decision makers—who, let's not forget, entered the fray bound and determined to fight for Rely, to keep a bunch of bureaucrats from trying to dictate corporate and consumer policy based on insufficient data—gathered the facts, analyzed them, and did a complete 180-degree turn on their previous position.

That weekend "was the turning point," Harness said. "I knew Sunday night what we had to do."[131]

The next day, Monday, September 22, Procter & Gamble announced the withdrawal of Rely tampons from the marketplace and the immediate recall of all packages in the hands of consumers and retailers.

"We didn't know enough about toxic shock to act," said Harness, "and yet we knew too much not to act. In a case like that, we did the conservative thing. It was, in the end, an utterly simple decision to make. But it was a very emotional one."[132]

Tough decisions, when made in a vigilant mode, do have a tendency in the final analysis to become "simple" ones. Obviously, this is not always the case, but in going through a vigilant decision-making exercise, once all of the facts have been assembled, certain previously considered options tend to fall by the wayside, unable to stand up under close examination.

Procter & Gamble's options were:

• To challenge openly the government findings as inconclusive and to present its own research. This would have intensified the crisis; P&G's findings would have been suspect; there would have been heightened negative publicity, a further erosion of the company's tampon market share, and additional damage to its name, image, other products, and bottom line. And worst of all, it almost certainly would have led to a forced government recall.

• To proceed with warning labels anyway. If the government was determined to keep the heat of "bad publicity" on P&G (as the FDA later indicated it was prepared to do), this option would have had the same effect as the first, unless the FDA agreed to the labels.

• To withdraw the product "temporarily" until more was known about the causes of TSS. The possibility of announcing this option at the time was removed from P&G's consideration with the news coverage given to its production stoppage. The public wouldn't have gone for it at the time. Of course, should a cure for TSS suddenly be found, P&G is certainly in a position to rekindle its now 25 years of catamenial product research and introduce a tampon product to the marketplace.*

• Or pull the product.

Once the facts were in, the last option was the only viable alternative. According to the *Journal:*

> The decision wasn't marked with eloquent speeches.
>
> The few executives gathered in Mr. Harness's office offered no rebuttal, but to make sure they agreed, Mr. Butler went around the room and asked each one, "Do you disagree?" None did.
>
> That afternoon, after the public announcement, Mr. Harness remembered feeling "as tired as I've ever been in my life. I ached all over."[133]

There are few, if any, who would argue that Proctor & Gamble did not act in a responsible manner. True, it did act slowly at times, but part of that molasseslike attitude is due to (a) the general nature of the giant, and (b) a marked disbelief on the part of P&G executives, managers, and researchers that the company's own findings could be faulty. That sort of thing just didn't happen. And they *did* eventually make their decision within a week.

But how should a company respond when confronted with evidence that its product—when used properly—kills?

Let's take a fast look at how two other international giants performed under strikingly similar circumstances. Firestone Tire & Rubber Company and the Ford Motor Company both had popular products that were accused of causing fatalities under normal operating conditions.

---

*In March 1984 P&G reentered the marketplace with Always feminine napkins.

The Firestone 500 series of steel-belted radial tires had been a popular line for the Akron, Ohio–based company. But according to federal authorities at the Traffic Safety Administration, the tires were prone to blowouts, tread separations, and several other dangerous conditions and deformities. There had been thousands of consumer complaints to the company as well as to the government, which launched an investigation.

At one point, there had been at least 34 deaths associated with the tire and hundreds of accidents. These statistics were supplied *by* Firestone to congressional and government investigators.

But Firestone insisted that there was nothing wrong with the tire design and chose to blame "consumer neglect and abuse. . . . Consumers damage their tires by overloading them, banging them against the curb, failing to keep them adequately inflated, and driving at excessive speeds,"[134] according to a Firestone executive quoted in *Fortune* back in 1978.

Repeatedly, and with moderate success at first, the company tried to block any investigation of the tire and publicly questioned the true motives of those doing the investigation. The company even tried to suppress the results of a Traffic Safety Administration–sponsored survey of Firestone tire owners.

A host of actions by Firestone resulted in a series of delays. F example, the Traffic Safety Administration asked the company to resp to a lengthy list of questions about (a) steel-belted radials, (b) any plaints Firestone had received about the tires, (c) any consumer-i lawsuits against the company as a result of tire failures, and (d) any implemented by Firestone in methods of manufacturing radial ti

Firestone, for its part, objected to all of the questions for reasons, even when demanded to answer under penalty of prosecution. The company bemoaned the length of time it compile all the answers, questioned the government's authority over certain issues, and even complained abo was being asked to send documents to Washington, rat them available at its Midwest plant.

But the champion of the stall has to be the Fo more than eight years, Ford was able to put standard known as Federal Motor Vehicle Stand forced the auto maker to redesign the apparer Pinto—a car that prior to and during this eig being responsible for between 500 and 900

The most prevalent theory was t according to a then-timely *Business ar* "How Ford Put Two Million Firetraps

reasons: the company's cost-benefit model showed it would not be profitable to redesign the Pinto model and change the location of the gas tank.

Ford masterfully used three delaying tactics that had the government running in circles:

• First, Ford made its arguments in succession, one at a time. After the government spent months performing necessary research to refute one of Ford's arguments, the company would simply make another.

• A second technique was merely to claim that the problem was the consumer (similar to the Firestone charge) and not the car. At one point, for example, Ford claimed that most of the people who died would have died anyway from the force of the impact, not from the gas-tank explosion. The government then had to go back and reexamine its own data.

• Third, Ford simply accompanied every single argument with a mountain of highly technical assertions, often running into thousands of pages, which the government then had to spend additional months, or years, perusing.

In addition to charging the government with unfair testing methods (also a Firestone ploy, as well as a gambit that Procter & Gamble considered but rejected), Henry Ford threatened to close the company down entirely if new government standards proved too costly to implement.

Had Procter & Gamble responded to its crisis with the same "fight-all-the-way" maneuvers as Ford and Firestone, the company might have suffered the same intensive negative consumer and media attention and government scrutiny.

But more than government scrutiny, had P&G tried to "tough it out," Rely could have counted on an official government recall. And as bad as it s to have to remove a product, a voluntary withdrawal is better than a rced recall. In a voluntary withdrawal you at least have a better chance to ntrol the message.

Here is how P&G moved to control the message on September 22, n it announced the withdrawal. The first paragraph of its news release

ter & Gamble Chairman Edward G. Harness announced today that the any has suspended sale of Rely tampons. "We are taking this action to ve Rely and the company from the controversy surrounding a new e called toxic shock syndrome (TSS). This is being done despite the fact e know of no defect in the Rely tampon and despite evidence that the wal of Rely will not eliminate the occurrence of TSS even if Rely's mpletely discontinued. For example, the disease has been identified la, where Rely has never been marketed, and was found in several he United States before Rely was introduced into those areas."[136]

This message is proactive when you consider the reactive manner in which the company would have had to respond had the government ordered a recall. As Harness himself said at the time, in offering advice for any other CEOs caught in a similar crisis, "Keep the ball in your own court, if you can. Do it right before somebody else does it wrong for you."[137]

The rest of the week of September 22 was spent in hammering out the details between P&G and the FDA, such as a debate on whether to call the move a "recall" (the FDA's choice) or a "withdrawal" (P&G's obvious choice); the signing of a consent decree, in which the company, while not admitting any wrongdoing, agreed to a massive public educational program via advertising on toxic shock; and so on. Another detail, naturally, was the actual withdrawal of the product, which took about two weeks.

And how did the American pubic respond? According to two public opinion studies undertaken at the time, there was a marked dissatisfaction with and negative attitude toward P&G immediately after the withdrawal; the public thought P&G had acted too slowly. However, just one month later, this negative opinion was replaced with a positive reaction to the company's *perceived* quick handling of the crisis, supported in no small measure by the massive advertising campaign.

Once again, in an advertising campaign, it is the paying advertiser—P&G—who gets to control the message. True, the government did have to pass on some of the advertising copy; but control was still in P&G's hands.

A few postscripts are in order:
• Although Rely was withdrawn in September 1980, new cases of TSS still continue to be reported at a rate of some 30 per month. Between 1980 and 1984, the CDC reported that 2,683 persons suffered toxic shock syndrome, and 114 of them died.
• More than 15 percent of TSS cases have occurred in men, children, surgery patients, and nonmenstruating women.
• There have been several lawsuits brought against P&G by victims and, in at least one case, the family of a deceased TSS victim. Three verdicts have been reached to date. In the first two, P&G was found guilty of negligence and producing a defective product; however, no punitive damages were awarded. In the third case, the jury found that P&G had not acted negligently, nor was Rely defective. In the case of the deceased's family suit, although no punitive damages were awarded, $300,000 in compensatory damages were awarded. P&G appealed the compensatory award and lost.
• P&G has so far committed more than $3 million in financial assistance to 25 outside, independent, university-based research groups to help sponsor TSS research.
• During and immediately after the crisis, P&G's toll-free 800 cus-

tomer service line was inundated with telephone calls. (The company states it does not have data on the number of calls that were actually related to Rely.) However, since this was the same 800 number found on the back of all P&G products, the company initially was insensitive to female callers who felt uncomfortable talking to male operators. After a number of complaints, however, all Rely calls were routed to women operators. No medical information was given out, though; callers were counseled to speak with their own gynecologist or physician.

• During the acute crisis, P&G's stock dropped almost seven points.

• During the crisis, Harness occasionally issued memos to "the Procter & Gamble Organization," keeping employees abreast of certain salient developments. This type of internal crisis communications can be every bit as important as external crisis communications. His communiqué to employees issued 48 hours after the withdrawal announcement contains two key sentences that are important reminders for anyone doing business in a manner that asks for the public's trust:

> The financial cost to the Company of Rely's voluntary suspension may turn out to be high, but we believe we have done what is right and that our action is consistent with the long-held Procter & Gamble view that the Company and the Company alone is responsible for the safety of our products. To sacrifice this principle could over the years ahead be a far greater cost than the monetary losses we face on the Rely brand.[138]

• Finally, in the late spring of 1985, researchers at Harvard Medical School, led by Dr. Edward Kass, announced what may turn out to be a breakthrough in the mystery of what causes toxic shock syndrome. The theory put forth is that two kinds of synthetic fiber used in some tampons—polyester foam and polyacrylate rayon—combine to rob the vagina of magnesium, thereby fostering the production of a bacterial poison that causes TSS. The researchers claimed that when magnesium is added to the tampon, it appears to be safe. But these effects have occurred only in an artificial culture in a lab, according to P&G spokesperson Sydney McHugh. P&G maintains that more independent studies are required, especially with menstruating women, and labels the results of this particular study—which was funded by Tambrand, the company that makes Tampax tampons—as "preliminary findings."

The Johnson & Johnson/ Tylenol Crisis

Everything has been thought of before, but the problem is to think of it again.

—Goethe

THE CRISIS IN BRIEF

Sometime during the fall of 1982, for reasons not known, a malevolent person or persons, presumably unknown, replaced Tylenol Extra-Strength capsules with cyanide-laced capsules, resealed the packages, and deposited them on the shelves of at least a half-dozen or so pharmacies and food stores in the Chicago area. The poison capsules were purchased, and seven unsuspecting people died a horrible death. Johnson & Johnson, parent company of McNeil Consumer Products Company which makes Tylenol, suddenly and with no warning—no prodrome at all—had to explain to the world why its trusted product was killing people.

KEY PLAYERS IN BRIEF

- James E. Burke, chairman and chief executive officer, Johnson & Johnson
- David R. Clare, president and chairman of J&J's executive committee
- David E. Collins, chairman of McNeil and vice chairman of J&J's executive committee
- Joseph R. Chiesa, president, McNeil Consumer Products Company
- Lawrence G. Foster, J&J's corporate vice president, public relations
- Robert Kniffen, director of public relations, J&J

September 30, 1982, began as a morning like any other, recalled Bob Kniffen. But then one of his public relations staffers, Jim Murray, walked into his office to report a bizarre telephone call he had just received from a Chicago *Tribune* reporter. The reporter initially asked some rather basic questions about Tylenol, about Johnson & Johnson, about J&J's relationship to its subsidiary McNeil Consumer Products Company. Then the reporter began asking for the spelling of "Tylenol" and "McNeil" and the companies' full names.

It didn't smell right to Murray, "and I didn't like it, either," said Kniffen. This reporter had been asking the sort of basics that any business reporter should have known. But this was not a business reporter.

Kniffen called the reporter and demanded to know what was going on. The answer changed his life forever: the reporter was investigating a suspicion by the Chicago medical examiner that there was some kind of link between Tylenol and a recent death.

Kniffen called his boss. Fast.

Larry Foster had been home that morning when the call came, and the corporate vice president for public relations wasted no time in alerting his boss, the chairman of the board, Jim Burke.

Foster's first thoughts were centered on some possible screw-up at a plant, and he was worried about the implications that suggested. But worry gave way to prayer as he sped to the office. He hoped this was all a mistake.

Dave Collins was new to his job. Until just two weeks before, he had been president of McNeil Pharmaceuticals* for about three years, and now he was in the international arena, heading up part of J&J's Latin American operations and serving for the first time on the executive committee. Collins recalled recently:

> I was on the phone talking with someone in Mexico, and I remember my secretary coming in to interrupt me to tell me that Jim Burke was on the line. And I told her to tell him I was tied up on an important call and that I would get back to him.
>
> It was when she came back into my office that I sensed something was wrong. "He says he wants to see you and he wants to see you *now*," she told me.
>
> I couldn't imagine what was going on. But I got off the phone immediately.

By the time Collins got to the chairman's office, where Kniffen had also been summoned, Burke already had been in touch with McNeil, which had gotten calls, too. And it seemed that whatever was happening was escalat-

---

*McNeil Pharmaceuticals is the sister company of McNeil Consumer Products. The pharmaceuticals firm supplies the medical profession with prescription drugs, including Tylenol and codeine. But it is McNeil Consumer Products that manufactures the over-the-counter Tylenol capsules and tablets.

ing rapidly. All that was known by a handful of J&J executives at that precise moment on September 30 was that there was some kind of wild talk or rumor or *something* going on in Chicago that was linking a Johnson & Johnson product, Tylenol, with death.

Johnson & Johnson! This is not a hazardous-chemical company, this is not a waste polluter, this is not a company that "kills." This is probably the world's leading health-care company. This is a company that *saves* lives, not *takes* them. But if anyone saw any irony in that fact, it was lost in the concerned and tense atmosphere in Burke's office.

Burke immediately got to the point before anyone had a chance to sit down. He told Collins and Kniffen what he knew so far. Kniffen, of course, knew some of it; Collins was shocked. He had no inkling.

Literally just moments ago, Dave Collins had been sitting in his new office, getting the feel of his new title and new responsibilities and talking on the telephone with part of the Latin American operations he oversaw. Now he was in the office of the chairman of the board of what has been called one of the 100 best companies in the world to work for, and he was hearing foreign words: words like "death" and "killings" and "poisonings."

And they were being said in the same breath with words that for years had represented comfort and trust and security: words like "Johnson & Johnson" and "McNeil" and "Tylenol."

"It was all so disorienting," said Collins, "a very disorienting experience. And I was scared. We all were scared."

Burke wasted no time in briefing Collins and Kniffen. It didn't take long, owing to the sparsity of information.

He told Collins and Kniffen that he had ordered a helicopter to shuttle the two of them immediately to McNeil's headquarters in Fort Washington, Pennsylvania—just a short helicopter puddle-jump from J&J's campuslike headquarters in New Brunswick, New Jersey, adjacent to Rutgers University.

Burke didn't believe in wasting time or words. He looked Collins in the eye and said, "Take charge."

Ninety minutes later, Dave Collins and Bob Kniffen were deposited by helicopter on the doorstep of one of the most heinous crimes and shocking crises in the annals of both criminology and commerce.

For the first time in history, terrorism had reached into American homes.

Let's pause here for a moment to consider what transpired.

The Johnson & Johnson/Tylenol crisis has been hailed as one of the best-handled corporate crises in history—despite the fact that the corporate executives who managed the acute crisis, in extensive interviews, made one thing clear: Johnson & Johnson as a company thought at the time that it was ill prepared to handle this crisis. But it was wrong, as you shall see.

J&J had done no planning for this sort of contingency—true. The thought of potential product tampering had never crossed anyone's mind, although any product company is always on the lookout for a manufacturing facility that might produce a defective product. This, certainly, is one reason for quality control.

While key J&J executives now have *two* copies of a written crisis management manual—one for the office and one for the nightstand at home—no such document existed before. Executives had to scramble for home telephone numbers or names of people they needed to reach.

Because of the saboteurial nature of the crime, the crisis had no prodrome. In one instant, a company that had built its reputation on health and health care was violently thrust into the sickness of a criminal mind that was threatening the stability of the company, as well as the sanity of many who initially said, "This *can't* be happening!" It is difficult at best to try to plan for a psychopath.

The point was made at the beginning of this book and will be made one more time here: a crisis in business can occur today with little or no warning, anywhere, anytime. And it can happen to any company, large or small, public or private.

This simple truth has been illustrated time and again throughout this book. However, all previous crises mentioned had prodromes of varying lengths. Normally, an acute crisis phase is preceded by a prodrome, but not always—especially not when your crisis is caused by a psychopath.

But prodrome or not, remember, too, that a crisis is merely a turning point in which you can find opportunity as well as danger. Johnson & Johnson turned tragedy into triumph.

Look at what was accomplished within the first hour and a half. Without knowing too much more than has been presented here so far—in fact, much less— Johnson & Johnson lost no time in elevating the crisis into the domain of the chairman, who:

- Appointed a senior executive to put all matters aside and "take charge" and find out what was going on. (Identify the crisis; isolate the crisis; or isolate someone or some team to manage it.)
- Directed the crisis manager to get on the scene. (Gather facts.)
- Directed a public relations professional to accompany the crisis manager. (Crisis communications.)
- Required that he (the chairman) be kept informed. (Also crisis communications.)

By accident or by design, Burke could not have picked a more qualified person to manage the acute phase of this crisis than Dave Collins. Collins knew Chicago; he had been born and raised there. One of the first things he did before boarding the helicopter was to call a lawyer he knew well in Chicago and tell him to try to get some reliable medical information from the coroner's office, from the police, from anywhere he could think of.

And Collins knew McNeil. Having served as president of the sister company, McNeil Pharmaceuticals, Collins knew his former counterpart well: Joe Chiesa, president of McNeil Consumer.

On the helicopter ride, Collins tried to make some sense of the situation. There were only two possibilities at that early stage: first, that it was all some kind of big mistake; if not, that somehow one of the plants screwed up.

Early on, Collins formulated a list of three priority goals:

1. Stop the killings.
2. Come up with the reasons for the killings.
3. Provide assistance to those in trouble.

Thinking initially that the cause of the deaths was internal, not external, stopping the killings would certainly qualify as identifying the heart of the crisis. If a piece of machinery malfunctioned and caused a defective product, or if an employee "malfunctioned" and sabotaged your product, then stopping the killings—stopping the malfunction—certainly is identifying the crisis.

But when it became known a few days later that the product had been shipped in perfect condition and that the tampering had been the result of external forces, then "stopping the killings" was no longer a crisis over which Johnson & Johnson had any control.

While the company certainly wanted the killings halted and the lunatic caught (two understatements, to be sure), and toward that end it did everything that law enforcement officials requested of it (with one notable exception, which we will mention later), it realized that apprehending the person responsible and stopping the killings was no longer *its* crisis. These were the responsibility of the FBI and the Chicago police.

But J&J didn't know that yet. It did know that as the death count climbed during the next few days, fear, apprehension, and uncertainty permeated its corridors.

And fear quickly spread across the nation. No one really knew for sure what was going on, but one of the most trusted corporate names in America's medicine chests was somehow being linked to some bizarre poisonings in the Midwest.

No pun intended, but Johnson & Johnson is the ultimate "cradle-to-grave" company. From the well-known line of Johnson & Johnson baby products to Ortho-Novum birth-control pills, from Band-Aids to surgical wound-closure instruments, from Reach toothbrushes to laser surgical devices—from the delivery room to the operating room, Johnson & Johnson has been with us and our loved ones for generations.

And now—so the world then thought—its Tylenol brand of over-the-counter analgesic, which, at the time of the crisis had had a commanding 35 percent share of the market and was outselling the next four brands *combined*—was killing people.

The ripple effect a crisis can have on people's lives is far-reaching.

Ann Marie Collins was confused. Her fifth-grade classmates taunted and teased her, saying her Daddy worked for a company that killed people.

Instead of being childishly happy when her Daddy appeared on television, she was upset by the things they said on the TV and in school. And her Daddy wasn't even home to talk to her. Daddy, of course, is Dave Collins, who was still at McNeil for the first few days, but then worked very late even when he returned to New Jersey. "Thank God for my wife," Collins said. "She was able to explain things to Ann Marie."

As for Collins, he admitted to having been tired and scared. "And I was afraid of the next phone call. When the phone rang at home at night, I was almost afraid to answer it; afraid someone would tell me that there had been another death. I couldn't sleep.

"It is a terrible responsibility to cause someone to die."

"One of the most important things in a crisis is authority," stated Larry Foster. "Either authority to act, or immediate access to authority." Foster, as corporate vice president for public relations, has—and had—both. He reports directly to the chairman of the board, Jim Burke, just as he reported directly to the previous two chairmen.

And as far as Foster was concerned, when a crisis hits, your first responsibility is to the consumer. Foster didn't go to Burke, nor did he have to, to work out the first, basic communications strategy of the crisis: to find out what the hell was going on and tell the truth to the consumers through the media.

The truth.

When asked for his own interpretation of why Johnson & Johnson performed so well in the crisis, Foster unhesitatingly said, "The company acted responsibly, and it acted fast."

His analysis of why J&J did so well with the public during and after the acute phase of the crisis boiled down to three points:

1. Openness to the press.
2. A willingness at all costs to withdraw the product.
3. And the American sense of fair play—"asking the public to trust us."

"We earned their loyalty," Foster said. "We earned it in the manner in which we have always treated our consumers: honestly and fairly. And we earned it by treating them honestly and fairly during the Tylenol crisis."

Foster was an integral part of the crisis management team in New Brunswick, which was headed by Burke and joined by Collins when he returned from McNeil a few days later. Also on the crisis management team, which met twice daily during the entire crisis, even when it was impossible to tell when one meeting ended and the next one began, was J&J president David R. Clare, company group chairman Wayne K. Nelson, executive committee member Arthur M. Quilty, and general counsel George S. Frazza.

Foster's key role on the team, most naturally, was coordinating crisis communications activities, and one of the first things he did in this regard was to send someone from the public relations staff, Bob Andrews, out to Chicago to be his "eyes and ears."

"It was the old newsman's instinct in me," said Foster. "Always get your own person on the scene as quickly as possible—someone you know, someone who you can count on for being reliable and not prone to exaggeration. Someone who knows how to get the facts."

The instinct—fact gathering—was right. But, as Foster admitted, in this case it really served little function.

"It wasn't like the scene of a crime; there wasn't action taking place in any one location," Foster lamented. As a result, there wasn't too much forthcoming in the way of useful information. But still, he felt more secure knowing he had his own person there.

He also had his own person in Fort Washington.

"I was depressed, really depressed," said Bob Kniffen. "To think that someone would hurt this company really depressed me."

Kniffen didn't have too much time to feel depressed, though. His job on the scene at McNeil was to "tell what we knew as soon as we knew it. The public interest was legitimate."

Handling the media was a nightmare for Kniffen at McNeil, although it was no better in New Brunswick.

J&J called it "something of a communications media monster."[139] During the crisis there were some 80,000 separate news stories in U.S. newspapers, hundreds of hours of national and local television and radio coverage, and more than 2,000 telephone calls to Johnson & Johnson seeking information on the Tylenol crisis.

The company reports findings that "more than 90 percent of the American population knew about the Chicago deaths due to cyanide-laced Tylenol within the first week of the crisis. . . ." The disaster was referred to by one newspaper columnist as "one of the most heavily covered news events since Vietnam."

In some instances, Kniffen had to go out and tenaciously track down inside facts for a reporter's story. One reporter who was working on a theory of possible sabotage after a shipment left the Texas facility asked Kniffen for the precise route the truck and the shipment took. Because of the quirks of interstate trucking, in which the trucker can split shipments for economic reasons, it took Kniffen about three days to track down the requested information. He did, but the reporter's theory was no good.

Foster's attitude was equally vigilant. When the news broke that the capsules had contained cyanide, reporters wanted to know if Tylenol manufacturing facilities contained cyanide. Foster checked, and was told no. And for the first three days of the crisis, Foster told reporters, and the world, "No cyanide."

But one of the by-products of a crisis is chaos, and Johnson & Johnson did not escape this, especially early on. As good as the company's crisis communications system was, it was not totally coordinated. As a result, late on a Saturday evening, the Associated Press in Newark called Foster to confirm a report it had that there was, indeed, cyanide at McNeil.

Foster followed up the lead, spoke to one of McNeil's facility operations managers, and was told, "Yes, we do have cyanide here. It is used in quality-assurance testing. But it is housed in a completely separate facility; there is very little ever kept on the premises; none of it is missing; and it could in no way have gotten into the capsules in the production facility."

Foster believed him; but the world's media had believed Foster for the past 72 hours, during which time he had said there was no cyanide. The AP was on deadline for Sunday morning editions and was waiting for his call.

Foster didn't hesitate to pick up the phone and get hold of the AP. There was no way he wanted to be in a position of having someone accuse him of covering up. He told the reporter precisely what he had just learned and then pointed out that people could get the wrong idea if the story were blown out of proportion.

Over the years J&J had built a reputation of dealing fairly with consumers, as well as with the media. This reservoir of good will served J&J well throughout the crisis. It was able to go back to the well several times without being turned away.

When, in the midst of the Tylenol crisis—a full-blown national panic—Lawrence G. Foster said to the Associated Press, in effect, "Trust me, this is *not* a smoking gun," the AP agreed. That is, it agreed to the extent that if any other reporter got the story, Foster would have to let the AP know. The deal was made.

Later, as fate would have it, a reporter for the Newark *Star-Ledger* got the story and called Foster for verification. Foster immediately confirmed the presence of cyanide in the same carefully measured explanation he had given to the AP. Again, he basically said, "Trust me." And, after the reporter talked it over with his editor, *they* agreed.

Foster, though, keeping to the strict letter of the agreement he had made with the AP, called the wire service merely to report that another reporter had the story but that he, too, had agreed that running the story could cause a panic. The AP agreed not to go with it—unless *another* reporter got the story.

Well, naturally, a third journalist—a science reporter from the New York *Times*—did get the story, and at this point Foster saw the handwriting on the wall.

"When three reporters have the same story," said the newsman in Foster, "you can't control it." The problem was compounded because when Foster found out about this third outlet, the journalist was on his way back to New York from Fort Washington, and Foster had no way to reach him.

Foster then called the AP and the *Star-Ledger* to release them from the agreement, telling them that the *Times* had the story, too, and that more media were sure to follow. He asked them to use discretion in their reporting of the facts.

All of the media buried the cyanide reference so low in their Sunday stories that it had little impact. They ran it just the way Foster had explained it: there was no possibility that it was connected with the poisonings.

Try, if you can, to recall the panic at the time over Tylenol. You may recall that once the story was out that there were cyanide-laced capsules floating around, the big question was where the cyanide had come from (assuming at the time that it had been "an inside job").

If your memory is good, and you can recollect the fear, then you will have a better appreciation of Larry Foster's accomplishments of that evening. The media thought they had found the cyanide, but Foster very calmly told them that they didn't have the story they thought.

It could have been the kind of story that sold papers, as the old newsmen used to say. But Johnson & Johnson had asked for the public's trust for a long time, and it had never violated it.

Its reservoir of trust had paid off.

In a classic telling of the "good news/bad news" story, the good news came in two forms. First, the police, the FBI, the Food and Drug Administration, and Johnson & Johnson itself had been unable to find any evidence of any internal product tampering at either of J&J's two U.S. plants, in Pennsylvania and Texas. Second, in recovering the doctored packages, J&J and law-enforcement officials were able to confirm that contaminated packages came from *both* the Round Rock, Texas, *and* the Fort Washington, Pennsylvania, facilities, not just one of them.

In brief, this news meant that the odds that the poisonings had been an inside job were reduced to virtually nil. The strange coincidence of Tylenol packages from Pennsylvania and Texas finding their way to Chicago was due to the quirks of the trucking industry splitting and piggy-backing shipments to always have trucks rolling with full loads.

So the good news was the company's innocence.

The bad news was that some malignant psychopath had gone into several pharmacies and stores in Chicago, purchased Tylenol packages, laced some of the capsules with cyanide, resealed the containers and the packages, then returned the Tylenol to the stores, making sure that each store received its own packages in order to maintain the difference in pricing labels.

It was October 2.

"I had been depressed before," recalled Kniffen, "but now I got angry. I was resentful that someone would do this."

Foster remembers feeling that way, too. "At first, I naturally had been worried about the possibility of accidental poisonings taking place *in* the plant; but then I got angry when it was discovered that someone intentionally had tampered with our product."

This anger was quickly felt by many J&J employees around the world who took the crisis personally. It may sound corny, but many employees consider Johnson & Johnson almost a family. Many felt that a family member had been violated, and they looked for ways to channel that anger into constructive avenues.

And, in large measure, the public got angry, too. "America's sense of fair play," as Foster had phrased it, was brought into sharp focus when Ted Koppel interviewed Dave Collins on ABC's "Nightline." The message the public heard was that Johnson & Johnson was a victim, too.

While it would not be *quite* accurate to say that prior to this time the company did not know what its real crisis was, it would be correct to point out how much time and energy had been misspent trying, as Dave Collins put it, "to make decisions out of chaos."

The real crisis had not been identified *and* isolated until it became clear what had—and had not—happened. Collins had been trying to determine whether the plants were safe and the plant workers were innocent. Foster had been spending large amounts of time discussing with reporters the discovery of a small amount of cyanide, which, as it turned out, had nothing to do with the crisis. And Kniffen had been tracking down truck routes from Round Rock, Texas, into the Midwest.

Had the truth been known all along, Collins's, Foster's, and Kniffen's painstaking and time-consuming actions would not have been necessary.

So with the discovery that Tylenol had been the victim of outside sabotage, the entire complexion of the problem changed, and the crisis management team was at last able to assemble in New Brunswick and address itself to the real crisis: *could Tylenol be saved?*

Even before it became known that Tylenol had been the victim of sabotage, the management of J&J and McNeil knew that the future of Tylenol was at stake. It just had been unable to focus its attention exclusively on this crisis issue.

But it certainly was not ignored. Market research studies were being done from the second day of the crisis to judge consumers' attitudes toward the product. And as the death count rose, so, too, did consumers' lack of confidence in Tylenol.

In the first week of the crisis, McNeil had established a toll-free 800 hotline for consumers to respond to inquiries concerning the safety of Tylenol. More than 30,000 calls were received through November.

Trying to do everything it could to keep the Tylenol name alive and in people's homes, on October 12 (one week following the product withdrawal), the company placed full-page ads in major newspapers across the country offering to exchange packages of Tylenol *capsules* for Tylenol *tablets*. There had been no tampering with tablets, and the exchange offer was considered a success.

"The survival of the company was never really an issue," said Collins. "The question was the future of the brand. Could Tylenol be saved?"

One week into the crisis, after the sabotage had been discovered, Jim Burke helicoptered to McNeil in Fort Washington and made an impromptu speech to all McNeil employees, who were jammed into the cafeteria.

"It was an emotion-charged speech," recalled Kniffen. "And it became an emotional day for everyone, even me. What he said—and he said it with conviction—is that 'We're coming back'; that Tylenol is coming back. *We* believed it because *he* believed it."

Burke believed it because his market opinion studies were starting to tell him that he *could* believe it.

Buttons carrying a thumbs-up sign and the message "We're Coming Back" appeared within a few days and were worn by McNeil employees.

"McNeil employees who were idled by the crisis were given jobs to do to keep them busy and their spirits up," Collins said. "We even shut down certain automated facilities and had the work done by hand. It was more than just busy work; we wanted McNeil [employees] to know that Johnson & Johnson was behind them all the way."

Johnson & Johnson is organized on the principles of decentralized management and conducts its business through operating subsidiaries that are, for the most part, autonomous operations. Direct responsibility for each company lies with its operating management, headed by a president, general manager, or managing director who reports directly or through a company group chairman to a member of the executive committee. In line with this policy of decentralization, most international subsidiaries are managed by citizens of the country where they are located.

This is how Johnson & Johnson described itself in one of its annual reports.[140]

Its operational style sounds like that of many companies of comparable size, including Union Carbide.

But note how J&J's parent-corporation response differed markedly from Carbide's. Whereas Carbide moved to distance itself from the Bhopal subsidiary, J&J moved to embrace and support McNeil. Even Procter & Gamble laid off workers when it halted production of Rely. Not J&J.

In the much-publicized Tylenol withdrawal, the cost to the company— the Cost of Intervention—was about $100 million.* Had McNeil had to bear that cost, it would have gone belly up. Johnson & Johnson picked up the tab.

One J&J executive, in explaining why he thought Johnson & Johnson was a better company today because of the crisis, said, "There is more of an appreciation today by subsidiaries that they have strength in being part of a real corporate family."

It became clear to Johnson & Johnson, to the FDA, to congressional investigations, and to the public at large that what was needed was tamper-resistant packaging—not just on Tylenol, but on all packaging.

America had entered a new age. Whatever innocence we still had in the summer of 1982 was quickly shattered that fall. No longer could we walk into our neighborhood pharmacies or supermarkets and feel secure about an innocuous little purchase. Anything that could be opened and reclosed too easily and without detection became a risky buy, a potential killer.

J&J immediately set out to devise tamper-resistant packaging for

---

*"It is well to remember," said Dave Clare, "that two unused bottles of poisoned Tylenol were recovered as a result of the withdrawal, so lives may have been saved."[141]

Tylenol. The crisis management team was convinced that the public still considered Tylenol a trusted name and that the brand could be saved.

The question of what to do with the supply still on hand and in stores outside the Midwest (Jane Byrne, Mayor of Chicago at the time, had ordered *all* Tylenol products—even tablets—off the shelves in Chicago) was interrupted by the receipt on October 2 of an extortion note demanding $1 million in return for an end to the tampering.

Prior to the receipt of this demand, J&J and McNeil had been cooperating with FBI and other law-enforcement officials in trying to identify a possible motive for the tampering, as well as a possible suspect.

All of the usual avenues were explored—possibly disgruntled workers, recently fired employees, and so on. A link was sought among the victims: did they have anything in common, any *person* in common in their pasts? The FBI even considered that only one of the victims was killed intentionally and that the others had been killed at random to cover up the real crime. Nothing panned out, though.

The extortion note held promise because it was the only plausible explanation for the tampering: target a big company (no other analgesic companies had experienced any product tampering) and demand money to stop the crime spree. Tylenol could have been chosen as the target because of the apparent ease with which its capsules could be opened and because it was a popular, leading brand.

While the FBI set out to catch the extortionist, J&J went about its job of managing the crisis. Dealing with terrorists and extortionists was out of its league. Although the publicity surrounding the extortion demand further served to increase the public's appreciation for how J&J had been victimized, it did not help in deciding what to do about the Tylenol packages still on the market.

William Webster, the director of the FBI, and Arthur Hayes, then commissioner of the FDA, both personally appealed to J&J executives not to remove the extra-strength Tylenol capsules, a tactic that J&J had been considering.

They made this request based on reasoning that can be linked to the Israeli posture of never giving in to terrorists. The FBI was concerned that if Johnson & Johnson did withdraw the product, a signal would go out to terrorists around the world that American business could be brought to its knees.

Webster's and Hayes's argument had a lot of merit and might have carried the day—until the first copycat crime occurred in northern California on October 5 (except with strychnine instead of cyanide).

(Soon after this, the FDA investigated more than 250 deaths "originally linked to Tylenol"—a connection, it turned out, that proved groundless in all cases.)

"It was really Burke and Clare who made the decision to pull the product," said Collins. "The FBI and the FDA were against it, but as far as we were concerned the health and welfare of the community was the only issue. Removing the product addressed that concern.

The product was withdrawn on October 5, five days after the acute crisis began. And, with the ordered withdrawal, the acute crisis ended and the chronic phase of the crisis began.

Once the acute crisis had been identified and isolated, managing the crisis boiled down to whether the brand could be saved. Having decided that it could be saved by pulling it off the shelves, management's only remaining decisions were how to repackage it and when to reintroduce it.

The innovative triple-seal safety packages were introduced to the world at a November 11 teleconference, which was beamed by satellite to meeting rooms in 29 hotels across the country, where local media people had been assembled.

On the subject of crisis communications, and in addition to the consumer hotline and the October 12 newspaper ad mentioned earlier, J&J did the following:

• A 1-minute national television commercial was aired in October and November. It featured Dr. Thomas Gates, McNeil's medical director, who notified consumers of the impending return of Tylenol to the marketplace. J&J estimates that 85 percent of all TV households saw the spot an average of 2.5 times just during the first week it aired.

• J&J executives were interviewed by such publications as *Fortune* and the *Wall Street Journal,* and they appeared on such television shows as "60 Minutes," "Donahue," and ABC's "Nightline."

• Four videotaped reports were prepared and shown to all employees, letting them know what was happening during the crisis.

• At the height of the crisis, approximately 450,000 electronic mail messages were distributed to the medical profession and distributors. Similar electronic messages were sent to retailers when the withdrawal was announced.

• In order to get the Tylenol name back into homes as quickly as possible, at the November 11 news conference, Burke announced that consumers could obtain a $2.50 coupon good toward the purchase of *any* Tylenol product. The coupon was carried in special advertising, but it also was available by calling a special 800 number that Burke gave out at the conference. Within three weeks, more than 210,000 calls were received; 136,000 were received in the first 11 days.

Tylenol, in triple-seal packages, began appearing on grocery and drugstore shelves within about ten weeks after the withdrawal. Today, backed by massive advertising dollars, Tylenol has regained more than 98 percent of the market share it had before the crisis.

What the Tylenol incident taught Johnson & Johnson is how unprepared it was to deal with a crisis. The written crisis management plan it now has, while far from complete, would still give it a tremendous advantage if the company ever again is struck by a crisis.

There are many in the company, however, who feel that J&J had a crisis management plan of sorts all along—and followed it—but never knew it because they don't call it a crisis management plan. They are referring to the Johnson & Johnson Credo, which carries a lot of weight with J&J managers. Written more than 40 years ago by the late Robert Wood Johnson (son of the company founder), the Credo has changed slightly over the years, but its basic message hasn't. It says that the company has four responsibilities and, *in order,* they are:

1. To the consumers.
2. To the employees.
3. To the communities they serve.
4. To the stockholders.

There are many in the company who say with sincere conviction that when they were faced with stressful, crisis-induced decisions during the Tylenol crisis they looked to the Credo for guidance and, specifically, to see if the decision they were about to make (such as whether or not to withdraw the product) was in keeping with the first line of the Credo: "We believe our first responsibility is to the doctors, nurses and patients, to mothers and all others who use our products and services. . . ."[142] To the extent that a crisis management plan is a blueprint that tells you where to go and how to get there, yes, the J&J credo is a crisis management plan.

Dave Collins, today vice chairman of J&J's executive committee, said it took him a long while to get reoriented to a normal existence. "I had trouble sleeping for a while. And every time the phone rang at home I jumped, almost afraid to answer it; afraid not to. . . ."

Larry Foster pensively stared out of his window and reflected on the crisis:

I'm glad that it happened to me. I'm not pleased that it happened to Johnson & Johnson; but I'm glad that I had the opportunity to play a role. Partly because I know we did a good job.

And partly because of the old newsman's instincts to never want to miss out on a story. When I was a newspaper editor, I went on vacation one time and missed the sinking of the *Andrea Doria*. I always regretted missing out on covering that story.

Foster gets calls "every couple of weeks or so" from corporations in crisis ("Yes, I had some calls from Union Carbide") asking for guidance or suggestions. "Sometimes I can offer a suggestion, sometimes not," he said. "But basically I tell them they can't go wrong with the truth."

And James W. Lewis, what of him? He was the guy captured by the FBI in a New York City public library on December 13, 1982, for sending the extortion note to Johnson & Johnson. He pleaded guilty to attempted extortion and is serving 20 years in federal prison, but he denied any complicity with the actual crime.

Some others are not so sure. They point out that Lewis knew a little *too* much about how the crime *could* have been committed. And, they point out, there haven't been any more similar crimes since he was caught.

But, if Lewis really didn't have anything to do with the random killings of seven innocent people by lacing Tylenol with cyanide, then who did?

And why?

And will he strike again?

18

Interesting Times

When the One Great Scorer comes to write against your name—
He marks—not that you won or lost—but how you played the game.

—*Grantland Rice*

The older a culture, the more colorful its curses. In the Middle East, for example, a well-turned curse may suggest that your daughter lie down with camels.

A good Irish curse would have the unlucky recipient reincarnated as a chandelier—to hang by day and burn by night.

America, a relatively new culture by comparison to the rest of the world, has yet to progress far beyond a hearty "Drop dead" or a belligerent "So's your old man."

But the best curse is one that is so effectively subtle that you don't even know you've been cursed until you stop to think about it. And in that category, no one has yet surpassed the Chinese, who say: "May you live in interesting times."

In the fall of 1984, at a UCLA-sponsored seminar I was asked to conduct on crisis management, the audience heard from several leading authorities on various aspects of crises. Psychologist Dr. Harriet Braiker, director of the Los Angeles–based Praxis Training Group, spoke on the effects of crisis-induced stress on decision making; Chuck Novak, United Airlines' corporate manager of public relations, spoke on crisis management plans; Judith Cronin, senior product manager for Western Union, addressed electronic communications; and three leading journalists—Martin Baron, business editor of the Los Angeles *Times;* Roy Neal, correspondent and deputy West Coast bureau chief for NBC-TV; and Ed Pyle, former news director for KFWB all-news radio in Los Angeles—explained what the media need during a crisis.

And at the conclusion of the all-day seminar, the audience—and the panelists, too—were given a fictional crisis to manage. It is reprinted here for your enjoyment.

One seminar attendee thought the crisis was a little far-fetched, and I had to assure him that it was not. You who have read thus far and have observed how crises can materialize and escalate will need no such assurances.

Everything you need to know to manage this crisis is in this book and in your head. No answers are provided.

The name of the crisis? What else:

INTERESTING TIMES

You are the executive vice president—the number-two person in charge—of Wei-Ji Pharmaceutical Labs, a privately held (but soon to go public) Los Angeles–based manufacturer of prescription drugs. The Food and Drug Administration is only days away from approving your firm's request to manufacture and market Sneezex, a time capsule that will cure the common cold. In fact, your contact at the FDA told you a month ago on the telephone—off the record, of course—that the formal approval was *pro forma* and would be issued in a month.

When you reported this good news to your boss, the president, he decided to begin manufacturing and distribution to pharmacies and physicians early, in order to be ready immediately when the FDA approval was issued. You pointed out that this was illegal, but he ordered you to do it anyway and told you to put carefully worded warning labels on the packages, stating that the medication was not to be dispensed until the official approval came from the FDA and the go-ahead was given by Wei-Ji Labs. Feeling only somewhat mollified by the warning labels, you followed your boss's orders.

As soon as the FDA approval is given, Wei-Ji Labs plans to go public. Because of the almost-certain success of Sneezex, as well as your own position in the company, you stand to make about $5 million and retire at an early age.

The prospect of this personal success—which you can almost taste—is about the only thing keeping you going. You dislike your job and hate your boss; you have long thought that he has a serious drinking problem that, on more than one occasion, you believe has clouded his otherwise sound business judgment. However, the ten years you have devoted to Wei-Ji Labs are about to pay off—big.

But outside pressures are wearing you down, too. You are having difficulty making ends meet financially. You suspect your wife is having an affair, and she's been nagging you about buying a larger, more expensive house. You think that if you buy the house, she will end the affair. You need to put your oldest daughter through college and get braces for your youngest daughter. And last night at dinner, your 16-year-old son announced that he is gay.

This morning your wife has been calling you incessantly: first to report that the college-bound daughter is pregnant; second, to scream at you for not being more of a male role model for your son and to blame you for his being gay; third, to hold you personally responsible if your youngest daughter is ridiculed by the boys in school for having crooked teeth; fourth, to tell you that the real estate broker just called to report that she had located a beautiful "fixer-upper" at the beach that was a steal at $1.5 million, but you had to act fast; and last, to warn you that you had better not be late for dinner again tonight.

A little while ago, your doctor also called to report that the results of your last physical examination could have been better and that you have to slow down. Your blood pressure, he reminded you, is too high and, he said, if you aren't careful, you could become a candidate for a coronary. The thought of slowing down made you laugh. Later you would recall that it was the only laugh you had that day.

You had lunch with your stockbroker, who tried to explain why your portfolio was in bad shape. On the way back to the office, you were involved in a minor fender-bender with an uninsured motorist.

Although the events that followed have become somewhat of a blur because they happened so fast, you recall that the sequence was as follows:

• 2:00—You returned from lunch to find a message to report to the president's office immediately.

• 2:01—Your wife called to tell you that your neighbors are coming for dinner and you'll be playing bridge tonight.

• 2:15—You take a call from the Canadian Testing Lab, which has been running tests on mice relative to Sneezex. The call should have gone to your boss, but they couldn't reach him. They just wanted to let you know that "another mouse died" and to ask "what should we do?" You had never heard of *any* mice dying, but they tell you that the president has known for two weeks. You'll get back to them.

• 2:30—Another "urgent" message from the boss's secretary. "Please report to the president's office at once."

• 2:45—A prominent doctor, whose name you know from all of the publicity he seems to generate about himself, reaches you on the telephone to tell you that two of his patients (one with asthma and one with bronchitis) have died and four more are in hospitals on the critical list after having taken Sneezex. You ask him why he didn't obey the warning label, but he sidesteps this issue, demands an explanation, and threatens to go to the press, even though he admits that his suspicions about Sneezex are just conjecture.

• 3:00—A security guard shows up at your office to "escort" you to the president's suite. On your way out, you tell your secretary to have the public relations director, the chief of testing, the head of production, the biochemist who headed the Sneezex research and development team, and your in-house legal counsel meet you in the president's suite.

• 3:15—You find the president passed out on the couch in his office, and his secretary is obviously quite distraught. He is in a drunken stupor, but is clutching a bunch of fancy brochures for yachts, cruises, expensive cars, and vacation homes. At his feet is a two-week-old report from the Canadian Testing Lab reporting the death of three mice involved in the tests. The deaths are "inconclusive, but suspicious." Periodically the president can be heard to be singing "We're in the Money."

• 3:30—The head of production and distribution arrives and demands to know what the president has decided to do about the "glue problem." You don't know what he's talking about. He explains that the warning labels came in from the outside supplier with a "substandard" glue that "doesn't stick too well" on the Sneezex packages. He's also afraid some of the packages were delivered without the labels.

• 3:45—The president's secretary relays a message to you from your wife. She has given the real estate broker a $15,000 check to open escrow on the beach house. Be sure to cover the check before 5 P.M. Oh, and is meat loaf O.K. for dinner?

• 3:47—The public relations director shows up and reports that he just got off the phone with the Associated Press. AP has "reason to believe that there is a problem with Sneezex" and demands to speak directly to the president for comment. They are on a 6 P.M. deadline to make the morning papers and must speak to the CEO immediately or they will go with the story they have: "Prominent Doctor Reports Death of Patients Due to Sneezex Pill."

• 4:00—The president's secretary sticks her head in to say, "I don't know if this is important, but the FDA called at 2 P.M. to say that they are holding a news conference tomorrow at 9 A.M. in Washington, D.C., regarding Sneezex." She does not know the nature of the press conference. You tell her to get the FDA on the phone, but she comes back to report that it is now 7 P.M. on the East Coast and no one is answering the phone there.

• 4:05—Everyone you requested to be in the president's office has arrived—the public relations director, the chief of testing, the head of production, the R&D biochemist, the in-house legal counsel, as well as the security officer, who is still hanging around, not to mention the incapacitated CEO.

• 4:06—You sit in the president's chair to take a call from a Midwest pharmacist, who wants to know when her next shipment of Sneezex will arrive. She's almost out of the initial shipment.

- 4:10—The chief financial officer shows up to report there is not enough cash in the bank to make the payroll tomorrow morning.
- 4:15—The security officer's walkie-talkie crackles out an urgent message that there is a bomb scare in the building, but it could be "another hoax." The question is whether or not to evacuate, and what to do about the second shift, which is due in an hour.
- 4:20—The personnel director strolls in to report that the switchboard is getting a lot of "weird rumor calls" about the safety of Sneezex. The switchboard operators are upset. What should he have them say to the callers?
- 4:25—Your wife barges in unannounced to tell you that your son has threatened to leave home, "or worse," if his gay lover cannot move in with him.
- 4:30—Your head is pounding, you are sweating profusely, you loosen your tie. Every light on the telephone is lit up. The president is now singing loudly and rolls off the couch with a thud. Everyone ignores him. Two and a half hours ago things looked pretty good. Now your life and your company may be coming down around your ears unless something is done soon. You realize for the first time that you are sitting in the president's chair, and all eyes are on you.

The time has come to act.

Conclusion

When I was very young, my father used to tell me a story about an emperor who was interviewing candidates to be the driver of the royal coach.

The emperor asked the first of the three finalists: "If you were the driver of my coach, and we were near a cliff, how close might we come to the edge?" Thinking the emperor was testing for driving skill and derring-do, the first candidate boasted, "I could drive you within twelve inches of the edge, your excellency."

The emperor repeated the question to the second candidate, who thought his only hope for the coveted position was to best the first candidate. He bragged, "I could drive you within six inches of the edge, your excellency."

But when the emperor asked the third candidate, "How close might we come to the cliff's edge?" this would-be coachman replied: "Your excellency, we mightn't come close at all. I would drive you as far from the cliff's edge as safety dictates."

He got the job.

The purpose of this book has been to give you—a potential crisis manager—an attitude adjustment about crises, about turning points; to give you a different way of thinking about crises; to show you that it is possible to capitalize on the capricious.

You can hope for the best, but prepare for the worst. Regardless of your rung on the corporate ladder, the area for which you are responsible and that you manage may suffer a crisis. Or a crisis can strike your personal life.

Whenever it happens, wherever it happens, however it happens: look for the opportunity that exists in every crisis.

And manage it, get control of it, benefit from it. Somebody will; why shouldn't it be you?

From royal coaches to stagecoaches: if you remember those old cowboy movies, you may recall the inevitable scene of the runaway stagecoach.

I encourage you to view a crisis as a runaway stagecoach, with yourself as passenger. You have the option of sitting in back, being bumped and jostled and tossed from side to side without a prayer of gaining control.

Or you can ride on top. You may not stop it, but you will achieve some very definite control over the speed, the direction, and the duration.

Where you sit is up to you.

Either way, when the inevitable crisis hits, you're along for the ride.

Source Notes

GENERAL NOTE OF EXPLANATION ON NEWS SOURCES

As the reader already knows, many of the crises cited in this book are quite timely and topical. By the author's definition of a crisis, many of the crises discussed are still raging—in the chronic crisis stage. The passage of time usually makes a retrospective analysis of any event easier and more exact; however, when events are so current, the luxuries of time and historical perspective are not always on the author's side.

For that reason, every care has been taken to help ensure complete accuracy of all facts and events described in this book. For the most current and timely of events, the news media were relied on heavily as suppliers of the day-to-day facts, with other sources (as appropriately noted) used to verify media facts and to supply in-depth background information.

The morning and evening news shows of ABC, CBS, and NBC, as well as the Cable News Network and National Public Radio's "Morning Edition" and "All Things Considered," were relied on primarily as sources of fast-breaking news. Also, these media outlets gave the author an "eye witness" perspective on news conferences and other timely events where sight and sound provided added dimensions to an observer's appreciation of an event. But the next day's print media were then used as a double-check on the accuracy of a particular story first reported by the electronic media. In particular, the New York *Times,* The *Wall Street Journal,* and the Los Angeles *Times* were used daily in combination as a check on the electronic news, as well as a check on one another. National news and business magazines also were used, but usually not as primary sources.

Therefore, in many instances below where only one news source is listed as a reference, the reader may assume that other sources have been double- or triple-checked for verification and for accuracy.

CHAPTERS 1–4

GENERAL NOTE ON SOURCES FOR THREE MILE ISLAND

In addition to the author's own first-hand accounts and recollections of the events pertaining to the Three Mile Island incident, additional sources not specifically cited in the text (especially pertaining to subsequent regulatory and criminal proceedings against Metropolitan Edison) include personal interviews with Douglas H. Bedell, manager of communication services, and John C. Micka, coordinator of media affairs, GPU Nuclear Corporation, Middletown, Pa.; Joseph J. Fouchard, director of public affairs (today and at the time of the incident), U.S. Nuclear Regulatory Commission, Bethesda, Md.; and Sally A. Lied, assistant U.S. attorney, Harrisburg, Pa., who was one of the government prosecutors of Met Ed. In

addition, the author has examined the full 11-count criminal indictment returned
against Met Ed, and the resulting plea agreement.

1. Personal interview with author, Harrisburg, Pa., fall 1985.
2. Personal interview with author, Washington, D.C., fall 1985.
3. *Report of the President's Commission on the Accident at Three Mile Island*
   (Washington, D.C.: U.S. Government Printing Office, 1979), p.101. Hereaf-
   ter referred to as *Kemeny Commission Report,* after its chairman, John G.
   Kemeny.
4. Ibid., p. 11.
5. Ibid., pp. 110–111.
6. Ibid., pp. 10–11.
7. *Wall Street Journal,* January 25, 1985.
8. *Ibid.*
9. Various news sources, including Philadelphia *Inquirer,* February 10, 1985,
   and *Wall Street Journal,* February 8, 1985.

GENERAL NOTE ON CHAPTER 4

The Begelman affair, or "Hollywoodgate," is virtually all a matter of public
record—specifically The People of the State of California v. David Begelman, Case
No. A-586983, Superior Court of the State of California, County of Los Angeles,
1978. Given the celebrated circumstances as well as the participants, numerous
accounts of the events abound, such as Peter W. Bernstein's enlightening piece,
"Alan Hirschfield in 'My Last Days at Columbia Pictures,' " *Fortune,* Vol. 98, No. 4
(August 28, 1978), pp. 38–42. But, for a thorough and well-documented reference
that provided a concise and convenient chronicling of events—such as the chrono-
logical listing of who saw the "Cliff Robertson check" and when—the author relied
on David McClintick's splendid work *Indecent Exposure—A True Story of Hollywood and Wall Street.* Many of McClintick's references and sources that were
applicable to this work were checked for accuracy. Therefore, for this author's
analysis of the *crisis* of "Hollywoodgate," McClintick's book stands as *the* reference.

10. David McClintick, *Indecent Exposure* (New York: Morrow, 1982), p. 337.
11. Ibid., p. 518.
12. Ibid., p. 504.

CHAPTERS 5–10

13. Personal interview with author, White Plains, N.Y., spring 1985.
14. Ibid.
15. Los Angeles *Times,* March 24, 1985.
16. Ibid.
17. Personal interview with author, Los Angeles, fall 1984. Novak also appeared
    on November 17, 1984, as a panelist at a UCLA-sponsored seminar on crisis
    management that the author chaired.
18. Personal interview with author, Chicago, spring 1985.
19. Personal correspondence with author, fall 1984.
20. The author was in attendnace and witnessed the exchange.
21. Personal interview with author, Los Angeles, summer 1985.
22. Personal interview with author, San Francisco, summer 1985.

23. Los Angeles *Times*, June 1, 1985.
24. Ibid., July 24, 1985.
25. *Kemeny Commission Report*, p. 11.
26. Personal interview with author, New Brunswick, N.J., spring 1985.
27. *Wall Street Journal*, November 7, 1980.

CHAPTERS 11–16

28. Personal interview with author, New Brunswick, N.J., spring 1985.
29. The author was the communicator mentioned.
30. Los Angeles *Times*, February 24, 1985, citing International Resource Development, Inc.
31. Survey results used with permission of the Western Union Telegraph Co.
32. *Wall Street Journal*, January 8, 1982.
33. From the official government transcript, and as cited in the prologue to Dan Rather's book *The Camera Never Blinks* (New York: Morrow, 1977), p. 11.
34. "Symbolism and Public Relations," *The New Republic*, Vol. 192, No. 19, (May 13, 1985), pp. 7–8.
35. Los Angeles *Times*, April 20, 1985. In addition, the author observed the ceremony and the remarks on news programs on several national television networks and cable channels between April 19 and April 21, 1985.
36. *The New Republic*, loc. cit.
37. Los Angeles *Times*, April 9, 1985.
38. Personal interview with author, Harrisburg, Pa., fall 1985.
39. *Kemeny Commission Report*, p. 140.
40. Confirmed by Buchanan's office, October 1985.
41. Los Angeles *Times*, April 21, 1985.
42. "General Dynamics Under Fire," *Business Week*, No. 2887 (March 25, 1985), pp. 70–76.
43. Los Angeles *Times*, May 22, 1985.
44. *Business Week*, loc. cit.
45. Remarks at the crisis management seminar at UCLA, November 17, 1984, cited earlier.
46. Los Angeles *Times*, April 13, 1985.
47. Ibid., October 30, 1985.
48. Ibid., June 2, 1985.
49. Official court transcript, and as reported in Los Angeles *Times*, May 18, 1985.
50. Investor Responsibility Research Center, Inc., *Antitakeover Charter Amendments: A Directory of Major American Corporations*, 1984.
51. Investor Responsibility Research Center, Inc., *The Impact of Antitakeover Charter Amendments on Contests for Corporate Control*, 1985.
52. Personal interview with author, Los Angeles, fall 1984. Braiker also appeared on November 17, 1984, as a panelist at the UCLA-sponsored seminar on crisis management, cited earlier.
53. Richard F. Fenno, *The President's Cabinet* (Cambridge, Mass: Harvard University Press, 1959), p. 36.
54. *Kemeny Commission Report*, p. 140.
55. Drs. Irving Janis, Peter Defares, and Paul Grossman, "Hypervigilant Reactions to Threat," *Selye's Guide to Stress Research*, Volume 3, ed. Hans Selye, C.C., M.D., Ph.D., D.Sc. (New York: Van Nostrand Reinhold Co., Scientific and Academic Editions, 1983), p. 7.

110. Los Angeles *Times,* August 13, 1985.

111. Ibid.

112. Ibid., August 14, 1985.

113. Ibid., August 13, 1985.

114. *Wall Street Journal,* August 14, 1985.

115. New York *Times's* Forum, "Put Teeth in the Laws on Toxic Leaks," August 18, 1985. An editorial in the *Hindustan Times* said, "Surely, the [Union Carbide] management cannot cook up another sabotage theory as it did in the case of Bhopal." And the Washington correspondent for the *Times of India* wrote, "leakage of the poisonous gas has given the lie to the Carbide management's oft-repeated claim that the Bhopal gas disaster was caused primarily by the inefficiency of the Indian management of the Bhopal plant." (Reported by the Los Angeles *Times,* August 15, 1985.)

116. New York *Times,* August 14, 1985.

117. *Wall Street Journal,* August 14, 1985.

118. Ibid.

119. New York *Times,* December 14, 1984.

GENERAL NOTE ON THE PROCTER & GAMBLE SECTION

In addition to specific sources cited, the author conducted general background interviews with Procter & Gamble personnel, exchanged correspondence with company managers, and reviewed research reports and statistics supplied by Procter & Gamble and by the government. Also reviewed were the Proceedings of the 41st Annual Meeting of the Academy of Management, San Diego, California, August 2–5, 1981, and, specifically, a paper (presented by Elizabeth Gatewood and Archie B. Moore, University of Georgia) entitled, "The Procter & Gamble *Rely* Case: A Social Response Pattern for the 1980s?"

120. *Wall Street Journal,* November 3, 1980.

121. Ibid.

122. Ibid.

123. Ibid., November 17, 1980.

124. Ibid., November 3, 1980.

125. Ibid., November 17, 1980.

126. Ibid., November 3, 1980.

127. Ibid.

128. Ibid.

129. Ibid., November 17, 1980.

130. Ibid., November 3, 1980.

131. Ibid.

132. Ibid.

133. Ibid.

134. Arthur M. Louis, "Lessons from the Firestone Fracas," *Fortune,* Vol. 98, No. 4 (August 28, 1978), p. 45.

135. Mark Dowie, "How Ford Put Two Million Firetraps on Wheels," *Business and Society Review,* No. 23 (fall 1977), pp. 46–55. © *Mother Jones* magazine, San Francisco.

136. Procter & Gamble news release, September 22, 1980. The author has examined a copy of the statement.

137. *Wall Street Journal,* November 3, 1980.

138. Correspondence from Edward G. Harness "to the Procter & Gamble Organi-

zation," September 24, 1980. The author has examined a copy of this communiqué.

GENERAL NOTE ON THE JOHNSON & JOHNSON SECTION

After having been interviewed by hundreds of writers and news reporters on the subject of Tylenol for 15 months, as well as having given countless speeches on the subject, Johnson & Johnson said, "Enough" on January 1, 1984. The company decided that after that date it would no longer talk about the poisonings. However, the firm lifted the self-imposed gag rule in May 1985, and allowed the author to tape-record almost an entire day of behind-the-scenes interviews with key executives who played crucial roles in the crisis: David E. Collins, chairman of McNeil and vice chairman of Johnson & Johnson's executive committee; Lawrence G. Foster, Johnson & Johnson's corporate vice president, public relations; and Robert Kniffen, director of public relations for Johnson & Johnson. The interviews took place at Johnson & Johnson's worldwide corporate headquarters in New Brunswick, New Jersey.

Any quotations in this section not specifically attributed to another source are from these interviews.

139. "The Tylenol Comeback," special report issued by Johnson & Johnson in early 1983 to detail portions of the company's response to the Tylenol crisis. Many of the statistics cited by Johnson & Johnson executives during the interviews were double-checked in this report.
140. Johnson & Johnson 1982 Annual Report, p. 29.
141. Ibid., p. 3.
142. Johnson & Johnson's "Our Credo," located in the offices of most J&J managers and executives.

Index

233